Analyzing Financial Statements

JOHN E. McKINLEY

ROBERT L. JOHNSON

GERALD R. DOWNEY, JR.

CHARLES S. ZIMMERMAN

MICHAEL D. BLOOM

EDUCATION POLICY & DEVELOPMENT

AMERICAN
BANKERS
ASSOCIATION

1120 Connecticut Avenue, N.W.
Washington, D.C. 20036

This publication is designed to provide accurate and authoritative information in regard to the subject matter covered. It is sold with the understanding that the publisher is not engaged in rendering legal, accounting, or other professional service. If legal advice or other expert assistance is required, the services of a competent professional person should be sought.

From a Declaration of Principles jointly adopted by a Committee of the American Bar Association and a Committee of Publishers and Associations.

Library of Congress Cataloging-in-Publication Data

Analyzing financial statements.—3rd ed./by Michael D. Bloom . . . [et al.]
    p. cm.
  Includes index.
  ISBN 0-89982-352-1: $45.00
  1. Financial statements. I. Bloom, Michael D.
HF5681.B2A6464 1988
657'.3—dc19   88-9399
                                        CIP

Printed in the United States of America
1989 Printing

Contents

Preface

Analyzing Financial Statements is intended to be a practical introduction to financial analysis from the viewpoint of the commercial loan officer. One of the key skills of an effective loan officer is the ability to analyze a company's financial statements so as to achieve an understanding of the company's past performance and then to use that analysis to make sound predictions about the company's future performance and credit-worthiness.

Chapters 1 and 2 serve as introductory chapters defining financial analysis and explaining its purposes and limitations. Chapter 1 provides an overview of the orderly sequence of steps involved in financial analysis. Chapter 2 emphasizes the importance of thoroughly understanding a company and its operating environment and describes the various cyclical patterns of businesses which provide a conceptual framework for financial analysis.

The remaining chapters focus on specific analytical techniques using examples based on actual companies and showing how the data might be interpreted. Chapters 3 through 6 focus on the four basic analytical techniques that enable a loan officer to analyze and interpret a company's past performance:

- analysis of income statements
- analysis of balance sheets
- preparation and analysis of funds flow statements
- calculation and interpretation of ratios

Chapters 7 through 9 focus on those analytical techniques that help a loan officer predict a company's future performance:

- analysis of pro forma income statements and balance sheets
- preparation and analysis of cash budgets
- more advanced analytical techniques, including working investment analysis, sustainable growth, sensitivity analysis, break-even analysis, and operating leverage

The text concludes with a case study showing how a comprehensive financial analysis would proceed step by step using all the foregoing techniques to reach a sound judgment concerning a borrowing company's credit needs and its repayment ability.

Throughout, the text emphasizes the importance of both technical analysis (manipulating the numbers) and interpretive analysis (getting behind the numbers to raise questions and draw conclusions about the financial viability of a company). It also stresses that financial analysis does not in itself provide answers, but rather helps the loan officer focus attention on the most vulnerable aspects of a company's operation and identify important questions requiring answers from management. The ultimate decision, however, still must take into account the loan officer's subjective judgment of such factors as management's capabilities and the market situation.

This text will provide beginning loan officers with an understanding of the fundamentals of financial analysis. However, to become a proficient lender, the loan officer will have to hone the basic skills presented here through diligent application, further study, and—perhaps most important of all—practical experience.

The American Bankers Association (ABA) is grateful to all those who made this publication possible. This third edition of *Analyzing Financial Statements* was revised and updated by three of the authors of the original text: Gerald R. Downey, Executive Vice President, C & S Florida Corporation, Fort Lauderdale, Florida; Robert L. Johnson, Senior Vice President of Commercial Real Estate, The Citizens and Southern National Bank, Atlanta, Georgia; and John E. McKinley, Senior Executive Vice President, The Citizens and Southern National Bank, Atlanta, Georgia. The manuscript was thoroughly reviewed and many helpful suggestions were provided by George E. Ruth, Senior Vice President, MetroBank, Bloomington, Minnesota, who also wrote ABA's *Commercial Lending* text and the *Commercial Loan Officer Development* self-study training manual. Finally, ABA is especially appreciative of the many instructors and students who suggested improvements and additions to help make this edition an even more useful resource for commercial lenders.

1 Financial Analysis: An Overview

Learning Objectives

After studying this chapter, you should be able to
- define financial analysis
- explain the importance of financial analysis in commercial lending
- discuss the technical and interpretive aspects of analysis
- list the basic steps of financial analysis
- identify the limitations of financial analysis

▌▐▌▐▌▐▌▐ Introduction

Banks obtain much of their income from loans made to commercial customers. For this reason, banks depend on their commercial loan officers to make sound and reliable judgments about the financial stability of the businesses applying for loans. Financial analysis gives the loan officer much of the information required to make sound lending decisions.

Since many of the businesses applying for loans will be owned or operated by members of the community that the bank serves, the loan officer must also display concern for both the needs of the business and the community when making loan decisions. Through careful financial analysis and sound lending decisions, the commercial loan officer can contribute to the profitability of the bank, the growth of local businesses, and the meeting of the needs of the community.

This chapter provides a broad overview of financial analysis as it applies to commercial lenders. Financial analysis is defined, the concept of risk is discussed, and the sequence of steps involved in analyzing financial statements is presented. Other uses of financial analysis—such as in assessing problem loan situations—are also discussed briefly.

▌▐▌▐▌▐▌▐ Definition of Financial Analysis

Financial analysis is a critical component of the commercial lending process which helps the loan officer decide whether a loan should be made and under what terms and conditions. The commercial lending process normally begins with an interview between the commercial client and loan officer and continues through the credit investigation, financial analysis, loan structuring and pricing, loan negotiation, loan documentation and closing, and loan follow-up. Thus financial analysis is not only an important factor in the lending decision, but continues as part of the monitoring process after the loan is closed.

The focus of financial analysis is on the company's past and current financial performance, rather than on such factors as management characteristics and the company's credit history. Nevertheless, such nonfinancial considerations do help establish the direction and depth the financial analysis should take.

Financial analysis involves the systematic examination and interpretation of information to assess a company's past performance, present condition, and future viability. Financial analysis helps the commercial loan officer pinpoint unique characteristics—operating or financial—that affect a business's likelihood of success or failure. It presents a picture of the company that includes the following:

- financial structure—the assets the company maintains and the liabilities it has incurred to acquire and keep those assets

- operating cycle—the stages the business goes through to bring its products or services to the market

- trends—the direction that the business operation is going, as evidenced by comparison of financial results from more than one year

- flexibility—the company's capacity to deal with both planned and unplanned change

TECHNICAL VERSUS INTERPRETIVE ASPECTS OF ANALYSIS

Commercial loan officers examine the financial information available to them by applying techniques based on sound logic and mathematical or accounting principles. The loan officer performs many technical operations that include calculating ratios, reformatting information for clarity, evaluating the company's goals, comparing statistics with those of other businesses, and projecting future operating results.

This technical manipulation of the data is only a small part, however, of what is needed to complete a comprehensive and effective financial analysis of a company. Once the loan officer has "crunched" the numbers (calculated ratios, analyzed trends, and compared information), the results must be interpreted to determine the reasons behind the numbers (not only what is happening, but why) and how past and future events affect the company's potential repayment ability.

The crux of financial analysis then is to understand and correctly interpret the results of the technically manipulated data. To accomplish this, the commercial loan officer first needs considerable background information on the business. For example, the loan officer needs to know about the company's ownership, its management, its lines of business, its competition, and other operational aspects of the company. Information about the business's external environment helps the loan officer understand the characteristics of the industry in which the company competes. This includes the company's position within the industry, markets in which the company operates, pertinent government regulations, and the company's susceptibility to adverse changes in the general economy. Additionally, the lender should know to what extent demographic trends and consumer preferences are factors that may affect the company's operations.

Understanding these organizational and environmental factors provides meaning to the abstract numbers derived in the technical analysis. This information, along with the financial information, helps the loan officer reach a conclusion as to the riskiness of a proposed loan.

ANALYSIS OF RISK

The bank's role as commercial lender provides limited return. It earns its contracted rate of interest on the loan regardless of the company's profitability. This limited return—coupled with the thin margin between the bank's interest return and its cost of funds and its typical high leverage—requires the bank to take only a limited risk in the extension of credit.

Nevertheless, risk is an inescapable part of commercial lending. The principal risk—called *credit risk* by bankers—is that the borrower will not meet the terms of the loan and that secondary repayment sources, such as collateral, will be insufficient to cover the losses. Financial analysis attempts to minimize the credit risk involved in lending money by assessing the likelihood that companies will be able to repay their loans as agreed. The loan officer can lessen the risk by accurately appraising a customer's creditworthiness and then ensuring that the loan is properly secured, structured, and monitored.

To evaluate risk, the loan officer attempts to identify the many uncertainties the commercial borrower faces and to weigh its financial strengths and weaknesses. If the borrower's strengths exceed its weaknesses by a margin sufficient to cover the perceived uncertainties, the loan should represent an acceptable credit risk. This concept is often expressed as a formula:

Some of the areas of uncertainty that should be taken into consideration by a loan officer include the following:

- new or unproven aspects of a business—such as new products, production techniques, or management

- economic fluctuations—the effect of the general overall economy on the company's operations

- technological obsolescence—which in some industries may result overnight from a competitor's technological advances

- managerial ability—capacity to cope with growth, losses, and changes in markets

- government regulation—legislation that controls pricing, limits markets, restricts product and service offerings, or requires major unplanned expenditures (for example, to comply with environmental protection laws)

- social change—which may help or hinder a company's operation. For instance, the migration of people from inner-city to suburban areas has resulted in loss of business for many retail firms operating in inner cities while creating new opportunities for retail operations in the suburbs.

PURPOSES OF FINANCIAL ANALYSIS

The scope and focus of financial analysis will vary somewhat depending on the specific purpose of the analysis—for example, whether the company is seeking long-term or short-term financing or whether the analysis is being done as part of the ongoing monitoring of an existing loan.

New Loan Request

Both the size of the requested loan and its terms affect the loan officer's financial analysis. Companies requesting loans generally need to finance either current assets (such as accounts receivable and inventory) or fixed assets (equipment, buildings, or land). A basic tenet of lending dictates that a temporary or seasonal increase in current assets should be financed by short-term loans, while increases in fixed assets should be financed by long-term loans. Short-term loans are payable within one year and are listed on the balance sheet as current liabilities; long-term loans have maturities of one year or longer and are reported as long-term liabilities. Thus the term of the loan will be determined by its purpose in most cases.

Monitoring Process

Financial analysis is not used by the loan officer only in reaching a decision concerning a loan application. Rather, financial analysis is an important part of the ongoing monitoring process during the entire period that a loan is outstanding. It is particularly useful in identifying problem loan situations early on—before the situation deteriorates to the point that the bank has no choice but to call in the loan and risk receiving less than the full amount owed. With early detection of a problem situation, the bank can often help the company take prompt action to turn the situation around. In addition, banks often monitor their larger borrowers even when they have no loans currently outstanding.

Sequential Steps of Financial Analysis

The essence of financial analysis is to move from a preliminary investigation of a company to an in-depth examination of its operating performance as evidenced by its historical and projected financial statements. Most banks have a systematic approach for obtaining the various documents, organizing and presenting the information contained therein, and then evaluating and interpreting the data using the standard analytical techniques. The basic steps in financial analysis will be presented in detail in the following chapters in the order in which they are normally considered. The text is arranged in such a way that each chapter presents an in-depth look at a different tool of financial analysis. A brief overview of the entire financial analysis process follows.

OBTAINING AND PREPARING THE STATEMENTS

Banks generally ask prospective commercial borrowers to submit detailed financial data in support of their loan requests. Most banks have established guidelines as to the type and number of financial statements that should be obtained to do a comprehensive analysis. For example, a bank might require 3 years' worth of income statements and balance sheets as well as any interim statements for the current fiscal year. A funds flow statement will normally be included as part of accountant-prepared financial statements. The lender will also specify the number of years of pro forma financial statements required and may also request a cash budget. Other financial data that lenders may ask commercial borrowers to submit in support of their loan requests include a comprehensive business plan, tax returns, and various management reports such as the company's operating and capital budgets, inventory summary or listing, accounts receivable agings, accounts payable agings, and sales and expense breakdowns. If any of this documentation is not readily available, it can usually be prepared at the loan officer's request. In some cases, the lender may have to construct some of the items—such as the funds flow statement or cash budget—on the basis of available data.

For start-up companies without an established operating record, the one essential document upon which a lender must rely is the business plan. This is a comprehensive document that provides the commercial loan officer with a clear picture of how the company will be run and what its goals and objectives are. Personal financial information may also be requested, especially in situations where the principal will be required to guarantee the debt. Resumés of key officers may also be in order, including background on any previous business ventures in which they have been involved.

SPREADING AND COMMON-SIZING THE STATEMENTS

Statement spreading is the process by which information from financial statements is recorded on a standard form, or spreadsheet. This enables the loan officer to easily scan the data, spot trends, and make comparisons. Many banks use a standard spreadsheet for income statements and balance sheets, as well as a designated format for funds flow statements and cash budgets. The more commonly used ratios may also be included on the spreadsheet.

Another important preliminary step in preparing financial data for analysis is common-sizing. This entails calculating each account in the income statement as a percentage of net sales, and each balance sheet account as a percentage of total assets (or total liabilities plus net worth). This enables the loan officer to spot trends over time in the company's profit margin, for example, or the relative size of a company's accounts receivable or accounts payable compared to its competitors.

In many banks, spreading and common-sizing of financial statements and ratio calculations are done by computer. Often industry averages are also included on the spreadsheets to facilitate comparisons of the company's performance with that of other companies in the same industry. Industry averages are compiled for this purpose by Robert Morris Associates in its *Annual Statement Reports*.

ANALYSIS OF PAST PERFORMANCE

Income Statement Analysis

Financial analysis begins with the income statement (also called a *profit and loss statement* or *earnings statement*). This most important source of information about a company begins with total revenues (or sales) and then categorizes the various expenses leading to the net profit (or loss) for the period—the so-called bottom line. Lenders normally ask potential borrowers to submit income statements for the past 3 or 4 years so that a company's sales, expenses, and profits can be compared over a period of time. The analysis basically consists of revenue analysis and expense analysis.

Balance Sheet Analysis

The balance sheet is the second major source of information about a company to be analyzed. Unlike the income statement, which shows how a company performed over a period of time, the balance sheet is a point-in-time financial picture of the company—usually as of the last day of the company's fiscal year. The basic structure of the balance sheet can be stated as a simple equation: Assets = Liabilities + Net worth. Balance sheet analysis entails an evaluation of the company's assets followed by an evaluation of its liabilities (debt) and its net worth (or equity). Again, lenders normally ask companies to submit balance sheets for the past 3 or 4 years so that comparisons over time can be made and trends identified.

Funds Flow Statement Analysis

The next major tool of financial analysis is the funds flow statement (sometimes called a *sources and uses of funds statement* or *sources and applications of funds statement*). As its name implies, it shows how a company obtains and uses its economic resources and thus helps the lender determine both the company's funding needs and its sources of repayment. The funds flow statement shows inflows and outflows of funds categorized as operating funds flows, discretionary funds flows, and financing funds flows. Like an income statement, it is a period statement (normally covering a fiscal year) and like a balance sheet, it is based on a simple equation: Sources of funds = Uses of funds. If a company fails to submit an accountant-prepared funds flow statement as part of its financial documentation, the lender may need to construct one.

Ratio Analysis

Ratios are not only the best known and most widely used of all the financial analysis tools, they are also the most overrated and most widely misused. Ratios allow the lender to study the relationship between various components of financial statements such as assets and liabilities or expenses and revenues. While ratios are easily calculated, their correct interpretation is more problematic. The specific ratios used by a particular bank may vary, but the major categories of ratios reflect the major aspects of a company's operations that a lender needs to consider:

- liquidity—the company's ability to meet current obligations and convert assets to cash
- leverage—the relationship between the company's liabilities and its net worth
- coverage—the capacity of a company to meet its continuing payment obligations
- profitability—the ability of a company to sell its products or provide a service at a price that exceeds its expenses
- activity—the efficiency with which a company uses its assets (which will vary over time, particularly for a company that is cyclical in nature)

ANALYSIS OF PROJECTED PERFORMANCE

Pro Forma Analysis

The analysis of pro forma income statements and balance sheets is similar to that of historical financial statements except that it focuses on the company's anticipated performance in the future. Analysis of pro forma financial statements involves evaluating the company's underlying assumptions, as well as the expected economic, competitive, and regulatory environment in which the company will operate. Normally, the lender will want to analyze projections for 2 or 3 years into the future, depending on the size and term of the requested loan. However, since management-submitted pro formas tend to be overly optimistic, loan officers often create their own pro forma financial statements for a company based on more conservative assumptions (such as lower sales projections).

Cash Budget Analysis

Cash budgets are another financial analysis tool based on financial forecasts. Cash budgets forecast a company's cash receipts and payments, generally on a month-to-month basis, thus enabling the lender to gauge a business's peak credit needs and its ability to generate sufficient cash to repay short-term loans over the term of its operating cycle. The cash budget also helps a lender determine whether a company's borrowing needs are long term or short term. Cash budgets are especially useful in determining the financial needs of borrowers with seasonal operating cycles (such as a toy store that rings up half of its total sales in the last 2 months of each year).

Other Advanced Analytical Techniques

Besides the basic analytical tools described above, several more advanced analytical techniques are available to the loan officer. These include working investment analysis (which measures the impact of sales growth on financing requirements and a company's ability to expand sales), sustainable growth analysis (which measures a company's ability to expand sales), sensitivity analysis (in which a company's areas of greatest vulnerability are examined using multiple scenarios), breakeven analysis (which compares a company's fixed costs to its variable costs as a means of predicting future profitability), and operating leverage (which measures the impact on profitability of changes in sales). These techniques are invaluable in refining and focusing the financial analysis process and in evaluating a company's ability to grow. With practice, loan officers will gain skill in using them and in interpreting the results, as well as in determining what types of advanced analysis are useful in a particular situation.

INTERPRETING THE DATA

The final step in financial analysis is the interpretation of a company's past financial performance and likely future performance in order to gauge a company's ability to repay the requested loan (or the existing loan in a problem loan analysis). Determining trends over time and making industry comparisons are two basic analytical techniques that will be discussed in detail throughout the text. Ultimately, however, the key to financial analysis lies in the loan officer's ability not simply to determine what has happened in the past or even why it happened but what it bodes for the future. Thus even the most sophisticated calculations and projections are meaningless apart from an understanding of the context in which a company operates. Moreover, it cannot be overemphasized that financial analysis does not purport to be an exact science that can be used to predict with certainty a company's future. Unknown factors abound, and subjective judgment is necessarily involved in drawing conclusions from the analyzed data and making the final credit decision.

Ideally, sound conclusions should be reached efficiently—that is, with minimum effort. The amount of work entailed will vary greatly with the commercial loan officer's level of experience. For instance, a senior loan officer with 25 years of experience may be able to quickly scan and understand financial information, do technical and interpretive analyses mentally, and quickly reach a conclusion. The beginning loan officer, by contrast, can afford few shortcuts.

▌▌▌▌▌ Limitations of Analysis

Although financial analysis is a critical tool in commercial lending activities, it has some important limitations. First, its success depends

upon the reliability and completeness of the information being analyzed. Yet, even with completely accurate information, financial analysis
is not an exact science that can be used to arrive at absolute conclusions.
Because it deals with future uncertainty, analysis is much better at
formulating questions and projecting possibilities than it is at providing
definitive answers.

Moreover, technical analysis alone cannot provide a complete understanding of the borrower. Banks do not make loan decisions based on
financial analysis alone; the nonfinancial strengths and weaknesses of
the borrower must also be considered. In addition, pricing, negotiation
of specific terms, the bank's willingness to assume risk, and the availability of funds are also important aspects of the decision to extend or deny
credit.

Facts to Note:

Generally accepted accounting principles (GAAP) prescribe methods of
reporting accounting or financial information in order to facilitate
comparisons between companies. These principles have been established by various authoritative organizations.

Four of the most influential organizations that contribute to generally
accepted accounting principles are the American Accounting Association, the American Institute of Certified Public Accountants, the Financial
Accounting Standards Board, and the Securities and Exchange Commis-
sion.

ACCOUNTING METHODS

In preparing financial statements, many different accounting techniques are accepted. For example, financial statements can be prepared
on a cash or accrual basis, using the LIFO (Last In, First Out) or FIFO
(First In, First Out) inventory valuation method and using accelerated
depreciation or straight-line depreciation of fixed assets. Although the
accounting methods used are usually described in the footnotes to
accountant-prepared financial statements, differences in accounting
methods can make it difficult to make valid comparisons between com-

panies even in the same industry. Comparing financial statements of a company over time may also yield invalid conclusions if it has changed any of its accounting methods during the period being analyzed.

ADEQUACY OF INFORMATION

There may be relevant information that does not show up on the company's financial statements. For example, a listing of order backlogs, proposed capital expenditures, or unfunded pension liabilities may be important considerations that only an experienced loan officer or one knowledgeable about the company or industry being analyzed might know to look for.

Often the data in financial statements are aggregated. For example, a company with various product lines usually shows a single total sales figure on the income statement. The loan officer may need to request breakdowns of sales and expenses by product line or by geographical area.

Moreover, many important factors cannot be quantified and listed on a financial statement. Thus loan interviews and credit checks supplement the financial analysis of a company to assess such nonfinancial characteristics of the borrower as evidence of the company's willingness to repay past debts and an overall consideration of character traits of management.

▌▌▌▌▌ Summary

Financial analysis involves both the technical manipulation and interpretation of financial information to assess a company's past performance, present condition, and future viability as a means of determining the amount of risk involved in a lending situation as expressed in the formula: Strengths − Weaknesses > Uncertainties. The scope of the loan officer's analysis may be influenced by the size, purpose, and term of the loan or, in the case of a problem loan, the specific circumstances surrounding that loan.

Financial analysis involves a number of sequential steps beginning with such preliminaries as obtaining the requisite financial statements and spreading and common-sizing (expressing as percentages) the various income statement and balance sheet accounts—including, in many cases, industry averages. The analysis of a company's past performance centers on a company's operations as seen in its income statements and its financial structure as seen in its balance sheets. This analysis also includes trend analysis (comparing a company's results over time) and comparative analysis (comparing a company's results with that of other companies in the same industry). The next step is the analysis of a company's funds flow statement to assess a company's sources and uses of funds, followed by the analysis of ratios comparing key elements from a company's income statement or balance sheet.

Only after analyzing a company's historic record does the loan officer attempt to predict its future performance and hence its ability to repay the loan in question. This prospective analysis involves the analysis of a company's pro forma financial statements, the value of which depend in large part on their being based on a realistic sales projection. Often the loan officer will rework the pro formas using more conservative assumptions. The loan officer will then analyze the company's monthly cash budget (its projected receipts and expenditures) in order to determine whether the company is likely to have seasonal or other short-term funding needs that were not apparent from the pro forma analysis. Finally, the lender may select from several more advanced analytical techniques which may show, for example, a company's ability to undergo rapid growth. After completing all of these analytical steps, the loan officer must interpret the information in light of the company's nonfinancial strengths and weaknesses and the total environment in which the company operates.

Financial analysis has certain inherent shortcomings of which loan officers must be aware. Financial analysis is only as good as the quality of the information being analyzed, which may vary greatly even for accountant-prepared statements. Financial statements may also fail to disclose important information or may not be comparable because of inconsistent use of accounting methods.

Finally, financial analysis, in and of itself, cannot give the loan officer an adequate basis on which to approve or deny (or make early demand for) a loan. The ultimate decision remains a subjective one that must take into account management's strengths and weaknesses and the company's larger operating environment.

Questions

1. Define financial analysis. What aspects of a business does financial analysis consider? How does risk assessment fit into the overall picture?

2. What purposes does financial analysis serve from the standpoint of a lender?

3. What is the difference between technical and interpretive analysis?

4. List the principal consecutive steps involved in a comprehensive financial analysis.

5. How does financial analysis take into consideration the past, the present, and the future?

6. What uncertainties might a company face? What factors determine the company's ability to deal with these uncertainties?

7. What are some limitations of financial analysis? What can be done to overcome these limitations?

Exercises

E-1

To better understand the concept of financial analysis, imagine that you are a doctor using an electrocardiograph on a patient. The machine prints out a chart showing how the patient's heart is performing, and you interpret the chart to diagnose the patient's health. What other methods might you use to interpret the likelihood of the patient remaining healthy? Compare this analysis to the factors you might consider in determining the likelihood of a business remaining healthy. Finally, list several factors that might have an unexpected adverse effect on the health of the patient and the business.

E-2

Consider how the concept of uncertainty affects a loan officer's assessment of risk. What aspects of society can be accurately predicted? For example, can the economy, weather, or election results be accurately predicted? List some historic trends that can be studied to narrow the uncertainty gap, such as leading indicators, pressure zones, or opinion polls. Next, draw some conclusions as to how well historic trends predict the future and compare them to the accuracy of predictions you might reach when analyzing the financial statements of a company.

E-3
Prepare a list of factors that contribute to the stability of an organization seeking a loan. For example, a company with little or no debt can better withstand an increase in interest rates than a company with significant debt.

2 A Conceptual Framework

Learning Objectives

After studying this chapter, you should be able to

- explain the characteristic operating cycles of different types of business operations

- explain why a company's type of business, legal structure, size, and management strategies, as well as its external environment, are important considerations in financial analysis

- explain how a company's funds flow cycle affects its loan requirements and its ability to repay debt

- explain how a company's fixed asset cycle affects the repayment of debt

- explain how a company's profit cycle differs from its cash flow cycles

▌▌▌▌▌▌▌ Introduction

As described in Chapter 1, financial analysis is the process whereby the commercial loan officer determines the creditworthiness of potential or present borrowers. Even before beginning the analysis of specific financial data, however, the loan officer should have a good understanding of the company and its operating environment. This provides a context for the financial analysis and enables the loan officer to put the figures in a meaningful perspective.

Some of the factors that a lender should take into consideration from the outset include what type of business the loan applicant is engaged in—that is, whether it is a manufacturing, wholesaling, retailing, service, or agricultural enterprise. Each category of business operation has certain operational characteristics in common, and companies in a given category have similar operating cycles and characteristic types of credit needs and sources of financing or repayment. Another important distinction among companies is their legal status—for example, whether the company is organized as a proprietorship, a partnership, or a corporation. The size of the company is another factor that must be taken into consideration. The lender should also have enough knowledge of the company to understand its management objectives (for example, whether the goal is short-term profit or long-term maximization of wealth) and management style. Finally, the marketplace in which a company competes is a significant factor in setting the stage for financial analysis. This includes an understanding of the industry in which the company competes, its vulnerability to economic downturns, and the regulatory environment in which it operates.

Besides an understanding of the company and its operating environment, a loan officer must understand the company's funds flow cycle and how it affects the need for outside financing and the timing of loan repayment. A company's fixed asset cycle and profit cycle are other key concepts underlying financial analysis that will be presented in this chapter.

▌▌▌▌▌▌▌ The Company and Its Operating Environment

TYPE OF BUSINESS OPERATION

Most businesses can be categorized either as manufacturing, wholesaling, retailing, service, or agricultural enterprises. Businesses of the same type tend to have certain similarities such as similar operating cycles, similar uses of cash or credit, and similar asset and liability structures. The fact that many businesses today are integrated—that is, they operate in more than one of these five categories—complicates the analysis somewhat. For example, a company that manufactures suits may also retail them. In this situation, the loan officer may need to analyze the various components of the company separately.

Understanding the type of business in which a company is engaged is important because a company's operating cycle affects the riskiness of a loan and will thus enter into the loan officer's decision as to the amount, term, and structure of a loan. Furthermore, the lender must be aware of any factors that may disrupt the operating cycle, and therefore the company's cash flow. In addition, an experienced loan officer will come to know what to expect, and hence what is out of line, when looking at financial statements for a given type of company.

Manufacturers

Manufacturers make products for sale by changing raw materials or purchased parts into salable goods. For example, a paper mill is a manufacturer that converts wood pulp, a raw material, into paper. A furniture company, on the other hand, might purchase wood, glue, nails, and screws to produce desks or tables.

The operating cycle of manufacturers starts with cash (or trade credit), which is used to finance the purchase of raw materials. Using these raw materials, inventory is manufactured and then sold to create accounts receivable. When the accounts receivable are collected, cash is generated, which is then used to purchase more raw materials, thus beginning the cycle again.

In general, manufacturers are capital intensive, requiring a large amount of debt and equity to carry out their operations (which typically entails buying and equipping a plant). Manufacturing companies usually hold most of their assets in inventory, accounts receivable, and fixed assets.

Manufacturers request loans for many reasons, such as to purchase equipment related to their production process, fund inventory purchases, carry accounts receivable, or make plant improvements.

Wholesalers

Wholesalers do not produce goods, but purchase marketable goods—either manufactured or nonmanufactured—for resale at a profit to retailers, to other wholesalers, or to major users of the product. The operating cycle of a wholesaler begins with the use of cash or trade credit to purchase inventory. When the inventory is sold, accounts receivable are created, which upon payment are converted to cash, thus completing the cycle. A notable characteristic of the operating cycle of wholesalers is the large amount of inventory that is purchased and sold. This high rate of inventory turnover means that a wholesaler's profit as a percentage of sales is usually low. Accounts receivable typically constitute an important asset and accounts payable an important liability for wholesalers. Since wholesalers do not typically require substantial amounts of equipment or other fixed assets, the majority of loan requests relate to working capital requirements—that is, amounts required to carry inventory and accounts receivable.

Retailers

Retailers purchase finished products from wholesalers or directly from manufacturers for sale to consumers. Retail businesses are diverse, ranging from department stores to restaurants. The operating cycle of retailers begins with cash used to purchase inventory (a finished product) which in turn is generally sold directly to the public for cash. Thus accounts receivable are usually minimal. The cash is then used to purchase more inventory.

A key factor in evaluating a retailer is inventory turnover. Depending on the type of retailer, inventory may be the primary asset or fixed assets may be more significant. Retail businesses typically request loans to increase their inventory or expand their retail outlets. The amount of capital required to finance a retail operation varies greatly according to sales volume and the particular industry involved. High sales volume usually requires a significant amount of inventory and numerous retail outlets—both of which require capital.

Service Businesses

Service businesses—which include hospitals, law firms, and banks, just to mention a few types—do not sell tangible products, but instead provide a service. The operating cycle of a service business differs from that of other companies in that no inventory of salable stock is involved. Instead, cash is used in the performance of a service, which generates accounts receivable. When the accounts receivable are paid, cash is created, beginning the cycle again. In analyzing the operating cycle of a service business, the loan officer should focus on accounts receivable since a concentration of accounts receivable or a large number of uncollected receivables can disrupt the operating cycle, thereby posing a risk to the lender.

Most service companies have few physical assets and thus relatively low capital requirements. Accounts receivable is usually a significant item and inventory an insignificant item. The fixed assets of some types of service firms (such as airlines), however, are very large.

Agricultural Businesses

Agricultural businesses produce crops or raise livestock. In many respects, the operating cycle of a farming operation is similar to that of manufacturers. Cash is used to purchase seeds, fertilizer, and equipment for the production of inventory—in this case, a crop, livestock, or a derivative product such as milk. The product is sold at market, creating accounts receivable which when paid generate cash.

Like manufacturing firms, agricultural businesses generally borrow for equipment needs and seasonal financing needs that arise from the timing differences between payment of cultivation costs and receipt of revenues from sale of the cultivated crops.

TYPE OF LEGAL STRUCTURE

Another important distinction among businesses is their legal status—that is, whether a company is set up as a proprietorship, a partnership, or a corporation. The company's legal structure can have profound implications for lenders. For example, officers of a corporation are not legally liable for the corporation's financial obligations to the bank unless they formally agree to accept such liability. The owners of a proprietorship or partnership, on the other hand, do assume responsibility for the company's financial obligations.

Sole Proprietorships

Most small businesses in the United States are sole proprietorships. For example, most doctors, lawyers, carpenters, and other persons working alone operate as sole proprietorships. These are the easiest type of business structure to form. The owners of such businesses assume complete responsibility for their operations, including any financial obligations to banks. The assets, debt, and income of the owner and the business are one and the same. Thus a loan officer can take into account both personal and business assets in evaluating the creditworthiness of a sole proprietorship.

Partnerships

A partnership is a business that is jointly owned by two or more individuals. In a *general partnership*, the profits and losses are divided among the partners according to the terms of the partnership agreement (often based on each partner's equity contribution), and all of the business income is regarded as personal income of the owners. All partners assume complete legal responsibility for all the liabilities of the partnership, and lenders can look at the personal assets of each partner as well as those of the partnership when evaluating creditworthiness.

In a *limited partnership*, certain owners may be designated as general partners and others as limited partners. General partners are liable for all partnership debts, whereas limited partners are liable only if certain legal requirements are met. Limited partnerships are particularly common in real estate investment ventures.

Corporations

Corporations are business organizations that are legally treated as individuals. Thus, unlike sole proprietorships and partnerships, corporations pay taxes, buy and sell assets, and incur liabilities. They are also highly regulated. Corporations are owned by their stockholders—which may be one or a few individuals or hundreds of thousands of shareholders in the case of a large publicly held company. Most corporations, however, are privately held—that is, their stock is not publicly traded.

A corporation's income is taxed at corporate rates and is not considered to be the personal income of the owners. In a publicly held corporation, much of the income may be distributed as dividends (which are then taxed again at individual rates). Privately held firms normally either reinvest their profits (that is, retain them as equity) or distribute them in the form of salaries or other benefits to the owners.

An advantage of the corporate setup is that it protects its owners from personal exposure to indebtedness. Shareholders stand to lose no more than their investment in a company, even in the case of bankruptcy. For this reason, lenders may require owners of closely held corporations to personally guarantee any debt extended to the corporation.

SIZE OF THE COMPANY

A company's relative size, its stature in the community, and its clout in the marketplace may also affect its financing needs and its ability to repay debt. The sophistication (or lack thereof) of a company's financial statements may also reflect its size.

Small Businesses

The manager of a small business is generally the entrepreneur who began the business. The owner-manager typically has technical or sales expertise but lacks accounting or financial ability. Managers of small businesses often cannot afford to hire full-time financial experts and may instead use clerical bookkeepers or an accounting service. Therefore they may rely on their accountant and banker to provide financial expertise and direction.

Small businesses often direct their products or services to limited markets. The operation either introduces a new product to un-developed markets or is a minor participant in a larger, more established market. Additionally, the operations of a small company are often unsophisticated, and may comprise only one or two lines of business. Uncomplicated operational processes with little integration typically make up the organization of these businesses. Most small businesses have limited capital resources unless the owners are wealthy. Public equity markets are typically unavailable to them and, since the small business operation is unproven, owners may find that borrowing money is difficult even in the venture capital market.

Thus the bank usually serves a critical role in the funding of necessary capital for a small company's growth. The bank expects, in return, not only compensation for its risk (that is, payment of interest), but also substantial protection in terms of collateral, loan agreements, and continued information flow. Even then, a bank encounters a relatively high degree of risk simply because the failure rate of small businesses is so high.

Medium-Sized Businesses

A successful small business typically grows into a medium-sized business. To improve its management, the company will likely begin to hire specialists, such as a controller or marketing experts. Then, the company either enlarges its market or, if it is already operating in a large and established market, becomes a competitive factor.

As it becomes more sophisticated, the medium-sized company may diversify its lines of business. For example, a company that began by making paper cups may expand production to make milk cartons. Or a retailer of women's clothing may take on a line of men's clothing as well. Such diversification usually requires additional capital. The company may also obtain access to equity markets at this point or attract private investors. Access to private and public debt sources also increases.

As long as the company continues to grow, it will normally continue to have significant financing needs, and banks often continue to be a major source of funds. This funding role is often shared among several banks as the business outgrows the local bank's individual lending capacity and becomes, by virtue of its expansion or profits, a more desirable customer for other banks. As the company grows, it also typically begins to fine-tune its operations, may have larger or more complex cash flows, and may develop additional funding needs.

Large Businesses

A medium-sized company may eventually become a large company. By this time, its management is usually much more specialized. The company, for example, might have a treasurer, an assistant treasurer, and several financial analysts who not only deal with the company's ongoing capital needs, but also do long-range financial planning. Furthermore, the large company, as a major economic force, may be able to control or influence its industry's markets. For example, it may substantially affect product pricing and developmental trends.

Operationally, large companies tend to be more sophisticated with the latest and most complex technology, possibly including the use of robotics and computer-based cost accounting. Large companies generally have the capitalization, visibility, and operating record to enable them to draw from a wide variety of financial resources, including public debt or equity markets. At this point, the bank is likely to be a secondary provider of funds since public debt markets offer large, successful firms a pricing advantage over borrowing from commercial banks.

MANAGEMENT OBJECTIVES

Management policies and objectives are another factor that distinguishes companies and affects their need for financing and their ability to repay loans. A business with conservative operating policies emphasizes profits over growth, and generally has relatively strict accounts receivable and inventory controls. More aggressive companies tend to incur more debt and favor higher accounts receivable and inventory in their quest to capture a larger share of the market. Such a company might well cut the selling price of its product without a lowering of its costs in order to increase sales. Other companies are less concerned with short-term profits than with long-term maximization of equity. Understanding a company's objectives can help a loan officer put a company's financial statements in perspective and evaluate the company's success in achieving its goals.

Some companies are created because of legal and tax considerations. For example, to lower their taxes, many organizations set up separate companies for the sole purpose of owning property or other fixed assets that are then leased back to the organization. Other businesses, concerned with how their financial statements appear to creditors and investors, might create a separate company to provide off-balance-sheet financing for a portion of the organization's activities.

Only after understanding the objectives of the company can the loan officer begin to answer the questions vital to a financial analysis:

- How successful is the company?

- Can the company meet its objectives?

- What financial needs does the company have as a result of trying to meet its objectives?

- Should the bank attempt to satisfy all or part of the financial needs of the company, and if so, how?

EXTERNAL ENVIRONMENT

A lender must also understand the larger environment in which a company operates. This includes the marketplace in which it operates, the characteristics of the industry, the regulatory environment, the effect of the nation's economy on the business, and its vulnerability to the almost innumerable uncertainties that every company faces to some extent—be it the vagaries of the weather or technological and social change.

Market Characteristics

To put a company's financial results in perspective requires the loan officer to understand the structure of the market in which the company competes. Does it have many competitors or only a few? How easy is it for new competitors to enter the market? Does product differentiation play a major role in a company's success in this industry? To what extent can the company control the price of its products? Is the company an industry leader, or must it be ready to follow the leader's strategy on price, regardless of its own costs? To what extent do demographic and consumer preference trends affect the company? Is the market for the company's product expanding, stable, or contracting? Do sales fluctuate seasonally?

Economic Environment

Interest rates, inflation, tax policies, and the ups and downs of the national economy affect all companies to some extent. Some industries, however, are particularly vulnerable to changes in the general economy. For example, the automobile, construction, and capital goods industries are considered to be cyclical because they are so sensitive to economic downturns and recoveries.

Regulatory Environment

Another important consideration is the extent to which government regulations affect a company. Even industries that are not subject to a high degree of regulation may be subject to import quotas or export bans or price supports or subsidies. Other companies are subject to clean air and clean water regulations which have added tremendously to their cost of doing business. Besides federal regulations, state and local laws may be an important consideration for some companies.

▌ ▌ ▌ ▌ Funds Flow Cycles

The various characteristics of a business discussed in the first part of this chapter are important to financial analysis in part because they affect funds flow, which in turn affects a company's need for bank financing and its ability to repay debt. Most business enterprises rely to some extent on bank loans as a source of financing, or source of funds. These funds may be used to purchase inventory which in turn is used in the production of goods or the delivery of services and then returns to cash (or accounts receivable, and then cash). This cash enables the company to purchase more inventory, thus beginning the funds flow cycle again. An understanding of funds flows, including how funds are generated and used, is critical to the financial analysis process.

Funds include all the economic resources available to a company, not just cash. Although most business transactions do involve cash or cash equivalents, funds also include such noncash economic resources as trade credit and accruals. *Trade credit* results from the common practice of purchasing goods on account, meaning the goods are paid for sometime after they are received. During the time between the purchase and payment for a supplier's goods, trade credit serves as a source of funds.

Accruals are another noncash economic resource involving a promise to pay later for a service performed now. A restaurant owner, for example, may pay its dishwashers and busers weekly for work performed the previous week. Such owed, but unpaid, labor costs constitute another source of funds.

The concept of funds, therefore, includes not only cash and cash-equivalent assets, but other tangible resources or assets (such as inventory or machinery) and intangible economic power (such as the ability to incur debt in the form of trade credit and accruals). Because loans are always made and repaid in cash, a company's cash-to-cash cycle is of particular interest to a loan officer. Nevertheless, a company's

EXHIBIT 2.1 ■■■■■■■■■■■■■■■■■■■■■■■■■■■■■■■■■■

Funds Flow Cycle of Retailer

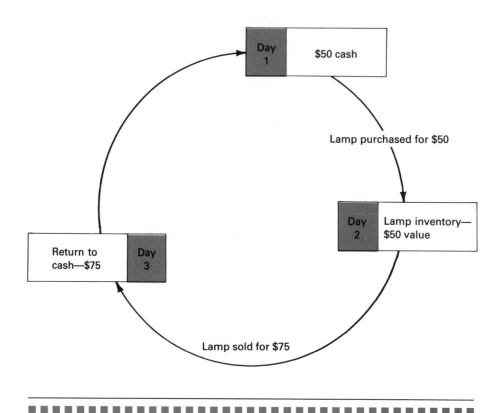

performance must be measured by taking into account all the resources employed in the business operation. By measuring both the amount of funds allocated and the efficiency of their use, the commercial loan officer can evaluate the success of the company's funds management and the risk associated with any loans made to the company.

SIMPLE FUNDS FLOW CYCLES

Funds flow in a business operation generally follows a repetitive pattern, or cycle. The cycle begins with cash (originally the owners' investment in the business and later cash representing profits) which is converted into other resources (generally inventory first and then accounts receivable), and then returns to cash (when accounts receivable are paid) within a specified period. In a retailing or wholesaling firm, funds move from cash to inventory and back to cash. In a manufacturing firm, labor that is applied to the inventory also is part of the funds flow cycle. In a service company, cash is used to perform a service, which results in cash (or accounts receivable and then cash).

Uses of Funds

To illustrate a simple funds flow cycle, consider the Anderson Light Company, a business that purchases and resells lamps at a profit. On day one, the Anderson Light Company has $50 in cash in its bank account. On day two, the company purchases a lamp from its wholesale suppliers for $50. Then, on day three, the company sells the lamp for $75 cash. Thus the company realizes a $25 profit for the work involved in purchasing and reselling the lamp. Exhibit 2.1 illustrates this simple funds flow cycle.

Most businesses, of course, involve more complex operations than simply purchasing and reselling a single product. Assume that Anderson Light Company buys unassembled lamp parts, employs people to assemble the lamps in its shop, and then sells the completed lamps. Exhibit 2.2 illustrates this slightly longer cycle. It shows that on day one the Anderson Light Company has $50 in its account. On day two, the company pays $35 for lamp parts. On day three, employees assemble the lamp and place it on the showroom floor. They are paid $15. On day four, the lamp is sold for $75 cash. Anderson Light still makes a $25

Funds Flow Cycle of Manufacturer

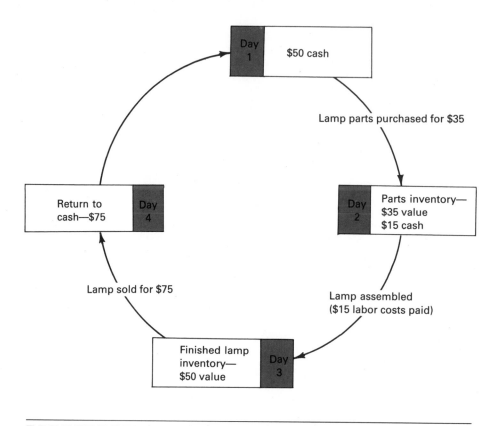

profit on its original $50 investment, but the length of its funds flow cycle is increased when it assembles as well as retails lamps.

The length of the company's funds flow cycle further increases if the lamp is sold on credit, as Exhibit 2.3 illustrates. In this example, the lamp is sold on day four on 30-day terms. This creates accounts receivable and greatly lengthens the funds flow cycle, assuming the customer waits until day 34 to pay for the lamp. In the meantime, the company has no cash to make more lamps or to pay its employees.

The preceding examples illustrate that the funds flow cycle reflects the type of operation in which a company engages (a retail operation versus a manufacturing operation). They also illustrate how management decisions can affect the funds flow cycle (in this case, by its decision to sell the lamps on credit).

Sources of Funds

Up to this point, the company's use of funds in its operation (to buy inventory and pay for labor) has been considered, but not the question of where those funds came from (the source of funds). It was assumed that the Anderson Light Company had sufficient cash to purchase parts, pay for labor, and wait 30 days to collect the proceeds of a sale.

Equity. The amount of money invested in the business's operation by the company's owner (the original $50) is considered *invested equity.* Invested equity is one of the major sources of funds available to businesses—and may be the only source available to a new business. But what happens if a company does not have sufficient equity to sustain its entire funds flow cycle? Specifically, what would happen if the Anderson Light Company started out with only $40 worth of equity? Exhibit 2.4 illustrates this situation.

After spending $35 on lamp parts, the company has only $5 left, whereas labor to assemble the lamp costs $15. The Anderson Light Company here faces a classic business dilemma—a shortage of funds. The *shortfall* is only $10, but the company needs that money to hire the necessary labor to assemble the lamp. Once assembled, the lamp can be sold for a profit and the workers paid. But if the company cannot complete its operating cycle, it fails. Failure to complete the operating cycle is a common cause of problem loans.

How can a company with insufficient equity raise money to enable it to complete its operating cycle? It could go to its bank and request a short-

Funds Flow Cycle with Accounts Receivable

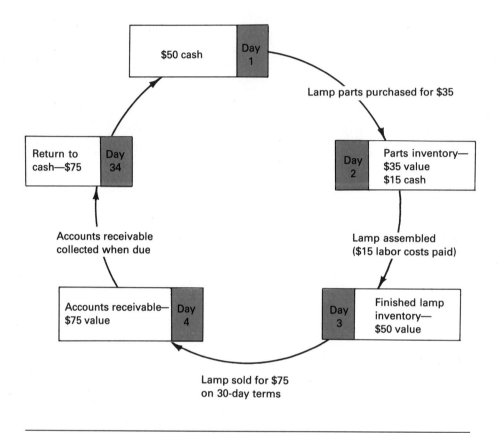

Incomplete Funds Flow Cycle

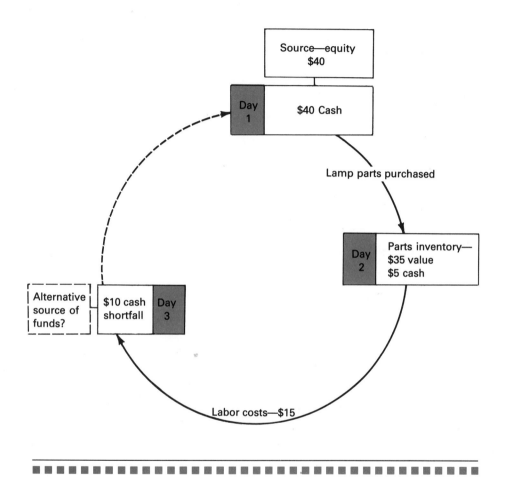

Incomplete Funds Flow Cycle: Use of Trade Credit to Delay Shortfall

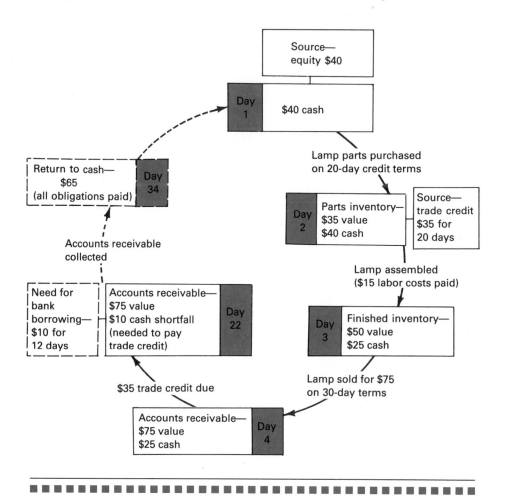

term loan. However, because loans cost money in the form of interest payments and thus reduce the company's profits, the company may consider other sources of funds first—such as trade credit, labor accruals, or a reduction of sale terms.

Trade credit. The Anderson Light Company might try to negotiate credit terms with its supplier of lamp parts. If its supplier will allow 20-day payment terms, for instance, the resulting funds flow cycle is that illustrated in Exhibit 2.5.

In this scenario, the Anderson Light Company has $40 in its account on day one. The next day, the company purchases $35 worth of lamp parts and promises to pay for them on day 22. Thus, the company still has $40 cash at its disposal. On the third day, Anderson Light Company uses $15 of its cash reserves to hire laborers to assemble the lamp parts. On the fourth day, the lamp is sold on 30-day terms. On day 22, the bill for lamp parts comes due at which point Anderson Light Company again faces a $10 shortfall. Unless the company can raise the additional $10, its supplier must wait for payment until day 34, when the customer's payment of $75 becomes due. If this fails to satisfy the supplier, the company may still need to request a short-term loan. However, the company now needs to borrow the $10 for only 12 days, rather than for 30 days (as required in the previous scenario).

Accruals. Another strategy Anderson Light Company might use to complete its funds flow cycle would be to adopt a policy of deferring the payment of its workers for a week. This is in effect a source of funds called labor accrual. The company's funds flow cycle would then look like that in Exhibit 2.6. Again, the Anderson Light Company begins with $40 in equity and spends $35 for lamp parts. Since it pays cash for the supplies, it now has a $5 balance. On day three, the employees assemble the lamp but agree to be paid one week later. On the fourth day, a customer purchases the lamp on 30-day terms. On day 10, the $15 labor expense comes due, but the company has only a $5 cash balance. Again, the company finds itself $10 short and must borrow from the bank for 24 days until the customer's $75 payment comes due. While this is preferable to borrowing for 30 days, it is not as effective a solution in this case as negotiating trade credit terms.

Reduction of credit sale terms. Another strategy that Anderson Light Company could adopt to alleviate its cash shortfall would be to reduce

Incomplete Funds Flow Cycle: Use of Labor Accrual to Delay Shortfall

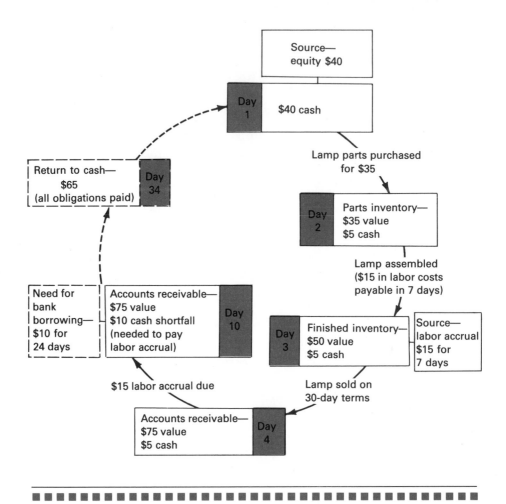

the credit terms offered to its customers. Suppose the company reduced the credit terms extended to its customers from 30 days to 18 days and was also able to negotiate 20-day trade credit with its supplier. The company's funds flow cycle would now look like that depicted in Exhibit 2.7.

On day one, the company has $40 in its account. The next day, the company purchases $35 in lamp parts on credit, promising to pay for them in 20 days. Employees assemble the lamp on the third day and receive $15 in payment. On the fourth day, a customer purchases the lamp for $75 on 18-day terms. On day 22, both the company's $35 bill for parts and the customer's $75 payment for the lamp come due, enabling Anderson Light Company to meet its debt obligation (assuming the customer pays by the due date). Moreover, the company still makes a $25 profit on its original investment.

REPETITIVE FUNDS FLOW CYCLES

The preceding examples illustrate some common funding needs and funding sources available to companies. For all businesses, the level of the owners' equity investment determines the need for and availability of funds. However, management policies such as the payment terms that it extends to customers and the terms that it negotiates with suppliers (trade credit) and employees (accruals) also affect a company's funding needs. Since businesses frequently ask banks to bridge their funding shortfall, it is important that loan officers understand the various factors that can determine both the amount and duration of the company's need for bank credit.

In all of the previous examples, it was assumed that the Anderson Light Company began with cash, initiated its operating cycle, and completed that cycle before initiating debt again. This is a useful way to show how a funds flow cycle operates, but is not very realistic. A company could hardly survive or prosper by selling only one lamp every 35 days at a $25 profit. Imagine, instead, that the company repeatedly initiates its funds flow cycle. That is, it buys parts for a lamp each day beginning with day two, hires workers to assemble a lamp each day beginning with day three, and sells one lamp each day beginning with day four. Exhibit 2.8 shows the resulting repetitive funds flow schedule assuming

Complete Funds Flow Cycle

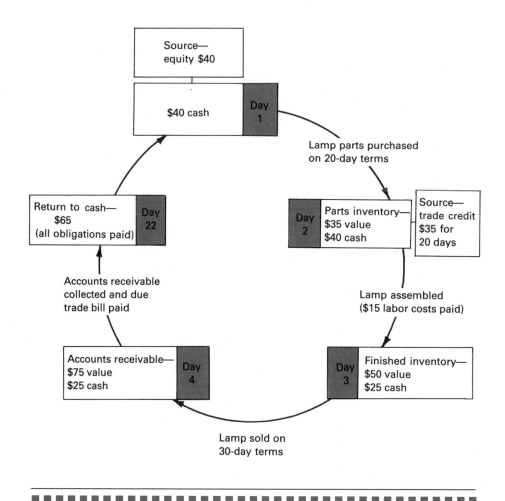

the company has negotiated a 7-day labor accrual, offers its customers 30-day payment terms, and negotiates 20-day trade credit terms with its supplier.

- *Day one.* The company has $50 in its account. This amount is shown in both the Beginning Funds and Net Funds Available columns.

- *Day two.* The company purchases $35 worth of lamp parts on 20-day terms. The company still has $50 in its account, and the $35 purchase is shown in the Accounts Payable column.

- *Day three.* Employees assemble the lamp in exchange for the company's promise to pay $15 one week later. This amount is shown in the Accruals column. The company also purchases another $35 worth of lamp parts, again on 20-day terms. (The company will pay its trade credit daily as it comes due.) The $35 purchase is added to the Accounts Payable column.

- *Day four.* The company sells the first lamp for $75 on 30-day terms. This amount is shown in the Accounts Receivable column. Employees assemble the second lamp, again in exchange for the company's promise to pay them one week later. (The company will pay wages daily, but with a week's lag time.) Thus another $15 is added to the Accruals column. The company buys a third set of lamp parts for $35, again on 20-day terms, an amount that is added to the Accounts Payable column.

- *Days five to nine.* On each of these days, the company sells one lamp on 30-day terms, assembles one lamp with a promise to pay its workers in 7 days, and purchases parts for one additional lamp on 20-day terms. These transactions are all reflected in the appropriate columns of the funds flow schedule.

- *Days 10 to 12.* The company pays the $15 daily labor expense incurred on days three to five. These transactions are shown in the Amount Disbursed (Labor) column. The Net Funds Available column is reduced each day in recognition of these payments. Each day's purchase of inventory continues to increase the Accounts Payable column. The amount in the Accruals column now remains unchanged as the amount disbursed for labor each day and the daily labor costs incurred cancel each other. The company's daily sales are added to the Accounts Receivable column.

EXHIBIT 2.8 ■■■■■■■■■■■■■■■■■■■■■■■■■■■■■■■■■■■■

Repetitive Funds Flow Schedule

Day	Beginning Funds	Amount Collected	Amount Disbursed (Parts)	Amount Disbursed (Labor)	Net Funds Available	Accounts Receivable	Accruals	Accounts Payable
1	50	0	0	0	50	0	0	0
2	50	0	0	0	50	0	0	35
3	50	0	0	0	50	0	15	70
4	50	0	0	0	50	75	30	105
5	50	0	0	0	50	150	45	140
6	50	0	0	0	50	225	60	175
7	50	0	0	0	50	300	75	210
8	50	0	0	0	50	375	90	245
9	50	0	0	0	50	450	105	280
10	50	0	0	15	35	525	105	315
11	35	0	0	15	20	600	105	340
12	20	0	0	15	5	675	105	375
13	5	0	0	15	(10)	750	105	410
14	(10)	0	0	15	(25)	825	105	445
15	(25)	0	0	15	(40)	900	105	480
16	(40)	0	0	15	(55)	975	105	415
17	(55)	0	0	15	(70)	1,050	105	440
18	(70)	0	0	15	(85)	1,125	105	475
19	(85)	0	0	15	(100)	1,200	105	510
20	(100)	0	0	15	(115)	1,275	105	545
21	(115)	0	0	15	(130)	1,350	105	580
22	(130)	0	35	15	(180)	1,425	105	580
23	(180)	0	35	15	(230)	1,500	105	580
24	(230)	0	35	15	(380) 280	1,575	105	580
25	(380) 280	0	35	15	(430) 330	1,650	105	580
26	(430) 330	0	35	15	(480) 380	1,725	105	580
27	(480) 380	0	35	15	(530) 430	1,800	105	580
28	(530) 430	0	35	15	(580) 480	1,875	105	580
29	(580) 480	0	35	15	(630) 530	1,950	105	580
30	(630) 530	0	35	15	(680) 580	2,025	105	580
31	(680) 580	0	35	15	(730) 630	2,100	105	580
32	(730) 630	0	35	15	(780) 680	2,175	105	580
33	(780) 680	0	35	15	(830) 730	2,250	105	580
34	(830) 730	75	35	15	(805) 705	2,250	105	580

Note: Negative numbers indicate borrowing needs.

- *Day 13.* The company owes $15 in labor costs but has only $5 in its account, as shown in the Beginning Funds column. Therefore, if employees are to be paid as promised, the company must borrow from the bank. The amount of shortfall is shown as a negative $10 in the Net Funds Available column. (Any negative amount in this column depicts borrowing needs.) All the transactions of previous days are again repeated.

- *Days 14 to 21.* On each of these days, the company owes $15 more for labor expense incurred the previous week, which it can pay only by borrowing. This is shown with a steadily increasing negative balance in the Beginning Funds and Net Funds Available columns. The company continues to repeat all of the previous transactions.

- *Day 22.* In addition to the daily labor expense coming due, the company's accounts payable now begin to come due. Specifically, it needs to pay $35 for parts it purchased on day two. Again, the company cannot pay this obligation without borrowing from the bank. Payment of this obligation is reflected in both the Amount Disbursed (Parts) column and as a negative increase to the Net Funds Available column. Note that the amount in the Accounts Payable column is no longer increasing since the company is both making new purchases on credit and paying the same amount to the supplier for parts as the bills come due each day.

- *Days 23 to 33.* All of the transactions on these days are the same as those on day 22. The Accounts Receivable column continues to increase, as does the amount owed (shown as negative increases in the Net Funds Available and Beginning Funds columns).

- *Day 34.* The company collects its first receivable—the $75 owed for the purchase on day four—and can now pay its $15 labor obligation plus its $35 parts obligation maturing this day without any further borrowing. The company also has excess cash (its $25 profit) from which it can begin paying back the bank loan that was incurred on days 13 to 33.

Consider what has happened. The Anderson Light Company began with $50 equity and used other financial sources (trade credit and labor accruals), but still came up with a funds shortfall that began on day 13 and increased daily until day 33. Some conclusions can be drawn from this ongoing scenario.

An ongoing business cycle requires much more funding than indicated by the simple funds flow cycles illustrated previously. In general, large operations require larger amounts of funding than small operations. Moreover, the funding requirements for *repetitive* business operations become permanent. In the single cycle described in Exhibit 2.5, the company initiated trade credit on day two and repaid it on day 22. In the ongoing cycle, the company initiates trade credit every day. Cumulative trade credit continued to grow each day until day 22, when it leveled off—for each successive day's new trade bill of $35, there was a $35 payment. Bank debt in this situation is considered to be permanent because the company will continue to require funding of its accounts receivable. Generally, in repetitive business operations, funding requirements not only vary with the company's size and rate of growth, but become permanent instead of temporary.

Of course, business operations generate funds as well as use them. In the single funds flow cycle illustrated in Exhibit 2.3, the $25 in excess cash generated on day 34 was of little immediate consequence insofar as the company also regained its original $50 investment and had no outstanding funding needs. However, in the repetitive cycle, the company has incurred extensive liabilities by day 34 that it would do well to begin repaying.

The $25 worth of excess cash generated each day thereafter becomes available to amortize the company's bank debt. The company now has another, and in the long run, the most important source of funds— funds generated by the business operation itself. If an operation cannot generate its own source of funds, it cannot hope to create a profit and repay debt. Also, outside sources of funds such as suppliers and banks do not like to increase their credit extensions to a company without first seeing proportional increases in the business's equity funding. Therefore, the proven ability of a company to generate excess cash not only of itself provides an additional source of funding, but may encourage outside credit sources to further finance the business. In other words, a company's own ability to generate funds is a major determinant of its ability to grow.

FUNDS FLOW ANALYSIS

A company normally begins its operation with cash. Later, that cash converts into a succession of working assets, such as accounts receivable, inventory, and labor accruals, before returning to cash. However, a company's funds flow cycle reflects both the complexity of the operation (the number and timing of funds flow steps), the practices typically associated with the particular business or industry (trade terms, manufacturing methods, and marketing practices), and various management strategies (such as offering credit to customers to encourage sales).

Business operations create many funds requirements, such as the purchase of inventory and the payment of labor. A primary rule of funds flow analysis is that all funds uses involve either the creation or purchase of an asset (for example, inventory—including the labor to assemble it) or the reduction of a liability (through payment of due obligations).

Normal sources of funds include owners' equity, trade credit, bank credit, accruals, and the reduction of assets (for example, by shortening the accounts receivable terms). The second cardinal rule of funds flow analysis then is that all sources of funds involve either the creation of an obligation (whether to creditors or equity owners) or the reduction of assets.

An analysis of a company's funds flows may show inappropriate sources or uses of funds. If a company cannot pay its suppliers or labor at the agreed time, then those funding sources are inappropriate because they are involuntary (and may lead to severe problems such as legal action by creditors). Sale of an asset required for the company's efficient operation would be another inappropriate source of funds. The purchasing of excess inventory would be an inappropriate use of funds if the funds could better be spent to reduce debt.

What is the lender's role in a company's generation and repayment of funds? In the case of the Anderson Light Company, its funds uses exceeded both its original funding source (equity) and its ability to generate other sources of funds (accruals and trade credit). Consequently, the company asked its banker to provide working capital funding. In the single funds flow cycle, this need was temporary in that the funding was required for only a short period—until the accounts receivable could be converted into cash. However, the single cycle illustrated in the example was unrealistic; funds sources of repetitive cycles usually need to be permanent rather than temporary.

Does this mean that the bank's role always involves *permanent* rather than *temporary* funding? No. Because repetitive cycles vary over time (for example, 25 lamps assembled and sold one month versus 30 lamps the next month), temporary needs are created within repetitive cycles. The classic example of this is a company's seasonal buildup of inventory and receivables before Christmas. The bank provides the funding for the shortfall between the level of buildup (funds usage) and the support of that buildup (funds available). The company then repays the debt all at once or over a short period after reducing or liquidating the level of buildup.

Moreover, the bank's role as a provider of permanent operating funds does not mean the company never repays the bank. It does mean that because the bank loan supports the company's continuing needs, the bank cannot look to the reduction or elimination of those needs over a short period as the basis for repayment. It must look instead to the company's ability to generate, over time, funds in excess of those expended that can be used to repay debt. In other words, the company must replace the bank as a funding source with another funding source—that is, additional equity in the form of excess cash generated by the funds flow cycle. Understanding whether funding is permanent or temporary enables the loan officer to understand a company's debt structure and the degree of risk entailed in lending it money.

A company's ability to grow often relates directly to the bank's willingness to provide permanent funds. As the business operation grows, so does its needs for funding, including bank debt. The need for bank debt will level off only when the size of the operation itself levels off and when the operation begins to generate its own funds. Generally, the size and importance of the bank's role in providing operating funds depends on at least four factors:

- the operation's rate of growth

- characteristics of the company's funds usage (for example, how long inventory is held)

- the availability of other external funding sources (such as trade credit or accruals)

- the ability of the company to generate its own funds internally

However, a business operation that is not growing can also have increased funding needs—either inadvertently or by design. For example, increased funding needs can result from a buildup of inventories beyond the level necessary to meet expected customer demands. Increased funding needs can also arise from a management decision to increase terms of credit sales in response to a similar move by the competition or in an attempt to increase its own competitive edge.

Because the bank's role is largely determined by the funding requirements of the company, it is critical that the commercial loan officer understand a company's funds flow requirements and their implications. Specific techniques for analyzing funds flows are discussed in greater detail in Chapter 5.

▌▌▌▌▌ The Fixed Asset Cycle

The discussion of funds flow thus far has been concerned with the *funds flow cycle*, which involved the conversion of cash into operating assets and then back into cash within a short period. But that cash conversion process does not take place in a vacuum. Businesses need facilities to house their operations and tools to perform their tasks. The Anderson Light Company, for example, might need offices for its sales and administrative staff, space for the assembly process, and a warehouse for its inventory. It might also need production equipment (such as a drill press) and other equipment (perhaps a delivery van). Assets needed to support a company's operation are referred to as *fixed assets* or *capital assets*. The acquisition, funding, use, and replacement of fixed assets is called the *fixed asset cycle* because the company uses the assets again and again through a number of operating cycles rather than expending them or converting them to cash within a single cycle. Most fixed assets are, however, eventually expended through their repeated use in the production process and must eventually be replaced. Because replacement is usually several years later, replacement lost is higher and needs to be considered in funds flow analysis.

The fixed asset cycle, like the funds flow cycle, begins with the expenditure of cash to acquire or create an asset. The company does not, however, convert the fixed asset back into cash. A manufacturer does not sell its drill press, for example, to create an account receivable that is later collected to produce cash. Nevertheless, fixed assets do play a critical part in the cash generation cycle. The company's products cannot be created or its services delivered without the support of the company's fixed assets. Thus, the company recovers the original cash expenditure for the fixed asset, but only over time and only through the profitable sale of the products that the fixed asset helps create. During this time, the fixed assets generally depreciate in value.

A company must have adequate fixed assets to support its funds flow cycle. Additionally, the company must structure its funding of those fixed assets to avoid disrupting the operation of the business. Funding for the fixed assets can come from three sources: excess cash, equity contribution, or debt. Of these, debt is the most common funding source for fixed assets. The company's funds flow cycle generates the funds to repay the debt. However, funds generated through the funds flow cycle must first be used to replenish the company's operating assets, such as inventory and receivables. Only the excess cash, or profits, are available to purchase fixed assets or service debt. Also, those profits are only available to the extent that they are not used for some other purpose, such as to fund growth. Therefore, the commercial loan officer should structure loans for the purchase of fixed assets in such a way that companies can repay these debts with profits generated through the use of the fixed assets in the funds flow cycle.

In summary, the funds flow cycle and the fixed asset cycle comprise all the funds movement related to a company's basic operations. Those cycles must generate sufficient funds to replenish working capital, provide for growth, and repay debt incurred to acquire fixed assets. Any other funds requirements are outside the company's primary operation, and management should consider these needs only after the company has adequately provided for the funding requirements of the funds flow and fixed asset cycles.

▌▌▌▌▌▌▌ The Profit Cycle: Accrual Vs. Cash Accounting

Besides the funds flow and fixed asset cycles, which provide the cash flow required to repay debt, another useful way of looking at a company's operations is in terms of its profit cycle. The components of the profit cycle involve a company's recognition of income and the expenses related thereto and the resulting profit or loss. It is important to understand that recognition of profit does not generally coincide with a company's cash flow. In fact, while all companies seek to maximize their cash flow (since this is the medium for paying bills, loans, salaries, dividends, etc.), not all companies try to maximize profits. In fact, many privately held companies try to minimize reported earnings. However, because most financial statements are earnings-oriented rather than cash-oriented, it is important to understand both the profit cycle and the cash cycle—and to be able to make the transition between the two.

Most companies prepare their financial statements using accrual accounting rather than cash accounting. Accrual accounting recognizes revenues as earned when sales are transacted, regardless of when the company actually receives payment. Expenses are likewise recognized when they are incurred rather than when payment is made. Cash accounting, on the other hand, recognizes revenues as earned when payment is received, regardless of the timing of the transaction. Likewise, the company expenses the cost associated with producing these revenues only when the funds are actually paid out. For example, if a company with a calendar-year fiscal period sold $2,000 worth of products on December 20, 1988, with payment due on January 20, 1989, the $2,000 would be recognized as 1988 revenue under the accrual method, but as 1989 revenue under the cash method.

Although cash accounting provides a clearer picture of a company's cash flow, companies use accrual accounting for financial reporting purposes because it matches related revenues and expenses, thus providing a more accurate measure of the company's earnings. To illustrate this, assume that the Photo Dealer, a wholesaler of photographic equipment, opened for business on November 1, 1988. Exhibit 2.9 shows the company's cash-basis income statement prepared for November and December. The company buys cameras for $125 each, paying for them at the time of purchase. It rents office and warehouse facilities for $500 per month and pays an average of $200 per month for utilities. The company pays both the rent and the utility bills on the 15th day of each month.

On November 1, the Photo Dealer purchases 40 cameras for $125 each (or a total of $5,000). The next day, the company sells 30 cameras at $200 each. The cameras will be delivered to Photo Dealer's retail customers during November. The cameras are sold on 30-day terms, due December 2. On December 8, the Photo Dealer sells 10 cameras at $100 each, a 50 percent pre-Christmas discount intended to clear remaining inventory. These cameras are delivered in December, with payment due upon receipt of the merchandise. On a cash basis, the business appears

Cash-Basis Income Statement

Photo Dealer
Income Statement (Cash Basis)

	Month Ended 11/30/88	Month Ended 12/31/88
Sales (revenues)	—	$7,000
Purchases	$ 5,000	—
Gross profit	(5,000)	7,000
Utilities and rent	700	700
Profit (loss)	$(5,700)	$6,300

Accrual-Basis Income Statement

Photo Dealer
Income Statement (Accrual Basis)

	Month Ended 11/30/88	Month Ended 12/31/88
Revenue	$6,000	$1,000
Cost of goods sold	3,750	1,250
Gross profit	2,250	(250)
Utilities and rent	700	700
Net income (loss)	$1,550	$ (950)

to have lost money in November, whereas December's profits were excellent.

Accrual accounting, which matches revenues with expenses, tells quite a different story. It shows that November was a profitable month for the Photo Dealer, whereas December was unprofitable. Recall that during November, the Photo Dealer sold 30 cameras for $200, resulting in a $75 profit on each camera. However, in December, the company sold 10 cameras for $100 each, for a $25 loss per camera. Although the business had excess cash in December (as shown in the cash-basis statement), the extra funds were not due to an effective sales strategy. Exhibit 2.10 shows the company's interim income statement calculated on an accrual basis.

In the two income statements for the Photo Dealer, the total profit for the 2-month period equals the amount of cash generated ($600 in each case). In an actual situation, the amount of profit or loss shown on an accrual-basis income statement would normally be quite different from the company's cash flow. That is why lenders use funds flow statements (discussed in Chapter 5) and cash budgets (discussed in Chapter 8) to determine the timing and amount of a company's cash requirements over time which may not be evident from an analysis of a company's accrual-basis financial statements. Nevertheless, the profit cycle, as reflected in a company's financial statements, is a better reflection of how efficiently a company has managed its assets to generate revenues and earnings. Thus both profit and cash cycles are important to financial analysis.

▌▐ ▐ ▐ ▐ Summary

From the outset, it is important that the loan officer have a good understanding of the company that is to be the subject of financial analysis. This requires first of all an understanding of the five basic types of businesses—manufacturers, wholesalers, retailers, service companies, and agricultural businesses—each of which has a characteristic operating cycle resulting in differing funding needs. Other factors that need to be considered include the legal structure of the business, its size and rapidity of growth, its management policies and objectives, and the company's external environment—that is, the marketplace in which it operates. Together these factors provide a meaningful context for the ensuing financial analysis.

An understanding of the company's business operations will also help a lender understand its funds flow cycle. As was illustrated by the various scenarios involving the Anderson Light Company, funds flow cycles may utilize various sources of funds—including equity, trade credit, accruals, and bank loans. The scenarios also showed how repetitive funds cycles tend to create the need for permanent financing—an important concept underlying financial analysis.

A loan officer must also understand a company's fixed asset cycle and how it relates to the funds flow cycle, as well as the company's profit cycle—including the distinction between profitability as shown by accrual-basis financial statements and actual cash flow. With this background, the loan officer is ready to tackle a company's financial statements.

Questions

1. Identify the five major types of business operations, and discuss how their operating cycles, financial structure, and need for funds differ.

2. Name the three principal legal structures a business may have, and explain how a business's legal status affects bank lending.

3. How can management's objectives affect a company's funding requirements?

4. How does business size affect a company's loan requirements?

5. Describe the concept of funds flow. What are funds? What are the principal sources of funds? How do businesses use funds? How does funds flow affect a company's ability to repay debt?

6. What is a repetitive funds flow cycle? How does it affect a company's loan requirements and its repayment of debt?

7. Describe the relationship between the funds flow cycle and the fixed asset cycle, and explain how these cycles affect the repayment of debt.

8. Explain the difference between accrual and cash accounting. Why is a company's profit cycle not the same as its cash-generating cycles?

Exercises

E-1

Diagram the funds flow cycle of a retail department store that sells on a cash basis. Assume the following: the beginning cash balance is $100, merchandise costs $135, the supplier grants 10-day terms, merchandise stays in inventory for 13 days, and the merchandise sells for $225 cash. Then answer the following questions:

a. How does this cycle differ from that of a manufacturer?

b. What is the amount of funding shortfall? How can the shortfall be alleviated?

E-2

Diagram a fixed asset cycle. Assume that the cost of a new loom is $100,000 and that it is funded at purchase by a $100,000 bank loan. The interest expense over the term of the loan will be $20,000.

The loom is used in a textile manufacturing process that averages 30 days in its cycle. The completion of each operating cycle produces cash flow of $3,000, which is used to service the debt and for the company's other cash requirements, which come to approximately $12,000 per year. Then answer the following questions:

a. How long will it take to repay the loan? [Hint: First calculate the amount of cash flow per year available to service the debt.]

b. What factors could affect repayment?

c. Explain how the fixed asset is "converted into cash."

E-3

Create a funds flow schedule (using the format shown in Exhibit 2.8), which tracks the first 25 days of operation of a wholesale company.

Assume that the company pays $25 per ton for its inventory and that purchases are on 5-day terms. One ton of the product is purchased on day one. Thereafter one more ton of the product is bought each day through day nine (that is, two tons are bought on day two, three tons on day three, etc.). Thereafter, purchase volume remains unchanged at nine tons per day.

All products are sold on the day after purchase for a selling price of $40 per ton. Therefore there is no inventory buildup. Sales are on 10-day credit terms.

Labor expense totals $40 per day and is payable in 7 days and daily thereafter. Beginning cash totals $100.

3 The Income Statement

Learning Objectives

After studying this chapter, you should be able to

- identify the basic components of an income statement
- spread and common-size an income statement
- apply the concepts of comparison, change, distribution analysis, and projection in revenue analysis
- differentiate between those expenses that are included in cost of goods sold and those that are included as operating expenses
- explain the difference between cost of goods sold and gross margin for a manufacturer and for a wholesale or retail operation
- explain the difference between LIFO and FIFO and how the inventory valuation method affects a company's profitability
- explain what kinds of income and expenses are categorized as nonoperating, or "other," income and expenses on an income statement

▌▌▌▌▌▌▌▌ Introduction

The income statement, also called a *profit and loss statement* or *earnings statement*, matches a company's total revenues with its total expenses over a stated period of time, usually a fiscal year. Because income statements represent the best measure of a company's ability to use its resources to earn profits, commercial loan officers rely on the income statement as the primary tool for evaluating a company's long-range viability. Generally lenders require prospective borrowers to submit both income statements and balance sheets for the past 2 or 3 years. These two basic financial statements are at the core of any financial analysis. The income statement and the balance sheet (the subject of Chapter 4) are closely related and thus must be analyzed relative to each other. But because sales are the primary basis for a company's existence, the analysis starts with the income statement.

Income statement analysis consists of two basic functions—revenue analysis and expense analysis. Companies are profitable when their revenues exceed the expenses incurred in generating those revenues. Since a company's profitability is a primary determinant of its ability to repay debt, this is a major factor in the lender's decision to extend credit.

▌▌▌▌▌▌▌▌ Preliminary Considerations

Before analyzing a company's income statement, the loan officer must first consider such factors as what method the company uses to recognize revenue and expenses, who prepared the statements, and whether they are fiscal year or interim statements. In addition, the loan officer must consider the income statement in the context of what kind of business the company is engaged in and the characteristics of the market in which the company operates (as discussed in more detail in Chapter 2).

PERIOD OF INCOME STATEMENT

An income statement covering a normal business cycle of 12 months is called a *fiscal statement*. Income statements prepared for periods of less than 12 months are called *interim statements*. It is a generally accepted accounting principle (GAAP) that businesses do not prepare income statements for periods of more than 12 months. The most common interim periods are semiannual (every 6 months), quarterly (every 3 months), and monthly. Year-to-date figures compiled at the end of any month during the year can also serve as interim statements. Therefore, the time represented by an interim statement can be from 1 to 11 months.

REVENUE AND EXPENSE RECOGNITION

As discussed in Chapter 2, most financial statements are prepared on an accrual basis, rather than a cash basis. Thus revenues are recognized when sales are made, not when payment is received, and expenses are recognized when they are incurred, not when payment is made. However, certain expenses that relate directly to sales—called *cost of goods sold* on the income statement—are not recognized until the inventory item or manufactured product is actually sold. Thus a buildup in inventory (for a wholesaler or retailer) or in raw materials, work-in-process, or unsold finished goods (for a manufacturer) does not affect a company's profits since inventory expenses are recognized only when matched to the revenues they help produce.

Accrual-basis accounting allows operating expenses to be recognized in one period (the period in which they are incurred), but paid for in a prior or a subsequent period. If an item is paid for in one period and recorded as an expense in a later period, the item is carried as an asset (called a *prepaid expense*) on the balance sheet. If, on the other hand, expenses are recognized before they are paid, they are considered liabilities (called *accruals*) on the balance sheet. Both prepaid expenses and accruals are discussed more fully in Chapter 4.

TYPE OF BUSINESS

As discussed in Chapter 2, manufacturers, wholesalers, retailers, service companies, and agricultural enterprises have distinctly different operating characteristics. These differences are reflected in their income statements. For example, relative to other types of businesses, manufacturing companies generally have a higher gross profit as a percentage of sales (the gross profit margin). A healthy gross profit margin is deemed more important for a manufacturer than for other types of companies because manufacturing is considered to be the riskiest of all types of businesses. A high gross profit margin helps alleviate the greater risk involved in lending funds to manufacturers. A manufacturer's operating expenses as a percentage of sales are also large due to distribution, marketing, and administrative costs.

The gross profit margin of wholesalers is usually not as large as that of manufacturers, and their operating costs are also usually relatively low. Because wholesalers merely handle merchandise (rather than producing it), there is less danger of a wholesaler absorbing significant losses if a product loses consumer acceptance or becomes obsolete, or if the wholesaler keeps inventory under control and with little concentration in specific items.

Retailers normally have a gross profit margin larger than that of wholesalers, reflecting the higher markup they take on purchased goods. This is necessary because their operating expenses generally include advertising costs, salesclerks' salaries, showroom decor, shelving, and other merchandising expenses not incurred by wholesalers.

Gross profit among service companies is the same as revenue since they have no inventory purchases (cost of goods sold) to be deducted from revenue. All expenses incurred by service companies are considered as operating expenses.

Agricultural businesses, like manufacturers, create products. Therefore, their gross profit margin should be comparatively large relative to other types of companies to compensate for the considerable risk involved.

MARKET CHARACTERISTICS

The framework for income statement analysis also requires an understanding of the company's markets. A loan officer should be able to identify both internal and external factors—that is, factors that can be controlled by the company and those over which it has no control—that contribute to the demand for its particular products or services.

External Factors

External factors that influence the demand for products and services but which normally lie outside the control of a company's management include the competitiveness of the market, government regulations affecting the industry, and the overall state of the economy. For example, the loan officer should determine whether the market for the company's product is expanding, stable, or contracting; whether current regulatory requirements are likely to change; what companies provide the principal competition and the basis for the competition; and to what extent general economic conditions tend to affect the company's profitability.

As mentioned in Chapter 2, if a company's sales fluctuate with the seasons, the company faces an external factor called *seasonality*. A boat dealer, for example, usually sees heavy sales from spring through summer, with business almost nonexistent for the remainder of the year. General merchandise retailers, on the other hand, encounter heavy sales in November and December due to holiday shopping. Recognizing seasonality is particularly important when analyzing interim (partial-year) income statements.

Cyclicality is another external factor characterized by fluctuations in revenues between operating cycles caused by a reaction to the expansion or contraction of general business activity. For example, the automobile, construction, and capital goods industries are considered cyclical because they tend to prosper in good economic climates and suffer during economic downturns.

Products and services also have their own life cycles. They begin as an idea, are transformed into an entity for sale, and are marketed until they stop selling profitably. The business then discontinues the product or service. The product life cycle may be very short for a fad product or very long for a staple product. The commercial loan officer needs to consider at what stage of their life cycle a company's products or services are. This may be difficult to determine because unforeseen consumer trends and new technology may shorten a product's life cycle. For example, the demand for citizens band (CB) radios skyrocketed in the 1970s, then dropped precipitously after a few years when consumer interest waned. Nevertheless, evaluating the probability of continued profitable sales for a company's product or service is critical to an effective analysis.

Income Statement Spreadsheet

Name

	Operations	Period Date		%		%		%		%	I.S.
1	NET SALES			100		100		100		100	100
2	COST OF GOODS SOLD										
3	GROSS PROFIT/REVENUES										
4	Officers' salaries										
5	Selling expenses										
6	General and administrative expenses										
7	TOTAL OPERATING EXPENSES										
8	OPERATING PROFIT										
9	Other income										
10	Other expense										
11	Interest expense										
12	PROFIT BEFORE TAX										
13	Income taxes										
14	NET PROFIT AFTER TAX										
15	R	Net worth—beginning									
16	E	Add: net profit									
17	C	Retained earnings credits									
18	O	Less: net loss									
19	N	Dividends—preferred									
20	C	—common									
21	I	Retained earnings debits									
22	L	RETAINED EARNINGS—Increase or decrease									
23		Paid-in surplus credits									
24	O	Paid-in surplus debits									
25	F	Capital accounts—Increase or decrease									
26	N	NET WORTH—Increase or decrease									
27	W	Net worth—ending									
28	Depreciation										
29	Annual lease obligations										
30	PREPARED BY										
31	DATE PREPARED										

Internal Factors

In contrast to external factors, internal market factors are those that a company can control—that is, managerial strategy and decisions that influence the demand for its products or services. For example, a company's management team may select a certain geographic area to target for particular products. Then, in order to gain acceptance in the market, it may decide to reduce the prices of those products. Bringing out a new product line may also affect profit adversely for a period of time because of the increased operating expenses incurred.

■ ■ ■ ■ Components of the Income Statement

The income statement begins with revenues or sales, subtracts the cost of goods sold and the company's operating expenses, takes into account any other categories of income and expenses, including taxes, and ends up with net profit after taxes—the so-called bottom line. An example of a comparative income statement spreadsheet is shown as Exhibit 3.1. When common-sizing an income statement, all accounts are shown as a percentage of sales. The last column, labeled I.S., is for industry averages. This income statement spreadsheet also includes a reconciliation of net worth, which will be discussed in Chapter 4 in relation to the loan officer's analysis of a company's balance sheet. Many banks have computerized the spreading function so that common-sized financial statements are generated by computer, rather than manually.

NET SALES

Every invoice issued by a manufacturer or every cash receipt of a retailer represents a sale. When totaled over a period of time, gross sales are obtained for the period. Sales (also called revenues) do not reflect the amount of cash taken in since sales for manufacturers, wholesalers, and service companies are generally credit sales. Moreover, not all sales result in full payment. Discounts, allowances, and returns must be deducted from gross sales. In some industries, it is common to offer *discounts* for large volumes of purchases. *Allowances* result when customers are compensated for faulty goods by receiving credit on future bills.

Returns result when merchandise is returned and the bill is canceled. Thus net sales, the first entry on most income statements, is calculated as follows:

Net sales = Gross sales − (Sales discounts + Sales returns + Allowances).

COST OF GOODS SOLD

The second entry on the income statement is cost of goods sold. Whenever a product is manufactured or sold, certain direct costs are incurred. These direct costs—called cost of goods sold—include the expenses of production (cost of materials, labor, and manufacturing overhead) in a manufacturing company. For a wholesale or retail company, cost of goods sold equals the cost of purchased inventory. Because a service company doesn't sell a tangible product, it has no cost of goods sold. The cost of goods sold that is shown on a company's income statement represents only the cost to the company of products that were actually sold during the period covered by the statement. The cost of any goods manufactured or purchased, but not sold, represents increased inventory. Therefore, to calculate the cost of goods sold, the company's beginning inventory for the period must be compared to the ending inventory. The basic formula then for calculating the cost of goods sold for a retailer or a wholesaler is this:

Cost of goods sold = Beginning inventory + Net cost of purchases − Ending inventory.

The net cost of purchases includes shipping costs and can be further refined by subtracting any volume discounts and returns and allowances on purchased goods. This is shown by the following formulas:

Net cost of purchases = Net purchases + Transportation costs.

Net purchases = Purchases − (Purchase discounts + Purchase returns and allowances).

For a manufacturer, the calculation of cost of goods sold is a bit more complex. Not only must the cost of materials (raw goods) be taken into consideration, but manufacturing expenses must be added in to determine the true cost of the finished product. This includes the cost of labor involved in the manufacturing process and manufacturing overhead. Again, these costs are recognized as expenses only when a company sells its manufactured products. Thus, for a manufacturer,

$$\text{Cost of goods sold} = \text{Beginning inventory} + \text{Cost of goods manufactured} - \text{Ending inventory}$$

where

$$\text{Cost of goods manufactured} = \text{Raw materials used} + \text{Direct labor} + \text{Overhead expense}.$$

GROSS PROFIT

The next item on the income statement is gross profit. It represents a company's profitability based only on its sales compared to its cost of goods sold. For a retailer or wholesaler, gross profit reflects the markup applied to the company's purchases as reflected in their selling price. For a manufacturer, gross profit represents the value added to the raw materials or parts in the manufacturing process. For a service company, gross profit equals net sales. Gross profit then consists of those funds available to the company to cover its remaining operating expenses and to provide a net profit. Gross profit is calculated using the following formula:

$$\text{Net sales} - \text{Cost of goods sold} = \text{Gross profit}.$$

OPERATING EXPENSES

Operating expenses are the expenses incurred by a company in the normal course of conducting its business, other than the expenses of purchasing inventory and direct manufacturing expenses (which comprise cost of goods sold). These operating expenses are often categorized on the income statement as officers' salaries, selling expenses, and general and administrative expenses. The latter is a catchall category including everything from salaries of office staff to postage stamps.

Officers' salaries + Selling expenses + General and administrative expenses
= Operating expenses.

OPERATING PROFIT/(LOSS)

An operating profit results when a company's gross profit exceeds its operating expenses. An operating loss results if a company's expenses exceed its gross profit. Operating profit is calculated as follows:

Gross profit − Operating expenses = Operating profit/(loss).

NET PROFIT BEFORE TAX

Some companies have sources of income other than sales, and expenses other than cost of goods sold and operating expenses, that must be taken into consideration in calculating net profit. Other income consists of income generated outside the normal operating activities of a company—such as from the rental of excess facilities or dividends from an investment in another company. Other expenses not related to the operation of the business could include a loss resulting from the sale of a fixed asset at less than book value or from the discontinuation of an unprofitable operation. Interest expense (the cost of borrowing) is often shown as a separate expense item on the income statement. Any such additional income and expense items must be taken into account in determining a company's net profit, as shown in the following formula:

Operating profit + Other income − Other expenses − Interest expense
= Net profit before tax.

NET PROFIT AFTER TAX

The bottom line of the income statement is net profit after tax—that is, what remains after deducting from net profit any corporate income taxes owed. A net loss results if the company's total expenses exceed its total revenues. If a company's income statement shows a net loss, the company has not operated profitably during that period.

$$\text{Net profit before tax} - \text{Income taxes} = \text{Net profit after tax.}$$

■ ■ ■ ■ Revenue Analysis

Exhibit 3.2 shows an income statement for Bud's Sporting Goods, a retailer of weight-lifting equipment, athletic shoes, and uniforms. It has been common-sized so that each account is shown not only in absolute dollar amounts but also as a percentage of net sales. This income statement, which includes comparative data for 3 years, will be analyzed in detail throughout this chapter. The loan officer begins the analysis by looking at the company's revenues (or sales) and then at its expenses.

To put in perspective the revenue figure shown on an income statement, the loan officer looks at sales growth by comparing current sales with sales in previous periods and with competitors' sales growth, analyzing changes in sales volume and price, looking at distribution of sales by product and location, and making revenue projections.

COMPARATIVE ANALYSIS

A company's annual sales figures take on more meaning when they are compared to previous years' sales and to sales of other companies in the same industry over the same period. This comparison may indicate increasing or stagnant sales or erratic sales behavior. Consistent behavior is key to favorable lending decisions. When analyzing a potential borrower's revenue, loan officers look at the company's record in developing consistent sales over time. This type of analysis is easy if the company's past income statements have been spread and common-sized. Comparative sales data for Bud's Sporting Goods, shown as Exhibit 3.3, show that the company's sales increased 60 percent in 1987 and 25 percent in 1988.

Besides making internal comparisons, the loan officer will want to compare a company's sales growth with that of comparable companies. Compared to previous periods, the company may show an improve-

EXHIBIT 3.2 ■

Income Statement

Bud's Sporting Goods
Income Statement for the Years Ending December 31, 1986–1988

	1986	%	1987	%	1988	%
Sales	$250,000	100.0	$400,000	100.0	$500,000	100.0
Cost of goods sold	75,000	30.0	160,000	40.0	250,000	50.0
Gross profit	175,000	70.0	240,000	60.0	250,000	50.0
Operating expenses	150,000	60.0	225,000	56.3	230,000	46.0
Operating profit	25,000	10.0	15,000	3.7	20,000	4.0
Other income	5,000	2.0	—	—	4,000	1.0
Other expenses	—	—	—	—	—	—
Interest expense	—	—	—	—	—	—
Profit before tax	30,000	12.0	15,000	3.7	24,000	5.0
Income taxes	8,000	3.2	5,000	1.3	6,000	1.2
Net profit after tax	$ 22,000	8.8	$ 10,000	2.4	$ 18,000	3.8

■ ■

EXHIBIT 3.3 ■

Comparative Dollar Sales

Bud's Sporting Goods
Comparative Dollar Sales

Year	Sales	Change
1986	$250,000	—
1987	$400,000	60%
1988	$500,000	25%

■ ■

ment whereas a comparison to the industry as a whole may show subpar performance. For example, a company that has increased its sales by 20 percent in a year's time looks good until one realizes that the market grew by 50 percent. In this case, a market study might yield information about specific competitors that would help the loan officer understand the cause of the company's relatively poor performance.

Facts to Note:

Robert Morris Associates, a national association of bank loan and credit officers, publishes the *Annual Statement Studies*, which contain composite financial information on manufacturing, wholesaling, retailing, service, and contracting lines of business. The studies show financial statements for each industry in common-size form, accompanied by widely used ratios.

When making either internal or external sales comparisons, the income statements must cover comparable periods of time because seasonality and other cyclical factors may cause wide variations in sales from period to period. For example, it serves no purpose to compare revenues for a 3-month period during the peak of a company's selling season with sales for a 3-month period at the low point of the company's seasonal cycle.

Similarly, for a company in a cyclical industry, comparisons of sales trends with those of other companies may be very misleading if different time periods are compared. In an economic downturn, sales figures of a cyclical company would be expected to be lower than in prosperous years. Similarly, such a company's sales should show dramatic increases as the economy emerges from a recession. Thus it may be difficult to assess the performance of a cyclical company except by comparing its performance with that of its competitors.

The loan officer also tries to determine whether a change in the company's sales figures reflects a change in the overall market for its products or in the company's individual market share. In a rapidly growing market, a company might achieve increased sales at the same time its market share is decreasing. In a market with little or no growth,

Comparative Unit Sales

Bud's Sporting Goods
Comparative Unit Sales

Year	Units	Change
1986	27,000	—
1987	32,400	20%
1988	36,288	12%

■ ■

a company's sales growth may be entirely the result of increased market share.

PRICE VS. VOLUME CHANGES

Sales volume (the quantity of products sold) and selling price are the two factors that determine a company's total revenues. Thus increases or decreases in sales may reflect a change in sales volume, selling price, or product mix. Depending on the product, sales volume may be measured in terms of the number of units, pounds, or some other volume measure sold. An analysis of a company's sales volume over time will reveal whether the revenue figures on the income statement indicate real growth. For example, Exhibit 3.4 shows total sales volume (number of units of merchandise sold) for Bud's Sporting Goods over a 3-year period. Whereas sales revenues were up 60 percent for 1987 and 25 percent for 1988 (as shown in Exhibit 3.3), *unit* sales increased only 20 percent in 1987 and 12 percent in 1988. Thus the bulk of the company's revenue growth in the last 2 years reflected higher selling prices, not an increase in sales volume. A comparative analysis of sales volume may indicate that real growth in sales is considerably less than total revenue growth (as in the case of Bud's Sporting Goods). It may even reveal an increase in sales revenues while unit sales volume fell.

If actual volume figures are not available, the loan officer can use the inflation rate for a particular year to obtain a general idea of the company's real growth. Exhibit 3.3 shows that total sales revenue for Bud's Sporting Goods increased by 25 percent in 1988. If inflation was 13 percent for the same period, then real growth was approximately 12 percent for the period, about the same as shown by the unit sales figures in Exhibit 3.4. If a company's total sales revenue increased by 10 percent when inflation was 12 percent, this would suggest a real decline in sales volume.

If the company manufactures or sells more than one type of product, the loan officer will want to compute price and sales volume changes for each product line, if possible, since a change in product mix can also affect revenues.

Upon identifying changes in price or sales volume as the underlying cause of increased or decreased revenues, the loan officer should determine why they occurred. Is the increased sales volume due to a more aggressive marketing strategy by the company, or does it reflect the introduction of new products? Does a decrease in sales volume reflect lower market demand, or have there been problems with product quality? A decrease in sales volume might result from a plant shutdown caused by fire, a union strike, or severe weather—factors that reduce the availability of products for sale. An increase in unit sales volume might result from an increase in market demand or might reflect the fact that a major competitor has left the industry. Thus changes in sales volume may result from both internal and external factors. Similarly, does a lower selling price reflect increased competition or an attempt to increase the company's market share? Does an increase in selling price make the company more vulnerable to new competition?

When comparing sales volume from period to period, an apparent decrease in volume may result from abnormally high sales volume in the preceding period. For example, if the company received a very large, one-time order in response to a special sale, this sale should be deducted before making any sales comparisons.

Again Exhibit 3.4 shows that unit sales steadily increased for Bud's Sporting Goods in 1987 and 1988. However, closer investigation and discussion with the company reveal a one-time sale in 1988 of 10,000 uniforms. When this sale is deducted from the 1988 total, normal recurring sales volume actually shows a decrease from 32,400 units in 1987 to 26,288 units in 1988. Without such an in-depth analysis, the loan officer might incorrectly evaluate the company's ability to maintain its sales level in the future.

DISTRIBUTION ANALYSIS

After analyzing the company's sales volume and price changes, the loan officer will attempt to attribute any revenue fluctuations to specific products or locations. This process is called *distribution analysis*. Many companies have several operating units, product lines, or sales territories. Distribution analysis can provide answers to questions such as the following: What or who contributes the most or least to the overall financial condition and productivity of the business? Which products sell the best, and where? Which products sell the least? Which are considered to be the new leaders? Which division sells the most or the least? Which location is the best producer? If the analysis shows that 20 percent of the company's products contribute 90 percent of the sales, the company should perhaps consider eliminating some products.

Exhibit 3.5 shows the distribution of sales by product line for Bud's Sporting Goods. Weight-lifting equipment and athletic shoes together contributed 90 percent of the company's sales, whereas uniforms accounted for only 10 percent of sales in 1988. Furthermore, the company's sales of weight-lifting equipment and athletic shoes have grown tremendously over the last 3 years, while the sale of uniforms has dropped precipitously. The loan officer might conclude that the life cycle of uniforms is nearing its end while the life cycles of weight-lifting equipment and athletic shoes are on the upswing.

The same type of analysis can be done with sales distribution by location, as shown in Exhibit 3.6. It shows that Bud's Sporting Goods has three retail outlets—designated uptown, downtown, and suburban. These figures show that sales at the suburban store, which accounted for 60 percent of the company's sales in 1986, accounted for only 8 percent of total sales in 1988. Upon investigation, the lender learns that the company's suburban store almost exclusively markets uniforms, sales of which have shrunk considerably during the last 2 years. Moreover, weight-lifting equipment and athletic shoes have not sold well in the suburban location. Unless the company finds replacement products that gain acceptance in the suburbs, the suburban location might be a candidate for closing.

REVENUE PROJECTIONS

The discussion up to now has dealt with the analysis of a company's past sales performance. However, loan officers want to base their lending decisions on how the company is likely to perform in the future. Therefore, the company's ability to maintain or increase its revenues in the future must be evaluated.

Well-managed companies use a planning process that includes *projections* of their operations. By comparing management's past projections to the company's actual performance in past periods, the loan

Sales Distribution by Product Line

Bud's Sporting Goods
Sales Distribution by Product Line

Product	1986	%	1987	%	1988	%
Weight-lifting equipment	$ 25,000	10.0	$150,000	37.5	$250,000	50.0
Athletic shoes	25,000	10.0	150,000	37.5	200,000	40.0
Uniforms	200,000	80.0	100,000	25.0	50,000	10.0
Total	$250,000	100.0	$400,000	100.0	$500,000	100.0

Sales Distribution by Location

Bud's Sporting Goods
Sales Distribution by Location

Location	1986	%	1987	%	1988	%
Uptown	$ 50,000	20.0	$175,000	43.8	$240,000	48.0
Downtown	50,000	20.0	150,000	37.5	220,000	44.0
Suburban	150,000	60.0	75,000	18.8	40,000	8.0
Total	$250,000	100.0	$400,000	100.0	$500,000	100.0

Note: Totals may not add to 100% due to rounding.

officer can better assess the accuracy of the company's current projections. The loan officer must also assess the reasonableness of the company's assumptions used to project sales. If the company's assumptions seem overly optimistic, the projections should be altered.

The management team at Bud's Sporting Goods has projected a 30 percent growth in sales, or sales of $650,000, in 1989. This initially appears reasonable since, according to Exhibit 3.3, sales growth for 1987 and 1988 was 60 percent and 25 percent, respectively. However, the loan officer knows that the industrywide market growth for those 2 years was 80 percent and 40 percent, respectively. Thus the company's growth rate has been below that of the market. Moreover, the market growth rate for 1989 is projected to be only 20 percent. In light of these facts, management's projection of a 30 percent growth rate looks unrealistically high. The lending officer should reduce the company's projected growth rate to less than the industry's projected growth rate based on the company's actual experience in 1987 and 1988. Thus the lender might project a 15 percent increase in sales for 1989, which would bring sales to $575,000, as shown in Exhibit 3.7 (Method 1).

Projecting year-end results based on a company's interim (part-year) statements is another common method of developing sales projections. By annualizing an interim statement, the loan officer can get an idea of what a company's fiscal year-end statement will look like compared to previous year-end statements. Exhibit 3.7 shows that the company's actual sales for the first half of 1989 came to $300,000. If the level of sales is assumed to be about the same all year, it is readily apparent that annual sales will come to about $600,000. If, however, significant seasonal fluctuations in sales occur, then simply annualizing interim results to a yearly figure may be very misleading.

Suppose that Bud's Sporting Goods has highly seasonal sales with the first 6 months of the year accounting for 75 percent of annual sales. In this case, the interim 6-month sales volume ($300,000) should be divided by the percentage of annual sales this period represents—in this case, 75 percent. Therefore, instead of projected yearly sales of $600,000, a projection of $400,000 would be more realistic (the revised projection shown in Method 2 of Exhibit 3.7).

Preparation and analysis of projected statements, also called pro forma analysis, is discussed in detail in Chapter 7.

Projected Sales

Bud's Sporting Goods
Projected Sales

Method 1: Projecting a Percentage Increase

	1989 Sales Projections			
	Company's Projection		Bank's Projection	
1988 Sales	% Increase	Sales	% Increase	Sales
$500,000	30	$650,000	15	$575,000

Method 2: Annualizing Interim Sales

Actual Sales— 6 mos. ending 6/30/1989	1989 Sales Projections	
	Straight Projection	Revised Projection
$300,000	$600,000	$400,000

▌▌▌▌▌ Expense Analysis

After analyzing the revenues shown on the income statement, the loan officer next analyzes the corresponding expenses incurred. The ultimate goal, of course, is to assess the company's past profitability and to be able to make an educated guess concerning the company's future profitability.

The analysis of expenses in relation to revenues begins with a consideration of the company's cost of goods sold and an analysis of its profit margins and then entails a detailed analysis of its operating expenses.

COST OF GOODS SOLD

Whenever a product is manufactured or a trading company buys a product for resale, certain direct costs are incurred. These direct costs—called cost of goods sold—include the expenses of production in a manufacturing company and of purchasing inventory in a wholesale or retail company. The markup and final price of the product must include these basic expenses. For example, if Bud's Sporting Goods purchases handheld weights at a cost of $2.00 and resells them for $3.00, the cost of goods sold is $2.00. The $1.00 markup represents the gross profit margin resulting from the sale of each weight. For a manufacturer, the cost of goods sold also takes into account the value added to the raw materials during the manufacturing process.

Calculation of Cost of Goods Sold

The cost of goods sold shown on the income statement is based on the many products purchased or manufactured during a business's operating cycle or interim period and available for sale. However, these costs are not recognized until the company sells its inventory. Therefore, to calculate the cost of goods for the products that were actually sold, a company's beginning and ending inventory must be taken into consideration. As discussed previously, the cost of goods sold for a wholesaler or retailer is calculated by adding a company's inventory purchases to beginning inventory for the period and then subtracting ending inventory. This gives the cost of the merchandise sold (or lost or stolen) during the period.

Cost of Goods Sold for Bud's Sporting Goods

Beginning inventory (Jan. 1, 1988)	$ 35,000
Purchases	+ 257,000
Cost of goods available for sale	$292,000
Ending inventory (Dec. 31, 1988)	− 42,000
Cost of goods sold	$250,000

Cost of Goods Sold for a Manufacturer

Raw material—beginning inventory (Jan. 1, 1988)	$ 10,000
Raw material purchases	82,000
Total raw material available	$ 92,000
Raw material—ending inventory (Dec. 31, 1988)	− 12,000
Raw material used	$ 80,000
Work-in-process—beginning inventory (Jan. 1, 1988)	$ 5,000
Raw materials used	80,000
Direct labor	75,000
Manufacturing overhead expense allocation	100,000
Total cost of goods manufactured	$260,000
Work-in-process—ending inventory (Dec. 31, 1988)	− 6,000
Total cost of goods manufactured and transferred to finished goods	$254,000
Finished goods—beginning inventory (Jan. 1, 1988)	$ 20,000
Cost of goods manufactured	254,000
Cost of goods available for sale	$274,000
Finished goods—ending inventory (Dec. 31, 1988)	− 24,000
Cost of goods sold	$250,000

Exhibit 3.8 shows the calculation of cost of goods sold for Bud's Sporting Goods for 1988. No labor or overhead expenses are allocated to the inventory since a retailer adds no value to the inventory. The inventory handling expenses, such as the wholesaler's labor, delivery, and warehousing costs, are not included in the cost of goods sold, but are included on the income statement as operating expenses.

Cost of goods sold for a manufacturer. The cost of goods calculation for a manufacturer is more complex because three types of inventory must be distinguished: raw materials, work-in-process, and finished goods. Moreover, manufacturing expenses (direct labor costs and certain overhead expenses) must be added in to determine the true cost of the finished products. Again, these costs are recognized as expenses only when the company sells its inventory, which means that beginning and ending inventory amounts must be considered.

Labor costs comprise the wages paid to production workers. Manufacturing overhead expenses are usually allocated according to a percentage method of space allocation. For example, if 60 percent of a manufacturer's facilities are used in the manufacturing process, then 60 percent of the total utilities, rent, general managerial expenses, and building depreciation (a noncash expense) would be allocated to manufacturing overhead. Exhibit 3.9 shows the calculation of the cost of goods sold for a manufacturer.

The analysis of a manufacturer's cost of goods sold must include not just pricing considerations, but an evaluation of the company's cost controls—that is, its efficiency in controlling the consumption of raw materials used in the manufacturing process to ensure minimal waste. Furthermore, analysis of its productivity (manufacturing as much product as possible from a given amount of labor and related overhead expenses) is critical.

Inventory Determination and Valuation

Inventory is a key component in the cost of goods sold for all companies. Two basic methods are used to determine the amount of a company's total inventory at any point in time. These methods are known as perpetual and periodic inventory systems. A *perpetual inventory system* keeps a daily count of inventory. When a business sells an item, it immediately deducts it from inventory so that the count remains up to date. Companies usually use this system for very expensive or large inventory items that do not sell very quickly. Thus automobile dealers, heavy equipment dealers, and jewelers have traditionally used a perpetual inventory system. However, with the increased use of computers at checkout counters, many department stores and supermarkets also have adopted a perpetual inventory system.

The *periodic inventory system* involves taking a physical count of inventory on a scheduled basis. This system is primarily used with inventories that are characterized by diverse or numerous products with low unit prices and rapid turnover. Department stores, supermarkets, and wholesale grocers traditionally have used a periodic system, although many retailers are now converting to a computerized perpetual inventory system.

Because of the importance of inventory values in determining the cost of goods sold, periodic physical inventories are necessary. Inventory costs and, hence, profitability can only be estimated until the manufacturer performs an inventory count. Inventory counts are normally taken once a year, at the end of an operating cycle. This means that interim statements are usually based on estimates of inventory. Thus cost of goods sold and profit figures found in interim statements must be considered only as estimates. Even with a perpetual inventory system, damaged or stolen goods will not show without a physical inventory. Interim period "profits" sometimes evaporate at fiscal year-end when a physical inventory is taken.

The loan officer will want to know not only how a company counts its inventory, but what method it uses to assess the value of each item of inventory. There are several methods of valuing inventory that conform to generally accepted accounting principles. The two basic valuation methods are known as *last in, first out* (*LIFO*) and *first in, first out* (*FIFO*).

LIFO assumes that the last unit of inventory purchased is the first unit sold. Thus the first unit of inventory remains unsold as long as there is any inventory remaining. Therefore, ending inventory is valued at old rather than recent prices. In inflationary periods characterized by rising prices, this valuation method keeps ending inventory values low and cost of goods high. Consequently, gross profits are lower.

FIFO assumes that the first unit purchased is the first unit sold. In inflationary times, this method results in ending inventory being valued at higher prices, resulting in lower cost of goods sold and higher profits. Although these *inventory profits* are largely an illusion (since they must be used to support the higher costs of ending inventory), real taxes have to be paid on them. Thus the LIFO valuation method, which results in lower profits, is preferable to FIFO during inflationary periods.

Exhibits 3.10 and 3.11 illustrate how the LIFO and FIFO methods of inventory valuation can affect a company's gross profits. Exhibit 3.10 shows the inventory purchases for Bud's Sporting Goods over a 4-month period for a new line of athletic shoes. It purchased 240 pairs of these shoes at four different prices for a total cost of $3,750. Exhibit 3.11 compares the resulting value of inventory using the FIFO and LIFO valuation methods assuming the company sold 100 pairs of the shoes for $35 each during this same 4-month period. The two valuation methods result in significant differences in ending inventory values, cost of goods sold, gross profit, and gross margin. Specifically, ending inventory value and profitability are lower with LIFO than with FIFO given the same sales price, number of pairs of shoes sold, and inventory purchase costs.

When a company sells more than it purchases, it reduces its inventory. When this occurs with a company using LIFO valuation, the reduction in inventory is valued at older, lower prices; thus, inventory profits are created when the lower-priced inventory is expensed through cost of goods sold. This reduction in inventory is referred to as "dipping into the LIFO layer."

It is apparent, then, that a loan officer needs to know what inventory valuation method a company uses in order to compare cost of goods sold (or profit margins) and that comparisons for companies using different valuation methods may be misleading. Since a change in valuation method can significantly affect the cost of goods sold and gross margin percentages, the loan officer must also be alert to a change in inventory valuation method and take it into account when analyzing a significant improvement or deterioration in the cost of goods sold as a percentage of total sales. However, as long as a company consistently uses the same valuation method over successive operating periods, improvement or deterioration in the company's profit margin can be a meaningful indication of the company's performance.

Gross Profit Margin

The cost of goods sold is often expressed as a percentage of total sales. The difference between this percentage and 100 percent is the gross profit margin. The gross margin represents the percentage of each

Inventory Purchases

Month	Pairs of Shoes Purchased	Cost Per Pair	Total Cost of Purchases
1	100	$10.00	$1,000.00
2	50	15.00	750.00
3	50	20.00	1,000.00
4	40	25.00	1,000.00
Total	240		$3,750.00

■ ■

Cost of Goods Sold—LIFO vs. FIFO Valuations

LIFO Valuation

		Amount	%
Sales (100 pairs of shoes at $35.00 each)		$3,500.00	100.0
Beginning inventory	$ —		
Add: Purchases (240 pairs, Exhibit 3.10)	3,750.00		
Cost of goods available for sale	$3,750.00		
Subtract: Ending inventory (140 pairs)			
100 pairs at $10.00 each	$1,000.00		
40 pairs at $15.00 each	600.00		
	$1,600.00		
Cost of goods sold		2,150.00	61.0
Gross profit		$1,350.00	39.0

FIFO Valuation

		Amount	%
Sales (100 pairs of shoes at $35.00 each)		$3,500.00	100.0
Beginning inventory	$ —		
Add: Purchases (240 pairs, Exhibit 3.10)	3,750.00		
Cost of goods available for sale	$3,750.00		
Subtract: Ending inventory (140 pairs)			
40 pairs at $25.00 each	$1,000.00		
50 pairs at 20.00 each	1,000.00		
50 pairs at 15.00 each	750.00		
	$2,750.00		
Cost of goods sold		1,000.00	29.0
Gross profit		$2,500.00	71.0

dollar of sales that is available to cover the company's other operating expenses. Thus to be profitable a company must sell enough inventory to generate a sufficient gross profit to cover a controlled level of operating expenses. Although the concept is a simple one, its application in the actual operation of a business can be difficult. For instance, most companies sell several products, each of which may have a different cost of goods sold percentage and gross margin. These percentages may vary, not only for different products, but for the same products over time if competition causes the company to hold prices low relative to costs. If, as is often the case, a company does not raise its prices as fast as its costs increase, the cost of goods sold will increase as a percentage of sales, creating a situation of steadily eroding gross margins. As gross margin decreases, the sales level needed to cover the same level of operating expenses increases.

If, instead, a company's gross margin increases, the sales volume needed to break even, given a certain operating expense level, decreases. Thus a company may actually initiate a price decrease and accept a lower gross margin in hopes of generating enough additional sales to increase the absolute level of gross profit. Companies continually look for the optimum price the market will support where gross profit can be maximized on a given sales volume.

Again, the loan officer can perform the same types of analysis with gross profits and gross margins as performed previously for sales. That is, the lender can look at trends over time, industry comparisons, and breakdowns of profitability by product line and location. By looking at the common-sized income statements for Bud's Sporting Goods (Exhibit 3.2), the lender can see that at the same time that its sales were increasing, the company's gross profit margin was eroding steadily— from 70 percent in 1986 to 60 percent in 1987 to 50 percent in 1988. This deterioration in profit margin means greater risk to the lender since higher total sales must be achieved to cover the same level of operating expenses.

Because breakdowns of gross profit are available by product line for Bud's Sporting Goods (as shown in Exhibit 3.12), the loan officer can see that the decreased profit margin reflects both a decrease in the profit margin for uniforms and a pronounced change in product emphasis from uniforms to weight-lifting equipment, which has a lower profit margin. The product line breakdown also shows that different markups were applied to each of the company's three product lines in 1988, resulting in gross margins ranging from 43.5 percent for athletic shoes to 65 percent for uniforms.

Exhibit 3.12 shows that even though total revenues from uniforms have dropped precipitously (from $200,000 in 1986 to $50,000 in 1988), the gross margin for the product has remained consistently high. This suggests that although the market for uniforms is decreasing, a base market exists that wants or needs uniforms and will pay a premium for them. Therefore, the company should probably keep selling uniforms as long as the profit margin can be kept high and a reasonable sales volume can be maintained. The retailer's other products, weight-lifting equipment and athletic shoes, apparently face greater price competition. Whereas total sales and gross profits are higher for these products, the gross margins are lower.

The lender next decides to look at a breakdown of gross profits and gross margins by location, as shown in Exhibit 3.13. Because the suburban location of the company primarily sells uniforms, the store's gross margin has equaled the high gross margin of uniforms each year. The other two stores, which sell primarily weight-lifting equipment and athletic shoes, have much lower gross margins. Despite its high gross margin, sales at the suburban location are so low that the operating expenses of the suburban store must remain very low if the store is to remain profitable.

OPERATING EXPENSES

Up to this point, the loan officer has analyzed a company's sales and cost of goods sold, the two determinants of gross profit. The next step is to look at the company's general operating expenses—those costs not directly related to the purchase of inventory or the production of goods. Operating expenses are generally categorized on the income statement as officers' salaries, selling expenses (salespeople's salaries), and general and administrative expenses. (Note that factory workers' wages are included in cost of goods sold while management salaries are considered an operating expense.) The resulting operating profit (gross profit minus operating expenses) represents the profit from the basic operation of the company—that is, the buying and selling or the manufactur-

EXHIBIT 3.12 ■ ■■■■■■■■■■■■■■■■■■■■■■■■■■■■■■■ ■■

Gross Profit and Margin by Product Line

Bud's Sporting Goods
Gross Profit and Margin by Product Line

	1986			1987			1988		
Product	Sales	Gross Profit	Gross Margin	Sales	Gross Profit	Gross Margin	Sales	Gross Profit	Gross Margin
Weight-lifting equipment	$ 25,000	$ 12,500	50.0%	$150,000	$108,000	72.0%	$250,000	$130,500	52.2%
Athletic shoes	25,000	12,500	50.0	150,000	72,000	48.0	200,000	87,000	43.5
Uniforms	200,000	150,000	75.0	100,000	60,000	60.0	50,000	32,500	65.0
Total	$250,000	$175,000	70.0%	$400,000	$240,000	60.0%	$500,000	$250,000	50.0%

EXHIBIT 3.13 ■ ■■■■■■■■■■■■■■■■■■■■■■■■■■■■■■ ■■

Gross Profit and Margin by Location

Bud's Sporting Goods
Gross Profit and Margin by Location

	1986			1987			1988		
Location	Sales	Gross Profit	Gross Margin	Sales	Gross Profit	Gross Margin	Sales	Gross Profit	Gross Margin
Uptown	$ 50,000	$ 31,250	62.5%	$175,000	$ 97,500	56.0%	$240,000	$115,110	48.0%
Downtown	50,000	31,250	62.5	150,000	97,500	65.0	220,000	108,890	49.5
Suburban	150,000	112,500	75.0	75,000	45,000	60.0	40,000	26,000	65.0
Total	$250,000	$175,000	70.0%	$400,000	$240,000	60.0%	$500,000	$250,000	50.0%

ing and selling of the company's products. Thus operating profit is a key figure in analyzing how efficiently and consistently management has used the company's resources in its primary operations to generate profits.

As mentioned previously, manufacturing firms normally allocate a percentage of the company's total overhead and administrative costs to cost of goods sold while the remainder are allocated to operating expenses. In general, a manufacturer's cost of goods sold consists of *variable costs*—that is, costs that change with product volume—such as raw materials, direct labor, and manufacturing supplies. In contrast, its operating costs are primarily *fixed costs*—that is, they vary in relation to plant capacity, not production volume. The loan officer may find that a manufacturer has changed the allocation of certain manufacturing costs from cost of goods sold to operating expenses, or vice versa, thus distorting trend comparisons between costs of goods sold and operating expenses. In such cases, the loan officer should be cautious about evaluating large swings in gross profit margins, either positive or negative, until a detailed analysis of the company's expense allocations is made. A more complete discussion of fixed versus variable costs is included in Chapter 9.

In analyzing a company's operating expenses, the loan officer should get a detailed breakdown of operating expenses if it is available, such as that for Bud's Sporting Goods which is shown as Exhibit 3.14. Ideally, operating costs will be shown for 2 or more years. These costs can be further categorized for in-depth analysis as *controllable costs* and *noncontrollable costs*. Controllable costs—which include such items as bonuses, profit-sharing contributions, and a company's travel and entertainment budget—are prone to excessive spending. Especially in closely held companies, these types of expenses can escalate because they directly benefit the owners. For example, charging excessive rental or lease payments to the company for facilities personally owned by the owner of the company is a common way of taking additional personal income out of the company's operations. If members of the owner's family receive compensation, the loan officer should determine that they make a meaningful contribution to the company's operations.

Noncontrollable costs include utility payments, office salaries, and long-term lease obligations—all the necessary costs of doing business that cannot easily be changed by management. For example, once an

Operating Expense Comparisons

Bud's Sporting Goods
Breakdown of Operating Expenses

Operating Expense	1986		1987		1988	
	Amount	% of Sales	Amount	% of Sales	Amount	% of Sales
Salaries—officers	$ 20,000	8.0	$ 31,000	7.8	$ 30,000	6.0
Salaries—other	40,000	16.0	60,000	15.0	65,000	13.0
Payroll taxes	4,500	1.8	6,000	1.5	8,000	1.6
Rent	24,000	9.6	24,000	6.0	24,000	4.8
Auto leasing	10,000	4.0	10,000	2.5	10,000	2.0
Insurance	5,000	2.0	6,000	1.5	7,000	1.4
Interest	1,000	0.4	2,000	0.5	2,500	0.5
Repairs and maintenance	2,600	1.0	3,000	0.8	3,000	0.6
Telephone	4,000	1.6	7,000	1.8	8,000	1.6
Travel and entertainment	12,000	4.8	20,000	5.0	30,000	6.0
Profit sharing	12,000	4.8	35,000	8.8	15,000	3.0
Legal	1,000	0.4	1,000	0.3	1,500	0.3
Accounting	2,400	1.0	3,000	0.8	3,500	0.7
Advertising	10,000	4.0	15,000	3.8	20,000	4.0
Depreciation	1,500	0.6	2,000	0.5	2,500	0.5
Total	$150,000	60.0	$225,000	56.3	$230,000	46.0
Sales	$250,000	100.0	$400,000	100.0	$500,000	100.0

■ ■

equipment lease is signed, that expense cannot be altered, at least in the near term. Segregating noncontrollable expenses and controllable expenses helps the loan officer identify the costs that must be met if the company is to remain in business as opposed to those that could possibly be reduced to improve profitability. Moreover, if management has shown consistent and effective control over its controllable expenses in the past, such control is likely to be maintained during a debt repayment period.

One way the loan officer can evaluate a company's effectiveness of control is to look at operating expenses as a percentage of sales. When sales increase faster than operating expenses, the expenses-to-sales ratio decreases, thus showing good expense control. Consistency should also be analyzed by comparing a company's expenses in relation to sales over time. In addition, comparing a company's operating costs-to-sales ratio with that of similar companies or with an industry average may be instructive.

Note that depreciation is considered as an operating expense even though it is a noncash expense. Since depreciation of fixed assets can be figured in various ways, the loan officer needs to know what depreciation method the company uses. This can also affect a manufacturer's cost of goods sold since depreciation of fixed assets directly used in production are normally included in cost of goods sold. Since accelerated depreciation results in a larger depreciation expense, it leads to a lower profit; this may be advantageous since the increased depreciation involves a noncash expense yet may result in lower taxes. Depreciation and its effect on profitability are discussed in more detail in Chapter 4.

Another type of noncash expense is amortization—the recognition of an intangible prepaid cost as an expense over some extended period of time. For example, when a company pays an amount over book value when acquiring another company, the excess amount—called *goodwill*—is amortized to zero over a period of years allowed by tax laws and GAAP.

The loan officer reaches the following conclusions about the operating expenses of Bud's Sporting Goods, as shown in Exhibit 3.14.

Salaries. Bud's Sporting Goods has one owner and hires a number of employees, mainly salesclerks. The owner's salary seems reasonable, and there do not appear to be any excessive salaries or unproductive salary expenses for family members.

Rent. Rental expense on the company's facilities is $2,000 per month, and has remained unchanged for 3 years. The sales growth during that period indicates an increasingly efficient use of the facilities. Because rent is a fixed expense, it does not increase or decrease, at least in the short run, with changes in sales volume.

Travel and entertainment. This is the only expense category that has consistently increased as a percentage of sales. In fact, while sales have increased by 100 percent in a 2-year period, travel and entertainment expenses have increased by 150 percent. The loan officer should investigate whether these expense increases are justified or whether they include significant unproductive personal expenses.

Profit sharing. The profit-sharing contribution is a major expense for this company. The expense appeared excessive in 1987 but was reduced considerably in 1988. Again, this is a totally owner-controlled expense for the benefit of the owner and possibly the employees. The loan officer should determine the owner's plans for profit-sharing contributions in the future.

Other operating expenses. The remaining expenses (all of which come under the category of general and administrative expenses) appear to be reasonable and controlled. As sales volume increased, these expenses increased less rapidly; thus they decreased as a percentage of sales. A greater test of expense control is required when the sales volume decreases. Evidence of such control is shown when expenses decrease at least at the same rate as sales decrease.

▌▌▌▌▌▌▌▌ Other Income and Expense Analysis

Some companies have income other than sales, and expenses other than those included in cost of goods sold or operating expenses. After evaluating the operating profit of the company, the loan officer must look at these other income and expense items which lie outside the normal operations of a business to see if they significantly affect the overall net profitability of the company and whether the probability exists of these items consistently recurring.

OTHER INCOME

Other income is income that is generated outside the normal operating activities of the company. This income does not result from sales of the company's products or services, but from some peripheral activity. For example, a company may generate other income by renting its excess facilities or equipment to another company. Interest income, profit on the sale of fixed assets, dividend income, discounts earned, and bad debt recovery are other examples of nonoperating income. Some companies have a dependable source of other income that should be analyzed as a recurring income source.

Some typical sources of other income include the following:

Rental income. Rental income is often generated from excess building facilities or equipment. A company with excess capacity that it can rent or lease without interrupting the efficient flow of its operation is wise to do so. The lender needs to consider whether the income will be a continuing income source or whether the company will soon need to use the space or equipment itself.

Interest income. Interest income can be generated from excess cash invested in savings deposits or from other investments, such as a loan to another company. If such investments recur, the level of market interest rates will affect the level of income generated.

Profit on the sale of fixed assets. A company can generate additional income by selling its excess fixed assets at a profit. For instance, after upgrading its fixed assets with more efficient equipment, the company may want to sell its obsolete equipment. However, if assets necessary to the company's operation are sold, this one-time source of cash could jeopardize the company's future operations. A profit results when the sale price exceeds the net book value of the asset sold. This net value is the asset's cost less accumulated depreciation. For example, in 1986 Bud's Sporting Goods sold some equipment for a net profit of $5,000, which is shown as other income for the year on its income statement (Exhibit 3.2).

Dividend income. Many companies own stock in related operating companies or in publicly traded companies. Any dividends received constitute a source of nonoperating income. Because dividends are based on the profitable operation of another company, they may not constitute a dependable source of income in the future.

Discounts earned. Suppliers often offer cash discounts for prompt payment of money owed. This can benefit companies having the ability to generate cash on a timely basis to meet their maturing obligations, although the level of discounts offered by suppliers is a factor over which the company has little control. Any discounts earned by the company are included as nonoperating, or other, income. Bud's Sporting Goods was able to pay several suppliers early in 1988 to earn $4,000 in other income, again as shown on its income statement (Exhibit 3.2).

Bad debt recovery. When accounts receivable that are owed to a company for credit sales are deemed uncollectible, they may be expensed against income. If a receivable that has already been written off is ultimately collected, it is recognized as other income.

OTHER EXPENSES

A company may have nonoperating expenses as well as nonoperating income. Although no such expenses were reported by Bud's Sporting Goods, such expenses might include interest expense (often shown as a separate item), loss on a sale of fixed assets, loss on a sale of stock or discontinued operations, discounts allowed, and bad debt expense.

Interest expense. The cost of borrowing money depends both on the company's overall level of borrowing and the market interest rate at any particular time. Thus interest expense can fluctuate dramatically depending on the company's borrowing requirements and interest rates. When making a new loan, the lender should consider the increased interest expense and its effect on the company's profits.

Loss on the sale of fixed assets. If a company sells any of its fixed assets for below book value, the loss associated with the sale is recognized as a nonoperating expense. When such losses show up on the income statement, the loan officer should determine whether the company is considering the sale of more fixed assets; if so, the company can expect further losses, and the loan officer will want to understand why.

Loss on the sale of stock or discontinued operations. A company often sells its ownership in another company when its stock value is dropping or to generate needed cash. When the stock is sold for less than its cost, a loss results. A company may also choose to discontinue some of its operations. This usually occurs when certain operations have not been as profitable as management would like and the assets can be more efficiently used in some other area of the business. When a company decides to discontinue an operation, a reserve is usually established on the balance sheet by estimating what losses will occur in liquidating that operation. If the company accurately estimates the anticipated losses, additional losses will not arise after final disposition. However, the loan officer should determine whether the company will face additional losses in the future.

Discounts allowed. A company may allow discounts on prompt payment of its customer accounts just as it can earn discounts by promptly paying its own suppliers. The resulting expense depends on the level of discounts allowed and the customers' response to it. A company that needs to generate cash more quickly may do so by allowing excessive discounts. Thus the loan officer should analyze the company's plans for future discounting to determine the probable cost.

Bad debt expense. Bad debts (such as uncollectible accounts receivable) may be classified either as an operating expense or as a nonoperating, or other, expense. If it is a necessary cost of doing business, it is considered an operating expense. However, when bad debts result from a company's overly generous credit policy, then it is considered an expense unrelated to operations. Many companies establish a reserve to provide for losses based on actual and projected experience. This amount is then recognized as an expense each period. A related entry appears on the balance sheet as allowance for bad debts. Other companies recognize bad debts as a direct write-off in the period when an account is recognized as uncollectible. The loan officer should evaluate the adequacy of the company's method of recognizing bad debts.

INCOME TAX ANALYSIS

Income taxes are deducted from a company's profit figures to get to net profit after tax. Because financial statements are prepared using generally accepted accounting principles, whereas tax returns are prepared using the rules and regulations of the Internal Revenue Service, the tax expense shown on the income statement and the actual taxes paid usually differ. Many factors affect the amount of taxes reported on the income statement, making useful comparisons between companies difficult. Analysis of a company's ability to manage its tax burden and to project the impact of taxes on future profitability requires a detailed understanding of many complex tax issues.

NET PROFIT AFTER TAX ANALYSIS

After deducting corporate income taxes, net profit after tax—the bottom line—remains. Tracing the trend in net profits over a period of years provides insight into the consistency with which management has operated the company in the past, giving some basis for assessing the likely future profitability of a business. A company's profit record should also be compared with that of similar businesses and with industry averages. This can help the loan officer put the company's results in perspective.

▌▌▌▌▌▌▌▌ Summary

It is no accident that financial analysis begins with the income statement. It is of key importance in any analysis because it shows both sales, which are the basis of a company's existence, and profits, which determine a company's long-range viability. Income statement analysis provides insight into the effectiveness of management in generating sales, pricing its products or services, controlling expenses, and most importantly, making a profit. A loan officer begins by spreading and common-sizing a company's past income statements to facilitate comparisons over time and with industry averages. All income statement accounts are shown as a percentage of sales. Before beginning an in-depth analysis of a company's revenues and expenses, the lender should already have a good understanding of the type of business in which the company is engaged and the marketplace, including cyclicality, seasonality, and product life cycles.

Income statement analysis begins with revenue analysis. This entails comparisons of sales over time and sales of competitors, changes in sales volume (number of units sold) and price, distribution of sales by product and location, and revenue projections.

Expense analysis, the next step, involves an assessment of two basic categories of expenses—cost of goods sold and operating expenses. The cost of goods sold consists of inventory purchases for a wholesaler or retailer and of inventory, direct labor, and certain manufacturing and overhead expenses for a manufacturer. In analyzing a company's cost of goods sold, the loan officer must consider how the company counts its inventory (perpetual versus periodic inventory systems) and how it evaluates the inventory (FIFO versus LIFO methods of evaluation). The calculation of cost of goods sold enables the lender to calculate the company's profit margin, a key figure in assessing the company's efficiency and consistency of operation.

The loan officer next looks at the company's operating expenses—including officers' salaries, selling expenses, and general and administrative expenses—to see whether any expenses appear excessive and to capture trends over time by comparing changes in sales to changes in expenses. Once changes are isolated, the lender must seek explanations for the changes. The lender will also analyze a company's expenses in terms of controllable versus noncontrollable costs.

The loan officer then looks at any nonoperating income and expense items that are unrelated to the company's basic operations to determine whether any significant amounts are likely to be recurring or nonrecurring. Interest expense, often shown separately on the income statement, is an expense to which the lender should pay particular attention.

Finally, the lender analyzes the company's income tax expense and its after-tax profits, the crucial bottom line of the income statement that reflects all of a company's expense and revenue items. Income statement analysis provides the loan officer with a basic understanding of a company's operating performance, which assists in the next step of the financial analysis—an understanding of the company's financial structure, as shown by balance sheet analysis.

Questions

1. Explain how revenues and expenses are recognized for income statement purposes.

2. Explain the difference between fiscal and interim income statements.

3. What is a common-sized income statement? What is a spreadsheet?

4. Describe how income statements typically differ for manufacturers, retailers, wholesalers, service companies, and agricultural enterprises.

5. List the basic components of an income statement in the order they appear on the statement.

6. What are the two basic causes for changes in total revenues of a company from one period to another?

7. Explain the purpose of analyzing revenue distribution by product line and by location.

8. Describe two ways of projecting revenues, and explain the importance of such projections in analysis.

9. Discuss the concept of noncash expense recognition and how it affects a company's tax liability.

10. Explain what expenses are included in cost of goods sold. How is it calculated differently for a manufacturer than for a wholesale operation?

11. How do LIFO and FIFO methods of inventory valuation differ?

12. Give several examples of controllable and noncontrollable costs. Why is this distinction important in the analysis of operating expenses?

13. Explain why *efficiency* and *consistency* are important concepts in expense analysis.

14. How should individual operating costs be analyzed?

15. Name several types of income and expense items that would be shown as "other income" or "other expenses" on an income statement. Discuss whether they would likely be recurring or nonrecurring.

16. Why is net profit after tax called the bottom line?

Exercises

E-1

Convert the following income statement for 1985, 1986, 1987, and 1988 to a common-size statement, and answer the questions that follow.

Thompson Manufacturing Company
Income Statement

	1985	1986	1987	1988
Sales	$3,553,894	$2,811,867	$2,450,772	$2,666,196
Cost of goods sold	3,377,357	2,570,680	2,218,368	2,460,995
Gross profit	$ 176,537	$ 241,187	$ 232,404	$ 205,201
Selling expenses	44,336	67,671	51,318	66,987
Warehouse and handling	25,314	40,161	39,069	44,462
Delivery expense	30,764	62,360	52,463	33,561
Administrative expense	64,778	63,875	80,676	52,730
Total operating expenses	$ 165,192	$ 234,067	$ 223,526	$ 197,740
Income before taxes	11,345	7,120	8,878	7,461
Taxes	5,445	3,418	4,261	3,581
Net income	$ 5,900	$ 3,702	$ 4,617	$ 3,880

a. What can be said about the consistency of Thompson's sales, gross profit, and operating expenses during the last 4 years?

b. Given the following information for the industry, how does Thompson Manufacturing Company compare?

	1986	1987	1988
Sales growth (reduction)	(10%)	(6%)	1%
Gross margin	10%	11%	12%
Operating profit (percentage of sales)	1.0%	0.7%	1.1%

E-2

Given the following information, determine if a company's increased sales between 1987 and 1988 reflect price or volume changes.

	1987	1988
Average unit price	$ 2.50	$ 3.00
Total sales	$100,000	$150,000

E-3

A company's distribution of sales and gross margins by product and location for the past 3 years follow:

	1986		1987		1988	
	Gross Sales	Margin	Gross Sales	Margin	Gross Sales	Margin
Product X	$100,000	50%	$ 75,000	45%	$ 50,400	40%
Product Y	100,000	60	200,000	50	249,800	50
Product Z	100,000	55	175,000	45	349,800	40
Eastern division	50,000	55	75,000	47	75,000	46
Southern division	75,000	57	100,000	46	200,000	43
Northern division	75,000	56	125,000	45	175,000	44
Western division	100,000	55	150,000	46	200,000	42

a. What conclusions can be drawn as to the possible viability of this company's various product lines and locations?

b. If average fixed costs for each division are approximately $80,000 per year, how will this affect the analysis of revenue distribution by location?

c. What are the alternatives available to the company to keep all its divisions operating?

E-4

Using the following information, calculate the gross profit for a company using both LIFO and FIFO inventory valuation methods.

	Units	Cost/Price Per Unit
Beginning inventory	1,000	$ 20
Purchases	500	23
	600	25
	700	28
Units sold	1,500	50

E-5

A manufacturer provides the following income statement information. What questions should the loan officer ask about the company's operations?

	1986	1987	1988
Sales	$500,000	$600,000	$750,000
Cost of goods sold	175,000	240,000	337,500
Gross profit	325,000	360,000	412,500
Operating expenses	300,000	300,000	375,000
Operating profit	$ 25,000	$ 60,000	$ 37,500
Cost of goods sold			
Raw material	$ 52,500	$ 84,000	$128,250
Direct labor	52,500	64,800	87,750
Manufacturing expense	70,000	91,200	121,500
Total	$175,000	$240,000	$337,500
Operating expenses			
Salaries, officers	$ 80,000	$100,000	$120,000
Salaries, others	40,000	45,000	45,000
Rent	24,000	24,000	36,000
Auto leasing	20,000	30,000	30,000
Travel and entertainment	25,000	30,000	40,000
Profit sharing	20,000	30,000	36,000
Other	91,000	41,000	68,000
Total	$300,000	$300,000	$375,000

4   The Balance Sheet

Learning Objectives

After studying this chapter, you should be able to

- understand both the overall structure and the individual accounts on a balance sheet
- explain the typical distribution of assets and liabilities for manufacturers, wholesalers, retailers, and service companies
- evaluate asset accounts in terms of quality, liquidity, and potential collateral for loans
- explain the various methods for depreciating fixed assets
- evaluate each liability account in terms of its repayment requirements
- identify the various types of equity accounts and their availability as sources of financing
- explain the importance of equity to a lender

▐▎▌▐▎▐▎▐ Introduction

Balance sheet analysis is the next major step in financial analysis after income statement analysis. Whereas the income statement shows a company's performance over a period of time (usually a year), the balance sheet provides a financial picture of a company at a given point in time. It categorizes all of a company's resources as assets, liabilities, and owners' equity: these items are what the company has available to generate sales or revenues. The company uses its assets, including facilities and equipment, to manufacture or purchase products for inventory that, when sold, convert to cash or create accounts receivable. A company's *assets* are financed by the company's *liabilities* (also called *debt*) and *owners' equity* (also called *net worth* or simply *equity*).

The basic structure of the balance sheet is represented by the simple equation:

$$\text{Assets} = \text{Liabilities} + \text{Equity}.$$

This equation helps the loan officer understand the constantly occurring changes in the operation of any business. Since the equation must always be in balance, a change in one part of the equation must be offset by an equal change in another part to maintain the balance. Thus an increase in assets (whether fixed assets or inventory) must be balanced by a decrease in another asset account (such as accounts receivable) or an increase in liabilities (such as bank debt) or equity. Thus a company can obtain assets by liquidating other assets or by financing the new assets with liabilities or additional equity. Liabilities can be paid by liquidating assets or by increasing other liabilities or equity. Any combination of increasing or decreasing assets, liabilities, and equity can complete a transaction, provided the equation remains in balance.

In analyzing a balance sheet, the loan officer should recognize that the type of business, the industry, and the company's managerial style each affects the distribution of assets, liabilities, and equity in characteristic ways. The balance sheet analysis consists of evaluating each asset account in terms of its quality and liquidity—that is, as potential collateral in a lending situation. Each liability account is evaluated in terms of its repayment requirements and the expected sources of repayment. Each equity account is evaluated in terms of the form of equity investment and the general availability of equity as a source of financing.

Additionally, the loan officer can use comparative analysis to evaluate major changes in the company's balance sheet over time to determine the company's strengths and weaknesses, the effectiveness of its managerial strategies, and its responsiveness to general market trends.

■ ■ ■ ■ Preliminary Considerations

The asset and liability structure of a company's balance sheet depends on numerous factors. For example, the type of company, the nature of the industry, the company's objectives, and managerial decisions all affect the company's balance sheet mix. These same factors, as well as the conditions in the company's markets, the stage in the company's development, management's financing philosophy, and the availability of financing—debt and equity—also affect the company's balance sheet structure.

TYPE OF BUSINESS

The five basic types of companies—manufacturers, wholesalers, retailers, service companies, and agricultural companies—each have characteristic balance sheet structures reflecting the kinds and amount of assets and liabilities that are normal for that type of operation.

Manufacturers and Agricultural Companies

Manufacturing and farming operations generally require heavy fixed assets as well as large amounts of raw materials to produce finished goods for sale. Inventory levels and the resulting accounts receivable (since credit terms are normally offered) also tend to be high. Both long-term debt and equity are significant financing sources for the fixed assets manufacturers require. Short-term liabilities typically consist of bank debt and trade payables which are used to finance accounts receivable and inventory.

Wholesalers

As a trading operation, wholesalers have a concentration of current assets (or working assets) primarily consisting of their accounts receivable and inventory. Wholesalers generally hold only small amounts of fixed assets relative to their working assets. Their working assets are normally financed with short-term liabilities, primarily bank and trade debt (accounts payable). Their capital requirements for fixed assets are usually small; therefore, a wholesaler's equity and long-term debt requirements are generally smaller than that of a manufacturer or an agricultural company.

Retailers

Retailers generally need to invest more in fixed assets than wholesalers do. Because retailers must draw customers into their stores and create a favorable buying mood with pleasant surroundings, they usually invest in an easily accessible building, decor, shelving, and display-related fixtures. Many retailers are small and undercapitalized with both short-term and long-term debt, each of which usually exceeds equity. Trade debt is often a retailer's most important source of inventory financing. For a small retailer, accounts receivable may be virtually nonexistent; for a large retailer, they might be significant. Since retail sales are often seasonal, many retailers require short-term financing to support their seasonal buildup in inventory.

Service Companies

It is more difficult to generalize concerning typical balance sheet characteristics for a service company because service companies are so diverse—encompassing as they do large utilities, transportation companies, restaurants, laundries, and professional firms. Nonexistent or very low inventories are common to them all, however, since these companies provide a service, rather than sell tangible products.

Fixed assets make up a very large part of the balance sheet equation for utility and transportation companies, as well as laundries, restaurants, and other service companies that require specialized equipment. Fixed assets comprise a small part of the balance sheet for many other service companies. Many service companies provide services for cash, making their accounts receivable very small or nonexistent as well. Some service companies such as professional firms offer credit terms and thereby have significant accounts receivable. Therefore, fixed assets are generally a service company's most significant asset account although, in absolute dollars, it may not be large.

Equity and long-term debt generally finance the large capital commitment required by companies in the transportation and utility industries. Other service companies may have short-term debt if they have accounts receivable, but generally long-term debt and equity support their fixed assets.

INDUSTRY CHARACTERISTICS

Companies in a given industry also tend to have recognizable asset and liability structures. Industries vary particularly in the type and amount of financing that is characteristic. Although airlines and trains both provide transportation service, the balance sheet structures of airlines and train companies vary due to differences in the life cycles of their respective industries. Railroads are a mature industry with plenty of equity generated over many years to finance the expansion and replacement of fixed assets. Airlines, on the other hand, comprise a relatively young industry and have massive amounts of debt to finance their fixed asset requirements.

Another industry characteristic that affects a company's asset-liability balance is cyclicality (that is, the extent to which changes in the economy affect business). Highly cyclical companies (such as textile firms) require higher equity to sustain themselves through poor economic times. In contrast, a company in a staple food industry can operate with less equity because it is less vulnerable to recessions.

MANAGERIAL POLICIES

Generally a company's management policies can be characterized as conservative or aggressive. Companies of the same type in the same industry can have quite different balance sheet characteristics if their basic managerial policies differ. Companies with conservative management philosophies tend to emphasize profits rather than sales growth. Avoidance of risk-taking generally results in a balance sheet that is well capitalized with limited borrowings. Such managers usually take very strict control of their accounts receivable and place less reliance on trade credit as a marketing tool. Such conservatively operated companies often have significant holdings of cash and short-term investments. When management places most of its emphasis on equity, the company's growth is limited by the availability of internally generated equity (through profits) and external equity sources.

EXHIBIT 4.1 ■

Balance Sheet Spreadsheet

Name

		Type		%		%		%		%	I.S.
		Date									
53	ASSETS										
54	Cash										
55	Marketable securities										
56	Accounts receivable—net										
57	Notes receivable										
58	Inventory										
59	CURRENT ASSETS										
60	Fixed assets—net										
61	Due from officers, partners										
62	Due from affiliated concerns										
63	Investments in affiliates										
64	Other investments										
65	Deferred charges/prepaid expenses										
66	Intangibles										
67	NONCURRENT ASSETS										
68	TOTAL ASSETS			100		100		100		100	100
69	LIABILITIES										
70	Notes payable to banks										
71	Commercial paper outstanding										
72	Notes payable to others										
73	Accounts payable—trade										
74	Due affiliated concerns										
75	Due officers, partners, etc.										
76	Accruals										
77	Current maturities of long-term debt										
78	Current-year income taxes										
79	CURRENT DEBT										
80	Long-term debt—secured										
81	Long-term debt—unsecured										
82	Subordinated debt										
83	TOTAL LONG-TERM DEBT										
84	TOTAL DEBT										
85	Reserves—deferred income taxes										
86	Reserves—other										
87	TOTAL RESERVES										
88	MINORITY INTEREST										
89	Capital stock—preferred										
90	—common										
91	Paid-in surplus										
92	Retained earnings										
93	Less: Treasury stock										
94	NET WORTH										
95	TOTAL LIABILITIES AND NET WORTH			100		100		100		100	100
96	WORKING CAPITAL										
97	R	Quick/current									
98	A	Debt to worth									
99	T	Sales to receivables (days)									
100	I	Cost of sales to inventory (days)									
101	O	Purchases to payables (days)									
102	S	Contingent liabilities									

A more aggressive managerial philosophy would emphasize revenue growth and increased market share. The resulting balance sheet would probably show higher debt, lower equity, greater investments in accounts receivable and inventory, and low liquidity. Less stringent credit requirements and more liberal credit terms invite a significant increase in accounts receivable. A management team that emphasizes the importance of never losing a possible sale usually winds up in a heavily inventoried position. Such policies in turn require financing, which often is accomplished with liabilities rather than with equity because most companies cannot generate equity quickly enough. In general, new and smaller businesses take a more aggressive stance because of their limited access to capital.

■ ■ ■ ■ Analysis of Balance Sheet Accounts

In evaluating a company's balance sheet accounts, a loan officer needs to keep in mind the basic balance sheet equation: Assets = Liabilities + Equity. Each element of this equation can be further broken down as follows:

$$\text{Assets} = \text{Current assets} + \text{Noncurrent assets.}$$

$$\text{Liabilities} = \text{Current liabilities} + \text{Long-term debt.}$$

$$\text{Equity} = \text{Capital stock} + \text{Paid-in surplus} + \text{Retained earnings} - \text{Treasury stock.}$$

Exhibit 4.1 shows a sample spreadsheet useful for common-sizing and comparing a company's balance sheets over a period of years. This spreadsheet also facilitates industry comparisons. Exhibit 4.2 shows the balance sheet for Bud's Sporting Goods, the same company whose income statement was analyzed in Chapter 3.

Balance sheet analysis begins with a detailed analysis of a company's assets and continues with its liability and equity accounts.

ASSETS

Since few borrowers merit unsecured loans, lenders evaluate assets in terms of their value as collateral. This is largely a function of their liquidity. *Liquidity* measures how quickly a company can convert its

Comparative Balance Sheet

Bud's Sporting Goods
Balance Sheet as of December 31, 1987 and 1988

	1987	%	1988	%
Assets				
Cash	$ 8,000	7.5	$ 12,000	9.1
Accounts receivable	2,000	1.8	3,000	2.3
Inventory	35,000	33.0	42,000	31.8
Current assets	45,000	42.5	57,000	43.2
Fixed assets—net	58,000	54.7	71,000	53.8
Deferred charges/prepaid expenses	3,000	2.8	4,000	3.0
Noncurrent assets	61,000	57.5	75,000	56.8
Total assets	106,000	100.0	132,000	100.0
Liabilities and Net Worth				
Notes payable to banks	7,000	6.6	10,000	7.6
Accounts payable—trade	20,000	18.9	31,000	23.5
Current maturities—long-term debt	5,000	4.7	5,000	3.8
Current-year income taxes	3,000	2.8	4,000	3.0
Current debt	35,000	33.0	50,000	37.9
Long-term debt—secured	25,000	23.6	20,000	15.2
Total long-term debt	25,000	23.6	20,000	15.2
Total debt	60,000	56.6	70,000	53.0
Capital stock—common	10,000	9.4	10,000	7.6
Retained earnings	36,000	34.0	52,000	39.4
Net worth	46,000	43.4	62,000	47.0
Total liabilities and net worth	$106,000	100.0	$132,000	100.0

assets into cash. Assets on the balance sheet are presented in order of their liquidity—that is, in terms of their convertibility to cash. *Current assets*, defined as assets that should convert to cash within 12 months, are shown first. *Noncurrent assets*, including fixed assets, are listed next.

Current Assets

Current assets are shown on the balance sheet in order of their liquidity—cash first, followed by marketable securities, accounts receivable, notes receivable, and inventory. A company's working assets (including accounts receivable and inventory) are normally converted into cash through the operations of the business.

Cash. In keeping with the priority of liquidity, cash is listed first on the balance sheet. Companies can hold cash in various forms. For example, some companies may keep only a small amount of petty cash on the premises to take care of small disbursements that cannot be paid by check or credit card. Retailers require more cash to be on hand for making change. Retailers that sell products predominantly for cash must have adequate controls over their cash. If a company's cash controls are inadequate, this could indicate that its other controls are also inadequate; thus the company may be a poor credit risk.

Cash is normally represented by deposits in checking accounts that are available for use in a company's operations or in temporary interest-bearing investments. In analyzing a company's cash account, the availability of the cash is the most important consideration. For example, restrictions may apply if the interest-bearing deposits are pledged against debt. Thus if a company pledges its accounts, the cash becomes unavailable for daily operations. Compensating balances, which may be required for support of bank credit facilities, may also be unavailable for operations. A company with foreign bank accounts may find it difficult to transfer deposits to domestic operations. Moreover, deposits of foreign currency are subject to exchange valuations and may decrease when converted to dollars. In assessing the assets available to a business, a loan officer should discount cash that is not readily available.

The amount of time that elapses between the disbursement and collection of cash (for example, between the purchasing of inventory or the payment of expenses and the collection of accounts receivable) determines a company's cash requirements. Companies with sufficient available credit lines or other liabilities need not be as concerned with these timing differences.

Marketable securities. The second category of assets on a balance sheet is marketable securities. Companies often make temporary investments of their excess cash in marketable securities to earn income in the form of dividends, interest, or appreciation until cash is needed in the business. As the name implies, a ready market exists for these securities. U.S. government and high-grade corporate bonds fit this description, as does stock actively traded on a major stock exchange. Stocks of major national companies are classified as marketable securities, whereas stock that is not actively traded, stock in closely held corporations, and stock held in affiliates are not shown as marketable securities on the balance sheet. The loan officer should carefully analyze the overall quality of a company's marketable securities account in terms of investment types and their relative liquidity. However, unless it is large, this account is normally not a significant consideration in financial analysis.

Accounts receivable. When a company sells merchandise or services on credit, it specifies credit terms that allow the purchaser to pay within a specified time and may offer a discount as incentive for early payment. Credit sales are shown as accounts receivable on the balance sheet until they are collected. Other receivables, such as those created by credit extended to company officers, employees, or affiliates, and by sales of other assets should not be included in this account, which is reserved for trade accounts receivable. There are two risks basic to any business—the risk of not selling its inventory or services and the risk of not collecting on an account receivable once the sale is made on terms. When a company makes a credit sale, the first risk disappears and the second risk comes into play.

Both the size and quality of this balance sheet account are of prime interest to a loan officer. Three factors influence the size of a company's accounts receivable: the amount of credit sales, the company's credit terms and collection policies, and customers' payment habits. The more liberal the credit terms offered, the larger the accounts receivable will be. For example, suppose a company's sales total $30,000 per month, terms are net 30 (that is, payment is required in 30 days), and all customers pay within the established time frame. The company's accounts receivable will never exceed $30,000. However, if the company were to extend terms to 60 days, then its accounts receivable could easily double to $60,000.

Furthermore, lax collection practices tend to result in delayed payments. In the last example, if the company ignored overdue accounts and allowed customers to pay in 90 days rather than within the stipulated 60-day terms, its accounts receivable could increase by another $30,000—to $90,000. Liberal extension of credit to noncreditworthy customers and lax collection policies can undermine the quality of a company's accounts receivable.

A lagging economy can also result in slowed payments on accounts receivable. When an overall downturn in economic activity occurs, companies generally earn less profits; thus their liquidity is reduced. A chain reaction of slowed payments results as companies, paid more slowly by their own customers, in turn slow their payments to creditors. Since a company's liquidity is reduced when its receivables convert to cash less readily, less cash is generated for the business's operations.

If accounts receivable have increased rapidly, the loan officer should look at the income statement to see whether there has been a corresponding increase in sales. If not, the increase in receivables may pose a threat to the timely repayment of bank debt.

From the lender's standpoint, accounts receivable normally represent a good source of collateral because they generally are more liquid than the inventory which they replace. With a large customer base, the repayment risk is spread out, and a company's credit terms give the loan officer an idea of the approximate time before their conversion into cash. Accounts receivable also represent good collateral because they can be collected to repay debt.

However, some amount of accounts receivable will usually remain uncollected and, therefore, constitute a loss or bad debt. The company should prepare for this by creating a reserve that is deducted from its accounts receivable. The company increases this reserve by expensing for bad debts through the income statement. When an account becomes uncollectible, it is charged against the reserve.

In assessing a company's accounts receivable, the loan officer should determine the adequacy of a company's bad-debt reserve. The reserve should be a set percentage of the company's receivables. Thus, as

EXHIBIT 4.3 ■

Accounts Receivable Aging

Sherwin Clock Company
Accounts Receivable Aging as of 9/30/88

Customer Name	Total	Current	1–30 Days	31–60 Days	61–90 Days	Over 90 Days
C. Kennedy	$ 10,000	$10,000	$ —	$ —	$ —	$ —
M. Fernandez	14,000	—	14,000	—	—	—
T. Puckorius	5,000	—	—	5,000	—	—
. . .						
. . .						
. . .						
F. Serpa	6,000	—	—	—	—	6,000
Total	$100,000	$75,000	$14,000	$5,000	—	$6,000
Percentage	100%	75%	14%	5%	—	6%

■ ■

EXHIBIT 4.4 ■

Comparative Accounts Receivable Aging

Sherwin Clock Company
Comparative Accounts Receivable Aging

Date	Total	Current	1–30 Days	31–60 Days	61–90 Days	Over 90 Days
3/31/88	$ 85,000	$51,000	$ 8,500	$4,250	$12,750	$8,500
		60%	10%	5%	15%	10%
6/30/88	90,000	63,000	6,300	9,000	4,500	7,200
		70%	7%	10%	5%	8%
9/30/88	100,000	75,000	14,000	5,000	-0-	6,000
		75%	14%	5%	-0-	6%

■ ■

accounts receivable increase, the reserve should increase proportionally. If the quality of the company's accounts receivable deteriorates, the reserve should also be increased. For example, if losses have historically been 1 percent of average accounts receivable, the reserve should represent at least 1 percent of average receivables. If losses in a particular year begin to escalate and this higher level is expected to continue, then the company should increase the amount expensed on the income statement for bad debts.

The loan officer can more easily evaluate receivables with an *aging* of accounts receivable. This is a means of determining the currency of a company's accounts in relation to the credit terms allowed, the success of the company's collection efforts, and the overall quality of the accounts receivable. The company should be able to supply a statement showing the aging of each account receivable, both individually and by category. This is important because the older the receivable, the less likely it is to be paid.

Exhibit 4.3 illustrates a sample aging of accounts receivable. Without knowing the company's credit terms, this accounts receivable aging shows that 75 percent of the receivables are current (that is, not delinquent), and 89 percent are less than 30 days past due, which appears to represent a good collection effort. The loan officer can also use the aging to identify any concentration in accounts receivable in one or a few accounts. Such concentration usually means increased repayment risk although this depends on the quality of the customer representing the concentration.

Companies should age their accounts periodically to monitor the quality of their receivables over time and to spot current repayment trends. In many service industries, the accounts receivable should be broken out into completed work and work in process. For example, a CPA firm may list accounts receivable for audits in process. Exhibit 4.4 shows a comparative aging of receivables for three consecutive quarterly periods for the same company presented above. Although the company's total receivables have increased, the timeliness of repayment has improved over the three quarters—that is, the past due receivables have become more current. If the trend were negative, the loan officer would want to determine the causes and investigate what actions management has taken to reverse the slowing trend.

Notes receivable. The next asset account on the balance sheet is notes receivable. A note receivable is an outstanding note with a specific repayment agreement. Notes receivable are not a normal part of the operations of most businesses, and thus do not usually constitute a significant asset account. However, some businesses accept notes for the sale of merchandise. For instance, a heavy equipment dealer may accept notes with extended payment terms for the sale of large pieces of equipment.

If a note is not due within 12 months, then only the maturities due in the next 12 months are included under the company's current assets. The remaining maturities are carried on the balance sheet as noncurrent assets.

An evaluation of the quality of any notes begins with their payment status. If a customer took the note out to pay a past-due wholesale account receivable, for example, then a collection problem already exists and the note may be of questionable value. The company's liquidity is reduced if it cannot collect the note on a timely basis. If the company's notes receivable start to become a significant account, the loan officer should investigate the company's credit policies.

Companies can also assign notes as collateral. However, before the bank accepts notes as collateral, the loan officer should obtain financial information on the debtor to determine whether the note will be paid within its specified terms.

Inventory. Usually the last current asset account on the balance sheet is inventory. Inventory comprises the products that a retailer or wholesaler has purchased for resale. For a manufacturing company, inventory includes both the raw materials used to manufacture finished products, work-in-process, and any finished products not yet sold. For service companies, consumable supplies used in the business of providing a service are considered inventory. For example, replacement tires kept on hand by a trucking company would be classified as inventory.

For a retailer or wholesaler, the possibility that inventory will not sell is a basic business risk. A manufacturer's finished inventory is subject to this same risk. Therefore, the loan officer should assess a company's inventory account in terms of the marketability of its inventory.

Some kinds of merchandise have predictable and long-term marketability. For example, undergarments are staple items that tend to hold their value because they are a basic clothing item subject to continuous consumer demand. If, however, a company's inventory consists of stylish, trendy, or special-purpose inventory, a sudden drop in market demand could render such inventory valueless. In evaluating a company's inventory account, the loan officer should determine if it includes obsolete inventory that failed to meet market demand. If so, the value of the company's inventory may be overstated. Obsolete inventory does not represent liquidity for the company, and it represents poor collateral value for a lender to liquidate to repay debt.

Inventory that the company does not own but holds for the supplier (that is, the company pays for it only after the inventory sells) is called *consignment inventory*. The company never takes title to such inventory and acts only as an agent for the supplier. This type of inventory has no value for collateral purposes. Consequently, the lender should deduct consignment inventory from the inventory account on a company's balance sheet.

Managerial policies directly affect the size of the inventory account. Management may decide to compete more aggressively by keeping inventory stock high—which could prove risky if a sudden drop in market demand for the product occurs. Sometimes companies keep large inventories because supplies are difficult to obtain or entail lengthy waits before delivery.

A large inventory account can also result from speculation in inventory. A company may try to hedge on prices by buying in bulk at a low price in hopes of selling large quantities later at a higher price. If the price of the goods decreases instead of increasing, a large loss may result when the company sells its inventory. Often companies are not in a position to hold onto excess inventory in hopes of a later price increase because they need liquidity. Moreover, holding onto inventory can be expensive, especially during periods of high interest rates if bank financing is required.

In addition to finished goods inventory, manufacturers typically have two other types of inventory: raw materials used in the manufacturing process and work-in-process. Loan officers evaluate these inventory accounts on the same basis as finished goods—that is, in terms of their marketability. The end use of raw materials determines their marketability. If the raw materials have multiple uses and could be liquidated by selling them to various manufacturing industries, their marketability is much better than that of a raw material that is only used in a single manufacturing process.

The amount of work-in-process inventory depends primarily on the length of the production process. If the production process is short, then the value of the company's work-in-process will be small in relation to its raw materials and finished goods inventories. However, if the process is complex, as for the manufacturing of large or heavy equipment, then a more significant proportion of a company's assets may be tied up in work-in-process. Partially completed products not only require additional investment before they reach the value of finished goods, but usually their value is less than the invested costs. Therefore, the lender should assign a low value to work-in-process inventory for loan collateral purposes.

A company that makes customized products on order usually has a large work-in-process inventory and no finished goods inventory since its products are delivered to the buyer immediately upon completion. Since the general marketability of custom-made products is very low, a company should require substantial deposits or progress payments while manufacturing the products in order to reduce the risk of custom orders not being accepted. Custom-made inventory has little collateral value in the eyes of a loan officer.

As discussed in Chapter 3, companies may account for their inventory using either a perpetual or periodic inventory system. In either case, an actual count of inventory is necessary periodically. Unless the inventory account on the balance sheet reflects an actual physical inventory, it can only be an approximation—a fact the loan officer will want to know. The loan officer should also determine the accuracy of the company's inventory system by comparing the physical count to the book account. This provides a general idea of the credibility of the company's book value inventory account when it is not based on a physical count.

The loan officer will also want to know what method the company uses to value its inventory. As discussed in Chapter 3, there are two basic methods of valuing inventory: last in, first out (LIFO) and first in, first out (FIFO). Since LIFO values the company's inventory at older prices, this method undervalues the inventory compared to current prices during inflationary periods. FIFO valuation, on the other hand, values the company's inventory at more current, higher prices.

Companies often reduce the value of their inventories at year-end to their perceived market value. These write-downs of inventory can involve substantial amounts if the marketability of a company's products has been greatly reduced.

Other current assets. This account is usually insignificant. For example, the company would list an income tax refund due in this account. Since tax refunds usually result from a previous operating loss, this is not an item the loan officer would hope to find. Nevertheless, tax refunds do represent a source of liquidity when received.

Cash-value life insurance, which represents cash deposits built up over time in a whole life insurance policy, is another item that might show up in the other current assets account. A company can use this available cash in the business if the cash value is unencumbered by a loan from the insurance company or other financial institution. The insurance policy's real liquidity depends on the death of the insured. A loan officer should determine who is insured, as well as the face value of the policies. The lender should also evaluate the adequacy of the insurance coverage in terms of the importance of the insured persons to the company and the liabilities that would need to be paid from the proceeds.

This account may also include some types of prepaid expenses. If so, the lender should determine when the expense was paid and when it will be recognized on the income statement.

Noncurrent Assets

The assets described up to this point are all classified as current assets. Noncurrent assets, in contrast, are not expected to convert to cash within 12 months. The principal category of noncurrent assets is fixed assets. Other noncurrent assets are loan repayments due from company officers and affiliates, investments in other companies, prepaid expenses, deferred charges, and intangible assets.

Fixed assets. Fixed assets include equipment, buildings, vehicles, tools, computers, office equipment, leasehold improvements, and furniture—that is, any items of a fairly permanent nature that are required for the normal conduct of a business. The fixed asset account may be highly significant or very small, depending on the type of business. The

Straight-Line Depreciation

Cost of asset: $10,000
Useful life: 5 years
Depreciation rate: 20% per year

	Depreciation Expense	Book Value of Asset
Year 1	$ 2,000	$8,000
Year 2	2,000	6,000
Year 3	2,000	4,000
Year 4	2,000	2,000
Year 5	2,000	-0-
	$10,000	

■ ■

valuation of fixed assets is an important consideration in analyzing this account.

Financial statements report the value of fixed assets at *book value*. This is an accounting convention which values assets based on their original cost (the purchase price paid by the company) minus allowable depreciation to date. However, the book value of assets is of little concern to lenders. They are concerned primarily with *liquidation value*—the amount that a company or creditor could realize if it had to dispose of assets quickly. Most assets have substantially less value in liquidation than their *market value*—defined as the price a company could reasonably expect to receive for an asset in the open market in good economic and business conditions. The liquidation value of assets may be either more or less than their book value.

With the exception of land, fixed assets are assumed to lose their economic value over time—both for financial reporting and tax purposes. A fixed asset is valued at cost, or book value, when it is purchased, but each year thereafter it is depreciated—that is, it is valued at a progressively lower amount—until it is considered to be without value. This reflects the fact that most fixed assets eventually wear out and must be replaced. However, there are various ways of figuring depreciation and the same company may figure depreciation differently for financial reporting purposes and for tax purposes.

The depreciation method that is normally used for financial reporting purposes is called *straight-line depreciation*. This method divides the cost of a fixed asset by its economic life and reduces the value of the asset each year by that amount. Exhibit 4.5 shows this calculation on a fixed asset costing $10,000 and having a useful life of 5 years. The annual depreciation expense, which is recognized on the company's income statement as an operating expense, is $2,000, and the value of the asset is reduced to zero over a 5-year period.

Since depreciation is a noncash yet tax-deductible expense, it is a tax advantage to write off the value of an asset as quickly as possible. However, the Internal Revenue Service dictates how fast companies can depreciate fixed assets for tax purposes. The Economic Recovery Tax Act of 1981 introduced a new depreciation system, called the *accelerated cost recovery system (ACRS)*, which eliminated the useful-life concept for tax purposes and replaced it with a shorter recovery period. The law

Accelerated Cost Recovery

Class (Years)	Declining Balance Percentage
3	200
5	200
7	200
10	200
15	150
20	150
27.5	straight-line
31.5	straight-line

Accelerated Cost Recovery

Cost of asset: $10,000
5-year class
Declining balance percentage: 200

	Rate*	Depreciation Expense	Book Value of Asset
Year 1	40%	$ 4,000	$6,000
Year 2	40	2,400	3,600
Year 3	40	1,440	2,160
Year 4	50	1,080	1,080
Year 5	100	1,080	-0-
		$10,000	

*Based on declining balance.

also allowed more cost recovery in the earlier years of the recovery period, which is why it is called accelerated cost recovery.

The Tax Reform Act of 1986 in turn modified the ACRS. The ACRS now differentiates eight classes of property, each with different allowable recovery periods, as shown in Exhibit 4.6. The depreciable percentage of the cost of an asset is now either 200 percent or 150 percent of the straight-line percentage for the respective periods. This accelerated write-off percentage is calculated on the declining balance of the cost of an asset as each year's depreciation is deducted. This is done until the straight-line depreciation amount for the declining balance over the remaining years of the recovery period exceeds the ACRS amount. Then the straight-line amount can be used to complete the write-off. The last two classes (27.5 and 31.5 years) are required to use the straight-line method only.

Depreciation for tax purposes can be figured either by the straight-line method or by ACRS. Exhibit 4.7 shows the allowable depreciation expense using ACRS for the same $10,000 piece of equipment depreciated by the straight-line method in Exhibit 4.5. The depreciation expense using ACRS is greater in the first 2 years than with straight-line depreciation. Although this results in lower profit figures, it is advantageous because the accelerated depreciation involves a noncash expense yet results in lower taxes. Because of the difference that results in taxable income, and hence taxes paid, companies that use the accelerated depreciation method for tax purposes and the straight-line method for financial reporting purposes create a *reserve for deferred taxes*, which appears on the balance sheet as a long-term liability.

Land is one fixed asset that does not depreciate on the balance sheet. If used in the normal course of operations, land is considered a fixed asset; otherwise, it is considered an investment. Since land is valued at cost on the company's balance sheet, its appreciation can represent hidden value. The same is true of buildings which depreciate on the balance sheet but may actually appreciate in value over time.

The loan officer should also assess the capacity, efficiency, and specialization of a company's fixed assets. Capacity is defined in terms of how much additional sales volume a company's existing fixed assets can support. For example, if a company produces $1 million in sales using one 8-hour work shift, it should have the capacity to produce $3 million in sales using three 8-hour shifts. However, if management expects sales to increase above $3 million, the company needs additional capacity and equipment.

A company's efficiency depends on the cost-effectiveness of the equipment it uses. More efficient equipment may or may not reduce the cost of manufacturing products or providing services to a point that replacing existing equipment is cost-effective. However, as less efficient equipment nears the end of its economic life, it may pay to replace it with state-of-the-art equipment. Old equipment can become technologically obsolete because of new production methods or because more advanced equipment comes on the market. A company with inefficient equipment may become less competitive in its pricing.

Specialized equipment may have a lower resale value than a more commonly used piece of equipment. The marketability of a company's fixed assets, rather than their book value (cost minus depreciation), determines their value as collateral. Thus multi-use fixed assets have higher collateral value than single-purpose fixed assets, the actual value of which could be less than their cost or book value. For example, if a company incurs a large cost preparing a building to accept a highly specialized piece of equipment, this increases the cost (book value) of the building. However, a prospective buyer who plans to use the building for a different purpose will not want to pay extra for these added features.

Any costs of improving a leased building—such as carpeting, special lighting, general renovations, and decorating—are not expensed on the income statement but are carried on the balance sheet as fixed assets and depreciated. However, these types of fixed assets, called *leasehold improvements*, stay with the building and become the property of the owner should the company ever move to a new location. For this reason, banks give leasehold improvements little or no value as collateral. It is not unusual for certain types of service companies to have leasehold improvements constitute their major category of fixed assets.

Capitalized lease equipment is another type of asset which is accounted for as a fixed asset. However, since the company does not own the equipment, this type of fixed asset has no liquidation value. The loan officer will want to be aware of any leased assets in the fixed asset account when making a lending decision.

Due from officers/partners. This noncurrent asset account represents a company loan to one of its officers or owners. Although such loans are usually shown as an account receivable on financial statements, such loans often do not represent a liquid asset convertible to cash and available for business operations. Company officers normally pay the company last because they own part of the company. Therefore, the loan officer should shift such loans from accounts receivable to the noncurrent asset category.

The loan officer should also determine why the loan was made and the prospects for repayment. For example, an officer may have taken a loan from the company in lieu of a salary or bonus. This loan is in effect an expense not recognized by the company, thus improving its profitability. Moreover, the company officer need not claim the loan as income, thus avoiding additional personal taxes. An officer may even purchase stock in the company through the use of a note.

Loans to company officers should be examined closely by the lender to determine whether the officer has sufficient personal liquidity to repay this receivable. This is particularly important if the company must depend on repayment of the loan for needed liquidity. Therefore, the loan officer must evaluate this account in light of the overall financial condition of the company. A company that is borrowing funds to lend to one of its officers should be closely watched.

Due from affiliated concerns. Affiliated companies are those related by common ownership, either one owning the other or both companies owned by the same individual or other company. Amounts due from affiliates, like those due from officers or partners, are usually disclosed as an account receivable on the company's financial statements. However, this receivable may be nonliquid because of the nature of the affiliation and the absence of pressure to pay such debts. Thus the loan officer should consider it as a noncurrent asset.

The bank's loan officer should also determine the purpose of this account. Do normal sales exist between the companies? Has one company lent money to the other? Regardless of the reason behind this account, does the affiliate have the ability to repay the receivable? If a company wants to borrow money from the bank in order to lend it to an affiliated company, the loan officer should obtain financial statements on the affiliate as well in order to evaluate its ability to back up repayment. Extensive intercompany borrowings or investments bear watching, particularly in a closely held company where the distinction between owner and company finances may be blurred.

Investments in affiliates. When a company owns 20 percent or more of the common stock of another company, it normally can influence the operations of that company. The equity method of accounting is required to record such investments. This account reflects the amount of the company's investment in the affiliate, as well as the company's accumulated share in the earnings or losses of the affiliate since the investment was made. Any dividends that have been received should be deducted from the investment. Thus this account represents the net book value of the investment. Any earnings or dividends will show up as "other income" on the income statement, as was discussed in Chapter 3. Investments of less than 20 percent in other companies are listed as other investments on the balance sheet.

Deferred charges. This account usually represents major costs that have not yet been expensed—which, if expensed, would reduce the company's profitability. This account is similar to prepaid expenses in that future benefits arise from these costs; however, the company expenses these costs as it receives their benefits. As a result, the company's balance sheet overstates its earnings when these costs are incurred but not expensed.

Some companies show their start-up expenses as deferred charges because they will result in future sales benefits, yet to expense them at the outset would jeopardize the company's profitability. Developmental expenses related to real estate, such as architectural fees and surveys, are usually carried as deferred charges. This account represents no value in liquidation nor liquidity for operations. For this reason, the loan officer should thoroughly investigate any sizable amount in this account.

Prepaid expenses. Other costs that have been paid but have not yet been expensed on the income statement are prepaid expenses. Examples of prepaid expenses include insurance premiums paid annually or rent paid one month in advance. Prepaid expenses provide no liquidity, although they do provide a future expense benefit. Companies usually report prepaid expenses as a current asset. However, since the account has no liquidation value, the loan officer should not recognize it for liquidity purposes and should consider it a noncurrent asset.

Intangibles. These are nonmaterial resources having no quantifiable value to the company. The intangible that most commonly shows up on balance sheets is goodwill, an accounting mechanism used when one company buys another. When the actual price paid to purchase another company exceeds its book value, the excess cost is called *goodwill.* It represents payment in consideration of the acquired company's established customer base, reputation, and future earnings potential. Tax law requires that goodwill be treated as a non-tax-deductible expense which is amortized over a 40-year period if the company was acquired after 1970. Because intangibles have no liquidation value and no liquidity value, the loan officer should deduct any intangibles from the company's net asset value to obtain a true value for the company in the event of liquidation.

Other noncurrent assets. Assets that do not fit into any other category are valued at cost although they may have significant market value. The loan officer should know what items are included in this account—usually patents, trademarks, or operating rights.

Patents give a company the exclusive right to manufacture a product. This account reflects only the cost of obtaining the patent although the value of a patent for a highly successful product will be far greater than its original cost.

A *trademark* represents the registered name of a product or service. Trademarks can be bought and sold, or used in exchange for royalty payments. Again, the balance sheet account reflects only the original cost of establishing the trademark, although the current value of a trademark may be far greater.

Operating rights are special rights granted by government regulatory agencies, that are required in certain industries to operate. For example, trucking firms, airlines, and television stations all must obtain operating rights for their areas of operation. Because companies can sell or lease these rights, they often represent a far greater value to a company than is shown on the balance sheet.

LIABILITIES AND NET WORTH

The loan officer is now ready to look at the other side of the Assets = Liabilities + Net Worth equation. Whereas assets represent the gross value of a business entity, liabilities represent claims against those assets. The company's total liabilities also determine the company's net worth (or equity). A company's liabilities and equity represent not only claims against the assets but reflect how the assets have been financed. Unlike assets, which can fluctuate in true value depending on their marketability, liabilities are fixed in value and must eventually be paid at that value.

The loan officer should evaluate the company's liabilities in terms of their repayment requirements and continued availability as a source of financing for the company and their sources of payment. Liabilities should also be evaluated in terms of their cost to the company and the assets that may secure them. The loan officer should also distinguish between current and long-term liabilities. Debts that will come due for repayment within 12 months are considered current, whereas those having maturities in excess of 12 months are considered noncurrent. Short-term debt is normally incurred to finance current assets (such as accounts receivable and inventory), whereas long-term loans are normally used to finance fixed assets.

In analyzing any liability, the loan officer should determine to whom the money is owed, why it was borrowed, its repayment terms, whether assets have been pledged, and whether any restrictive loan agreements are in force.

Current Liabilities

A company normally pays its current liabilities (or short-term debt) from the conversion to cash of current assets in the 12-month period following the balance sheet date. A company's current liabilities may include notes payable to banks, commercial paper, accounts payable, accruals, loan repayments to officers or affiliates, and current-year income taxes.

Notes payable to banks. This account represents the short-term financing of a company's current assets (accounts receivable and inventory). A company with seasonal financing needs may have a seasonal line of credit. For example, a retail company may use a bank loan to increase its inventory prior to Christmas. As the company sells its inventory, it creates accounts receivable or cash. When these accounts are collected or cash sales accumulate, the bank loan is repaid. Therefore, short-term bank debt may fluctuate depending on when in the operating cycle a company prepares its balance sheet.

If the bank debt represents a seasonal or revolving line of credit, the loan officer should determine its terms, including payout requirements, if applicable. Since the company may have loans from more than one bank, the loan officer's evaluation should cover the purpose, expiration date, interest rates, and security pledged on each credit line. The evaluation should also assess the adequacy of these lines of credit for the company's needs.

A company may have asset-based financing, which is usually maintained at a maximum level in relation to the assets financed (accounts receivable and inventory). Banks base their level of financing on a total loan advance rate as a percentage of the financed assets. The outstanding debt should always be at or below this advance rate.

Occasionally, a company's longer-term bank debt temporarily has a maturity within 12 months, although amortization over a longer period at maturity is intended. If this is known, the loan officer should analyze this debt as long-term rather than short-term debt.

Commercial paper. This account represents unsecured short-term borrowings from an investor for up to 270 days in amounts of $100,000 or more. Usually this form of financing is only available to well-regarded national companies with an established credit rating (as conferred by such investment services as Moody's or Standard & Poor's). Companies usually pay interest rates lower than bank prime rates for commercial paper.

Notes payable to others. This account includes any amounts borrowed from creditors other than banks and investors in commercial paper. The loan officer should determine the identity of such creditors, including the reasons for creating the note, its terms, and the security pledged. Because such notes may represent a significantly past-due trade account, existence of this account on the balance sheet should signal caution to the loan officer.

Accounts payable. This account represents normal trade credit extended by suppliers for purchases of inventory and services. Trade payables owed by one company are shown as accounts receivable on its creditors' financial statements. The loan officer should know the normal credit terms and the borrower's ability to take advantage of discounts.

Accounts payable represent a permanent source of "interest free" funding for the company because, as the company pays its accounts, financing always remains available for new purchases. If, however, a company does not pay its accounts on a timely basis, its suppliers may refuse to extend it credit for new purchases. The company then either has to pay cash or finds itself without a source of inventory to continue its operations. The loan officer can determine the current status of a company's trade payables by calculating *payables turnover*. Stretching the amount of time between making purchases and paying for them is referred to as "riding the trade" and could indicate mismanagement or inadequate liquidity. If accounts payable turns are slowing, this may indicate that cash resources have been diverted to other uses, such as to purchase fixed assets or to fund losses. Chapter 6 covers payables turnover in more detail.

The relationship between the size of a company's payables and its inventory should also be analyzed. Inventory turnover represents the average time required for a company to sell all of its inventory. Since payables normally have shorter repayment terms than the turnover of inventory, a company's inventory account will normally be larger than its payables account. As inventory levels decrease over time, payables should decrease proportionally. If this is not the case, the loan officer should investigate why.

Due to affiliated concerns, officers, partners, etc. Any amounts owed to company officers, partners, or other owners, as well as debts to affiliated companies, are properly carried as current liabilities, regardless of their term. This is prudent since management controls repayment and can pay such debts quickly at will. The loan officer should determine how this liability to officers or affiliated companies arose and its terms, including any interest payable. For tax reasons, a company officer may lend funds to the company rather than invest in additional stock as equity. This type of debt should always be subordinated to bank debt. A loan is subordinate if the officer or affiliate has agreed not to be repaid until the bank loan is repaid.

Accruals. This account represents unpaid costs that the company has expensed through the income statement. These expenses usually are those paid at regular intervals, such as salaries and wages, utilities, and withholding taxes. For example, if a balance sheet is prepared in the middle of a pay period, the wages owed as of that date are shown as an accrual. The loan officer should look for significant amounts in this account. If a comparative analysis reveals any unusual buildup in accruals, short-term debt, and payables, a liquidity crisis could result, making timely payments to short-term creditors difficult. Accruals of prior quarters' withholding taxes are especially crucial in analysis because of potential Internal Revenue Service priority to a company's assets. Most banks do not lend money to companies with delinquent tax liability.

Current maturities of long-term debt. This account represents the principal portion of installment payments on long-term debt due (annually, quarterly, or monthly) over the next 12 months. Unlike other current liabilities, which depend on the conversion of current assets for repayment, the company normally pays these current maturities from its profits. Analysis of installment debt should include identification of its terms, conditions, security, and to whom it is owed. Some loans are structured so that the entire balance of an amortizing loan will become due. The loan officer should be alert to any such *balloon payments* in this account since they may require refinancing. If so, the lender needs to determine the likelihood of such refinancing being available. In many cases, the terms of the loan may already require refinancing.

Current-year income taxes. This account represents the tax liability due from the just-completed fiscal year but not yet paid or deferred as of the statement date. The tax liability shown in this account seldom matches the income tax expense from the income statement for two reasons. First, companies pay estimated income tax on a quarterly basis. Thus their year-end tax liability is far less than their total tax liability. In fact, any taxes owed for previous quarters should put the loan officer on notice for potential IRS liens. Second, this account does not include any deferred taxes since they are not a current liability. Deferred tax liability is included as a reserve item (a long-term liability).

Other current liabilities. This account is usually insignificant in relation to total current liabilities. However, if a company manufactures custom-made or high-priced products, it may require large deposits before processing or shipping orders. Such deposits, which are classified as a current liability, can be an important source of financing for these products. However, such deposits reduce the assets included as accounts receivable when the company finally invoices the products as sales. In liquidation customer deposits can also affect the value of inventory if the deposits were for inventory in stock. Funds held for year-end disbursement to a profit-sharing plan would also be reported in this account.

Long-Term Liabilities

These accounts represent debt with maturities in excess of 12 months. Both long-term debt (with maturities in excess of 20 years) and intermediate-term debt (with maturities of more than 1 year but less than 20 years) are combined on the balance sheet. Long-term debt is usually used to finance land and buildings and sometimes expensive manufacturing equipment. Intermediate-term debt usually finances equipment and permanent increases in inventory levels and accounts receivable. The purchase of another company would also be financed with intermediate-term debt. Repayment of longer-term liabilities normally comes from profits and not from the conversion of current assets to cash. Therefore, a company's long-term debt burden must be analyzed in relation to future profitability. Again, the loan officer's debt analysis should cover terms, purpose, interest rate, and security pledged for all outstanding loans.

Long-term debt. When a business incurs long-term debt, it usually enters into a loan agreement, which the loan officer should obtain a copy of. It will detail such provisions as terms and conditions of repayment, including default provisions. The loan officer also needs to determine whether other creditors have restricted the company from incurring the proposed debt. The balance sheet may also distinguish between secured and unsecured debt. A secured loan is one against which a tangible asset has been pledged in case of default on the loan.

Subordinated debt. Subordinated debt is a junior liability (usually held by company officers or affiliated companies) that can only be repaid when specified debt obligations—the terms of the subordination agreement— have been met. For example, a bank may extend a loan to a company only on the condition that any debt held by the owner or other stockholders be subordinated to the bank debt. This may be advisable when lending to a privately held company. The loan officer should obtain copies of subordinated debt agreements or hold the original agreement and notes if debt is subordinated to the bank and thoroughly understand their terms.

Reserves. Reserves represent a liability of a business that will become due sometime in the future. Although they are not a formal debt currently owed to a creditor, they are recognized on the balance sheet as a liability that will theoretically become due sometime in the future. Deferred income tax liability, the most common reserve item, is usually created to reconcile discrepancies arising from the use of different fixed asset depreciation methods for tax purposes and financial reporting purposes. Many companies depreciate fixed assets faster for tax purposes than for financial reporting purposes although, over the long term, both methods result in the expensing of 100 percent of the cost of the fixed asset. The "extra" tax liability incurred by using the straight-line, rather than the accelerated, depreciation method for financial reporting purposes is carried as a reserve for deferred taxes.

For example, assume that a company shows $10,000 net profit before tax on its income statement. Included in its expenses are $2,000 of depreciation on a $10,000 depreciable asset, figured using the straight-line depreciation method. However, for tax purposes, the company uses the accelerated depreciation method which, as shown by Exhibits 4.5 and 4.7, enables the company to depreciate the asset far more quickly in the early years. Thus depreciation for tax purposes is $4,000 for the first year, and taxable income becomes $10,000 minus $2,000 (reflecting the additional depreciation), or $8,000. The resulting tax (at a 15 percent rate) is $1,500 (.15 × $10,000) for financial reporting purposes, but only $1,200 (.15 × $8,000) actually payable on its income tax return. The $300 discrepancy between the $1,500 tax liability reported on the income statement and the $1,200 tax liability reported on the company's tax return would appear on the company's balance sheet as a reserve for deferred income taxes.

As long as the value of the company's fixed assets continues to increase, the reserve remains stable or increases as additional depreciation is figured on an accelerated basis. Thus this tax liability can be deferred indefinitely unless there is a substantial drop in the company's fixed asset purchases. In that case, the reserve may convert to a current liability (income tax debt) requiring payment in the current year.

Other reserves may be created in recognition of costs that have not yet been incurred such as a bad-debt reserve. Expensing through the income statement creates and adds to the reserve. When the cost is actually realized, the reserve should be large enough that additional expensing will not be required.

For example, if a manufacturer plans to discontinue a product line requiring specialized equipment that is unusable in its other processes, the company may have to liquidate the equipment for less than its book value. This liquidation creates a potential loss that the company can recognize and compensate for in advance. The company can expense the difference between the book value of the equipment and the actual selling price through the income statement and create the reserve. When the company actually liquidates the equipment, the company charges any loss to the reserve rather than to its income statement.

Although the reserve does not represent a liability actually owed, fixed assets must be reduced in value by at least the reserve amount. The fixed assets are then worth less than book value for collateral purposes.

Minority interest. This account occurs only when the reporting company has a partially owned subsidiary. If a parent company consolidates the subsidiary into its financial statements (that is, show assets, liabilities, and net worth for the total organization), then the minority interest not owned by the parent company must be represented as a liability on the parent company's financial statements. This liability is not considered a debt, but represents a claim against assets of the subsidiary. Therefore, the loan officer should not use this account in calculating leverage for the company.

Net Worth

The difference between a company's total assets and its total liabilities is its equity, or net worth (also called *owners' equity* or *shareholders' equity*). The amount of equity represents the cushion available to a lender in liquidating assets to repay liabilities. Creditors enjoy more protection with loan collateral and repayment probability when the company holds fewer liabilities. Excessive liabilities result in higher principal and interest payments that erode a company's profits and its financial strength. A highly leveraged company (one with proportionally more debt), therefore, represents a greater credit risk than a company with relatively little debt (and more equity).

Stockholders, like creditors, have a claim against the assets of a company. However, stockholders can make their claims only after all the company's creditors have been paid. Stockholders must absorb any shrinkage in a company's asset values and take the most risk in financing a company.

For a sole proprietorship or general partnership, the net worth is simply the amount of equity invested by the owners or partners. For a corporation, equity or net worth may consist of *capital stock*, *paid-in surplus*, *retained earnings*, and *treasury stock*. Net worth is calculated as the sum of the first three components less the fourth component (treasury stock).

Capital stock. Capital stock represents the nominal value of the company's outstanding shares of stock, including both preferred and common stock. Capital stock is valued at par value, an arbitrary value established when a company authorizes shares to be issued. Separate accounts may be shown for common stock and preferred stock. Common stock entitles the holder to vote at shareholders' meetings and provides potential income to the investor through declared dividends and appreciation in value. Dividends are declared at management's discretion. Preferred stock often does not entail voting rights, but dividends accrue at a set rate (which is fixed at the time of issuance). However, the company does not have to pay the set rate unless common stock dividends have been declared. Preferred stockholders also have preference ahead of common stockholders to the company's assets in liquidation.

Paid-in surplus. This account represents the extra equity a corporation generates when it sells stock in excess of its nominal, or par, value. Companies usually issue stock for a price in excess of par value. The difference between the issue price and par value represents paid-in surplus. Although a company usually creates this type of account when issuing stock for cash, paid-in surplus also results when stock is issued in exchange for a note receivable or for an asset invested in the company. If the company accepts an asset in exchange for stock, the loan officer should determine how the company established value for the asset. The loan officer should also look at transactions involving stock issued in return for a note receivable. If the company is unable to collect on the note receivable, then no true equity exists. Thus until the company can collect the note receivable, its financial statement overstates its equity.

Retained earnings. This account represents the amount of net profit after tax that is kept in the company as a future source of financing. A healthy company retains some of its earnings to reduce its dependence on liabilities. It pays a reasonable dividend to its owners (the stockholders) so that its stock remains an attractive investment and thus a possible source of future financing. Excessive dividends, however, result in less retained income to build equity, thereby increasing the risk to the lender.

Treasury stock. This account consists of stock that has been issued and is later repurchased by the company. Thus it represents a reduction in equity. The value of treasury stock is subtracted from the other accounts that comprise a company's net worth. If a company later retires its stock (at which point it is no longer outstanding), it reduces the par value and paid-in surplus of the stock by the original issue value. Any excess paid for the stock is deducted from the company's retained earnings. These shares then return to an authorized but unissued status.

Tangible Net Worth

When analyzing a company's net worth, the lender will also want to look at its tangible net worth, a figure that does not show up on the balance sheet. This is important because any shrinkage in the value of a company's assets can only be absorbed by equity. A company's liabilities to its creditors do not shrink when asset values are reduced. Therefore, to obtain a true picture of the relationship between a company's debt and equity, the loan officer should compare its tangible net worth to its liabilities. The tangible net worth is calculated by deducting those asset values relating to goodwill, notes receivable for stock purchases, deferred charges, and prepaid expenses since these assets have no value in liquidation.

The loan officer should also take into consideration a company's investment in nonproductive assets, such as boats, planes, and recreational homes that may have been purchased for the pleasure of the company's owners and provide little benefit to the business. Some lenders also deduct the value of leasehold improvements and officers' receivables when calculating tangible net worth.

The true relationship between equity and debt can be determined when equity has been adjusted for these weak asset values. Thus tangible net worth gives the lender a true picture of a company's financial cushion in the face of shrinkage in its asset values. At the same time, sufficient values are identified to cover the company's liabilities.

Reconciliation of Net Worth

Like any other balance sheet account, a company's net worth can change from operating period to operating period. Ideally, this change results from increases in equity invested by stockholders or increases in retained earnings from operations. Companies usually present a detailed reconciliation of net worth to the bank as a part of their financial statements. If none is available, the loan officer should prepare a reconciliation showing any changes in the equity accounts (net worth) from period to period. A reconciliation of net worth for Bud's Sporting Goods, which ties together the income statement discussed in the last chapter (Exhibit 3.2) and the balance sheet presented in this chapter (Exhibit 4.2), is shown as Exhibit 4.8.

A company's net worth increases when after-tax profits are added to retained earnings. Increases may also result from new equity investments involving the sale of additional stock to shareholders. Additionally, a company's equity accounts may increase as a result of extraordinary credits to retained earnings not related to the company's operations, such as the life insurance proceeds from a deceased officer or a donation of assets to the company.

On the other hand, a company's equity accounts may decrease. For example, equity will decrease if the company shows a net operating loss after taxes. It will also decrease if earnings are paid out as dividends to stockholders, rather than held as retained earnings. Decreased equity may also result from the repurchase of outstanding shares of stock as treasury stock, as well as from extraordinary debits to retained earnings not related to the company's operations, such as asset value loss due to uninsured or partially insured accidents or thefts.

The loan officer should understand any changes to a company's equity accounts. By isolating these changes through a reconciliation of net worth, the loan officer can direct specific questions to the company's management about those changes and clarify the company's net worth.

EXHIBIT 4.8 ■

Reconciliation of Net Worth

Bud's Sporting Goods
Reconciliation of Net Worth
for the Year Ended December 31, 1988

Net worth—beginning	$46,000
Net profit	16,000
Retained earnings credit	—
Less: Net loss	—
Less: Dividends—Preferred	—
—Common	—
Less: Retained earnings	—
Paid-in surplus credit	—
Less: Paid-in surplus debits	—
Capital accounts	—
Net worth—increase	16,000
Net worth—ending	$62,000

■ ■

■ ■ ■ ■ Comparative Analysis

Comparative analysis is an important part of balance sheet analysis. This includes internal comparisons of a company's current and previous balance sheets and external comparisons of the company's results with those of other companies or with industry averages. However, because a company's balance sheet represents its financial condition at a given point in time, the loan officer must make sure that balance sheet comparisons are meaningful. An internal comparison of balance sheets prepared on the same day for consecutive years would be meaningful whereas comparison of a company's figures for one year with industry averages for a previous year might not be meaningful.

INTERNAL COMPARISONS

In analyzing the company's balance sheet accounts, the loan officer should spread and common-size the figures, as shown in Exhibits 4.1 and 4.2. Each asset account is shown as a percentage of total assets, and each liability and equity account as a percentage of the total liabilities and equity. The loan officer can thus evaluate each account in absolute dollar terms and also in terms of the relative distribution of assets and their financing sources: liabilities and equity. These comparisons can help the loan officer pinpoint changes that need to be further explained by the company's management. For example, if a company's balance sheet shows increased current assets (inventory and accounts receivable) without sales growth to justify it, the loan officer should seek further explanation.

The loan officer should also compare balance sheet accounts from period to period in terms of increases and decreases both in absolute dollars and percentages of the total. However, only balance sheets prepared on the same day for consecutive years allow a meaningful comparison of all accounts. Year-to-year increases in assets require corresponding increases in liabilities and equity since the company's balance sheet must balance. Therefore, a particular percentage change may not reflect a change in that account but changes in other accounts. Chapters 5 and 6 provide a more detailed discussion of the analysis of balance sheets using funds flow analysis and ratio analysis. Since balance sheet accounts also reflect anticipated or actual sales, comparative analyses of income statements and balance sheets should be done concurrently.

EXTERNAL COMPARISONS

Besides comparing current balance sheet accounts with a company's past statements, the loan officer should also compare the company's balance sheet to that of other similar companies and to the industry. Internal comparisons may show an improving situation, while external comparisons may show the company's performance to be relatively poor by industry standards. For example, assume that a company's inventory decreased by 25 percent compared to the previous year as the result of a more efficient inventory control system. But if the industry's average inventory decreased by 50 percent overall, the company did not perform as efficiently as other companies in the industry. Such comparisons permit loan officers to rate the company's performance as average, favorable, or unfavorable. As mentioned previously, Robert Morris Associates publishes industry averages which are very useful in this regard.

▌▌▌▌▌▌▌ Summary

A thorough understanding of a company's balance sheet and income statement provides a solid foundation for a comprehensive financial analysis. By knowing the type of company, its industry, and its general managerial policies, the loan officer should have a general idea of what the company's balance sheet will look like. The simple equation, Assets = Liabilities + Equity, prescribes the general changes that can occur in a company's operations since any changes must combine to keep the equation always in balance. By understanding the relationship between assets, liabilities, and equity, loan officers can better understand what these changes mean in terms of the company's candidacy for a loan.

An understanding of a company's balance sheet accounts enables the loan officer to better evaluate the financial condition of the company.

An evaluation of each asset account in terms of quality and liquidity assists the loan officer in determining the company's debt repayment capability and the need for collateral to secure debt. Furthermore, an evaluation of each liability account helps the loan officer determine the current repayment requirements of the company in relation to its possible new financing requirements. An evaluation of a company's liabilities in relation to its equity accounts enables the loan officer to compare the bank's overall risk as a creditor with the risk faced by an investor.

The loan officer must recognize that whereas asset values fluctuate (which means their book values do not represent real values), the value of liabilities does not fluctuate. Equity is important then for two reasons. First, the more equity a company owns, the more likely it is that its owners will work diligently to protect that equity and repay the company's liabilities. Second, equity represents the cushion between a company's asset book values and its liabilities. Greater uncertainty in asset values requires a larger cushion to protect liabilities. For example, if assets equal $200,000 and liabilities equal $100,000, then equity equals $100,000. This amount of equity is sufficient to protect the company's liabilities up to a 50 percent shrinkage in assets. This cushion may be sufficient if asset values are stable. However, the company may need an additional cushion if asset values are very unstable.

Once the loan officer has analyzed the company's individual balance sheet accounts and the reconciliation of net worth, the lender can begin making comparisons with the company's past operating periods. The loan officer must analyze both absolute changes in dollars and percentage changes in the distribution of assets, liabilities, and equity. The loan officer will also do a comparative analysis of the company's balance sheet accounts and trends over time with those of other companies.

Questions

1. Explain the significance of the balance sheet equation, Assets = Liabilities + Equity.

2. Describe the basic characteristics of balance sheets for manufacturers, agricultural companies, wholesalers, retailers, and service companies.

3. Define the term *current assets*. Then list and explain briefly the current asset accounts in the order they appear on a balance sheet.

4. Discuss three factors affecting the size of accounts receivable.

5. Explain how loan officers evaluate the quality and liquidity of a company's inventory.

6. List and explain briefly the noncurrent asset accounts on the balance sheet.

7. How do a company's *capacity* and *efficiency* relate to the evaluation of fixed assets?

8. Explain how depreciation affects the value of a company's fixed assets.

9. Explain the distinction between current and long-term liabilities. Then discuss the general repayment sources for current and long-term liabilities.

10. What are accounts payable, and what is their significance?

11. List the four components of equity, and explain their importance as financing sources to a company.

12. Explain the importance of equity to a company's creditors.

13. Describe the steps involved in comparative analysis of a company's balance sheet both on an internal and external basis.

Exercises

E-1

Compare the following companies by common-sizing their balance
sheets. (Recall that to common size is to represent as percentages.)
Which company is better capitalized? Which represents a better credit
risk?

Beall Products and Services
Balance Sheet
(in thousands of dollars)
December 31, 1988

Assets		Liabilities and Net Worth	
Cash	$ 54	Notes payable	$ 510
Accounts receivable	798	Accounts payable	504
Inventory	1,032	Accrued taxes	198
Total current assets	$1,884	Total current liabilities	$1,212
Plant and equipment	429	Common stock	450
Prepaid expenses	18	Retained earnings	669
		Total liabilities and	
Total assets	$2,331	net worth	$2,331

Higgins Products and Services
Balance Sheet
(in thousands of dollars)
December 31, 1988

Assets		Liabilities and Net Worth	
Cash	$ 9	Notes payable	$ 15
Accounts receivable	36	Accounts payable	12
Inventory	45	Accrued taxes	12
Total current assets	$ 90	Total current liabilities	$ 39
Plant and equipment	12	Common stock	30
Prepaid expenses	6	Retained earnings	39
		Total liabilities and	
Total assets	$ 108	net worth	$ 108

E-2

Using the following comparative balance sheets for Norton, Inc., and for the industry, prepare common-size statements in order to compare Norton, Inc. to the industry. Which accounts should the loan officer look at more closely?

Norton, Incorporated
Comparative Balance Sheets
December 31, 1984–1988

	1984	1985	1986	1987	1988
Assets					
Cash	$ 4,500	$ 5,100	$ 3,900	$ 4,600	$ 6,000
Accounts receivable	90,000	100,800	117,600	137,700	159,000
Inventory	55,500	62,100	74,500	87,200	100,000
Total current assets	$ 150,000	$ 168,000	$ 196,000	$ 229,500	$ 265,000
Fixed assets (net)	150,000	182,000	204,000	220,500	235,000
Total assets	$ 300,000	$ 350,000	$ 400,000	$ 450,000	$ 500,000
Liabilities and Equity					
Accounts payable	$ 50,400	$ 58,800	$ 70,800	$ 83,700	$ 96,700
Notes payable	21,600	25,200	38,200	51,300	59,300
Total current liabilities	$ 72,000	$ 84,000	$ 109,000	$ 135,000	$ 156,000
Long-term debt	42,000	59,000	63,000	72,000	84,000
Owners' equity	186,000	207,000	228,000	243,000	260,000
Total liabilities and equity	$ 300,000	$ 350,000	$ 400,000	$ 450,000	$ 500,000
Net sales	$ 696,000	$ 751,660	$ 844,400	$ 972,000	$1,075,000
Net income	$ 16,000	$ 19,000	$ 23,000	$ 27,000	$ 31,175

Industry
Comparative Balance Sheet
1984–1987

	1984	1985	1986	1987
Assets				
Cash	$ 20,100	$ 20,100	$ 21,500	$ 22,400
Accounts receivable	220,800	219,700	235,900	246,400
Inventory	160,600	159,800	171,600	179,200
Total current assets	$ 401,500	$ 399,600	$ 429,000	$ 448,000
Fixed assets (net)	328,500	340,400	351,000	352,000
Total assets	$ 730,000	$ 740,000	$ 780,000	$ 800,000
Liabilities and				
Equity				
Accounts payable	$ 132,000	$ 145,600	$ 136,500	$ 163,200
Notes payable	44,000	36,400	58,500	40,800
Total current liabilities	$ 176,000	$ 182,000	$ 195,000	$ 204,000
Long-term debt	95,000	90,000	110,000	110,000
Owners' equity	459,000	468,000	475,000	486,000
Total liabilities and equity	$ 730,000	$ 740,000	$ 780,000	$ 800,000
Net sales	$1,882,000	$1,963,000	$1,983,000	$2,200,000
Net income	$ 41,400	$ 45,100	$ 47,600	$ 53,000
Number of firms:				
Total reporting	30	29	26	31
With year-end				
December 31	25	25	22	20
June 30	4	3	3	8
October 31	1	1	1	3

E-3

Prepare a balance sheet as of December 31, 1988, for the John Robbins Corporation based on the following information. (Organize the accounts into current assets, noncurrent assets, current liabilities, long-term debt, and equity.)

Retained earnings	$1,216,000
Bank notes payable	1,200,000
Accounts receivable	2,520,000
Advances to Cox Corp.	568,000
Prepaid insurance	56,000
Capital stock—common	3,200,000
Cash	360,000
Other accruals	312,000
Land	320,000
Accounts payable	1,112,000
Inventories	4,968,000
Subordinated debt	1,360,000
Accounts receivable—officers	120,000
Capital stock—preferred	1,200,000
Accrued taxes	608,000
Buildings (net of depreciation)	3,008,000
Current mortgage maturities	400,000
Accounts receivable—employees	16,000
Capital surplus	840,000
First mortgage payable	3,200,000
Machinery and equipment	1,896,000
Investment in Cox Corp.	400,000
Unamortized organization costs	104,000
Cash-value life insurance	312,000

E-4

The accounts receivable aging for September 30, 1988, and the comparative accounts receivable agings for the last three quarters for Pat Gill and Associates are listed. Answer the questions that follow.

Pat Gill and Associates
Accounts Receivable Aging 1988

Account Name	Total	Current	1–30 Days	31–60 Days	61–90 Days	Over 90 Days
Bocknek Co.	$ 10,000	$10,000	$	$	$	$
Clark Co.	14,000	2,000	6,000	3,000	3,000	
Domurot Co.	5,000	5,000				
Marchant Co.	15,000	10,000		5,000		
Nyeste Co.	20,000	5,000	5,000		6,000	4,000
Smith Co.	50,000					50,000
Snowden Co.	6,000	3,000		3,000		
Wiley Co.	8,000			4,000	4,000	
	$128,000	$35,000	$11,000	$15,000	$13,000	$54,000

Comparative Accounts Receivable Aging

	Total	Current	1–30 Days	31–60 Days	61–90 Days	Over 90 Days
3/31/88	$110,000	$43,000	$13,000	$40,000	$ 8,000	$ 6,000
6/30/88	120,000	47,000	6,000	13,000	40,000	14,000
9/30/88	128,000	35,000	11,000	15,000	13,000	54,000

a. What general observations can be made regarding the quality of these accounts knowing that 30-day payment terms are allowed?

b. What specific information should the loan officer request regarding these accounts?

E-5

A company has purchased a $100,000 piece of equipment with an expected life of 10 years. Calculate and compare the straight-line depreciation and accelerated cost recovery depreciation for this fixed asset.

E-6

Prepare a reconciliation of net worth as of December 31, 1988, for the Shelton Company, based on the following selected financial information (using the format shown in Exhibit 4.8):

- Net profit after tax was $20,000 in 1988.

- Five thousand shares of additional common stock with a $1 par value were sold for $10,000.

- Dividends of $15,000 were declared.

- An estate was settled leaving the company $10,000 in cash.

- Total net worth on January 1, 1988, was $100,000.

5 The Funds Flow Statement

Learning Objectives

After studying this chapter, you should be able to

- prepare a funds flow statement
- use a funds flow statement in financial analysis
- explain why sources and uses of funds always equal each other
- determine when a funds flow statement is required
- identify the questions a funds flow statement should answer

▍▎▍▎▍▎▍▎ Introduction

The *funds flow statement* has many names and may be presented in many different formats. When an accountant prepares a company's annual financial statements according to generally accepted accounting principles (GAAP), the funds flow statement is usually called the *statement of changes in financial position*; this is a requisite part of any presentation of balance sheet and income statement information using GAAP. The funds flow statement is also known as a *sources and uses of funds statement, a sources and applications of funds statement,* a *cash flow statement*, and by various other names. Whatever the format, its purpose is to determine a company's capacity to generate funds internally and thereby its need for outside financing.

As discussed in Chapter 2, funds represent all of a company's economic resources. Similarly, the funds flow statement considers all the economic resources available to a company. Since a funds flow statement presents the flow of funds resulting from actions taken by a company's management in deploying economic resources over a given period, usually a year, it allows the lender to evaluate these managerial decisions. Thus, the loan officer uses the funds flow statement to determine what resources the company has employed in the past, how they became available, and how efficiently they were used.

This chapter explains both how to prepare a funds flow statement and how to use it in financial analysis.

▍▎▍▎▍▎▍▎ Statement Preparation

A funds flow statement is constructed using information contained in the income statement, the balance sheet, and the reconciliation of net worth. Although a company's financial statements normally will include an accountant-prepared funds flow statement, a loan officer should understand how to construct one. This basically entails categorizing all of a company's funds flows as either sources or uses of funds. A completed funds flow statement must balance—thus the basic equation for a funds flow statement is this:

$$\text{Sources of funds} = \text{Uses of funds}.$$

INFORMATION SOURCES

As discussed in previous chapters, the income statement is a period statement (reflecting the deployment of resources over a period of time, typically a year) whereas the balance sheet is a snapshot or point-in-time statement (presenting the value of all economic resources deployed in the activities of the business, usually as of the end of the company's fiscal year). Like the income statement, the funds flow statement presents funds flows over a period of time, normally a fiscal year.

All the economic resources of a company—its assets, liabilities, and equity—are reflected in the balance sheet. This includes the economic resources generated by the income statement. For example, the amount of equity shown on the balance sheet reflects the net income generated from the income statement. Since all the economic activities of a business result in a flow of funds, every flow of funds is also reflected in the balance sheet. However, this flow is only apparent when balance sheets for two consecutive periods are compared.

Although two consecutive balance sheets are the primary source of information for a funds flow statement, the balance sheet information is supplemented by information from the company's most recent income statement and the reconciliation of net worth. Company management may provide additional details, or other pertinent information may be found in the sources and uses of funds statement prepared by the company's accountant.

IDENTIFYING SOURCES AND USES OF FUNDS

The first step in creating a funds flow statement is to categorize changes in a company's balance sheet accounts as sources and uses of funds. For example, a reduction in an asset account (such as accounts receivable) constitutes a source of funds, while an increase in an asset account constitutes a use of funds. On the other hand, any increase in liabilities (such as bank debt) constitutes a source of funds while a decrease in liabilities constitutes a use of funds. Similarly, any increase in equity (such as an increase in retained earnings) constitutes a source of funds while a decrease in equity constitutes a use of funds. Exhibit 5.1 summa-

Sources and Uses of Funds

Sources of Funds	*Uses of Funds*
• Decrease in assets	• Increase in assets
• Increase in liabilities	• Decrease in liabilities
• Increase in equity	• Decrease in equity

■ ■

rizes how increases and decreases in assets, liabilities, and equity may be understood in terms of sources and uses of funds.

Sources of funds result from decreases in assets (such as a reduction in accounts receivable), increases in liabilities (such as an increase in accounts payable or in long-term debt), and increases in equity (such as the sale of capital stock or an increase in the reserve for deferred taxes). *Uses of funds* result from increases in assets (such as an increase in inventory or a purchase of fixed assets), decreases in liabilities (such as a reduction in bank debt), and decreases in equity (such as the payment of dividends).

Exhibit 5.2 illustrates the first step in preparing a funds flow statement. It involves comparing a company's two most recent fiscal-year balance sheets and labeling each change in the asset, liability, and net worth accounts as a source or use of funds. Exhibit 5.2 shows a comparative balance sheet for the Garcia-Duran Design Company as of December 31, 1987 and 1988. In the change column, the difference between the value of each account as of those two dates is shown and the direction of change is indicated. An increase in any account is shown as a positive number and a decrease is shown as a negative number (that is, in parentheses). Each change is also labeled as a source or use of funds (again based on the information summarized in Exhibit 5.1). Because the change column reflects the net result of all funds flows through a balance sheet account during the course of a year, the source or use designation represents the net change in the account for the period.

For example, Exhibit 5.2 shows that Garcia-Duran's cash balance declined from $31,000 at the end of 1987 to $12,000 at the end of 1988, a decrease of $19,000. This decrease in an asset account represents a source of additional funds to the company. The $163,000 increase in accounts receivable—from $543,000 to $706,000—constitutes an increase in assets and therefore a use of funds. The increase in inventory is designated a use of funds for the same reason. The increases in the liability accounts—notes payable to banks, accounts payable, and accruals—are all labeled as sources of funds. The decreases in liability accounts—such as the $1,000 decrease in long-term debt—are labeled a use of funds. Similarly, the $6,000 increase in retained earnings shown in the net worth section of the balance sheet is labeled a source of funds. Since there were no net changes in some of the company's accounts—for example, subordinated debt and most of the

EXHIBIT 5.2 ■■■■■■■■■■■■■■■■■■■■■■■■■■■■■■■■■■■

Presentation of Net Changes

Garcia-Duran Design Company
Presentation of Net Changes
Based on Balance Sheets for December 31, 1987 and 1988
(in thousands of dollars)

	12/31/87	12/31/88	Change	
Assets				
Cash	31	12	(19)	Source
Accounts receivable—net	543	706	163	Use
Inventory	400	525	125	Use
Total current assets	974	1243	269	
Fixed assets—net	91	80	(11)	Source
Investments in affiliates	29	35	6	Use
Other assets	11	12	1	Use
Total noncurrent assets	131	127	(4)	
Total assets	1105	1370	265	
Liabilities				
Notes payable to banks	230	410	180	Source
Accounts payable	237	290	53	Source
Accruals	30	42	12	Source
Current-year income taxes	8	5	(3)	Use
Total current liabilities	505	747	242	
Long-term debt	26	25	(1)	Use
Subordinated debt	101	101	0	
Total long-term debt	127	126	(1)	
Total debt	632	873	241	
Reserve for deferred income taxes	129	147	18	Source
Net Worth				
Preferred stock	9	9	0	
Common stock and paid-in surplus	105	105	0	
Retained earnings	261	267	6	Source
Less: Treasury stock	(31)	(31)	0	
Net worth	344	350	6	
Total liabilities and net worth	1105	1370	265	

Sum of Sources and Uses of Funds

Garcia-Duran Design Company
Sum of Sources and Uses of Funds
for the Year Ended December 31, 1988
(in thousands of dollars)

Source of Funds		Use of Funds	
Cash	19	Accounts receivable—net	163
Fixed assets—net	11	Inventory	125
Notes payable to banks	180	Investments in affiliates	6
Accounts payable	53	Other assets	1
Accruals	12	Current-year income taxes	3
Reserve for deferred taxes	18	Long-term debt	1
Retained earnings	6		
Total sources	299	Total uses	299

components of net worth—no net flow of funds occurred, and no source or use of funds was created, in these accounts.

At this point, the loan officer should verify that the sum of all sources of funds equals the sum of all uses of funds. In this calculation, as shown in Exhibit 5.3, both sources and uses of funds are shown as a positive number, regardless of whether the change in a particular account was an increase or a decrease. If total sources and uses of funds do not tally, a calculation error has been made. (Note that this summary statement lists only the individual balance sheet accounts, not the subtotals or totals.)

Not all funds flows are apparent from a presentation of net changes in balance sheet accounts. Certain other information needed to construct a funds flow statement must be picked up from the income statement or the reconciliation of net worth. The additional information required includes net profit after tax, dividends, and depreciation. A comparative income statement for Garcia-Duran for 1987 and 1988, which includes a reconciliation of net worth, is shown as Exhibit 5.4. For 1988 it shows net profit after tax of $27,000 (a source of funds), dividends paid of $21,000 (a use of funds), and depreciation of $10,000 (which, as will be explained, is considered a source of funds).

In creating a funds flow statement, it is necessary to separate out the effect of depreciation from the change in net fixed assets shown on the balance sheet. To illustrate, suppose a company both purchased a $10,000 piece of machinery and also expensed a total of $10,000 in depreciation for the year on all its fixed assets. The fixed asset account net of depreciation, as shown in a comparison of balance sheet accounts, would remain unchanged since the $10,000 source of funds attributable to depreciation would in effect cancel out the $10,000 use of funds created by the purchase of the new machine. The actual change in fixed assets, then, is calculated as follows:

Change in fixed assets = Ending net fixed assets
            − Beginning net fixed assets
            + Depreciation.

In the case of Garcia-Duran, the balance sheet comparison (Exhibit 5.2) shows a decrease in net fixed assets of $11,000 during 1988. However, depreciation amounted to $10,000 in 1988, according to the income statement (Exhibit 5.4). By treating depreciation as a separate

EXHIBIT 5.4 ■■■■■■■■■■■■■■■■■■■■■■■■■■■■■■■■■■

Income Statement

Garcia-Duran Design Company
Income Statement
for the Years Ended December 31, 1987 and 1988
(in thousands of dollars)

	1987	1988
Net sales	1,648	2,142
Cost of goods sold	1,125	1,500
Gross profit	523	642
Total operating expense	444	577
Operating profit	79	65
Other income	6	8
Other expense	21	30
Profit before tax	64	43
Income tax	26	16
Net profit after tax	38	27
Notes:		
Dividends	21	21
Depreciation	12	10
Reconciliation of net worth:		
Net worth—beginning	327	344
Add: Net profit	38	27
Less: Dividends	21	21
Retained earnings increase	17	6
Net worth increase	17	6
Net worth—ending	344	350

■■

source of funds, the actual decrease to fixed assets during 1988 is seen to be only $1,000 ($80,000 − $91,000 + $10,000).

The next step in preparing a funds flow statement is to categorize funds flows as operating, discretionary, and financing funds flows. Thus, it is important to break out depreciation in this way because depreciation is considered an operating flow while a change in fixed assets is considered a discretionary flow.

FORMATTING THE FUNDS FLOW STATEMENT

There are several accepted formats for presenting funds flow information. The funds flow statement that is presented in this chapter was selected because it is easy to understand and most clearly presents the data for financial analysis purposes when examining a company's funds flows for a single year. The two formats most frequently used by accountants and another format that is a modification of the one used in this text are presented in a Facts to Note section later in this chapter. Most banks will have a preferred format; in fact, many banks use computer programs to generate standardized funds flow statements.

All the raw data needed to prepare a funds flow statement for Garcia-Duran Design Company has already been developed using the company's balance sheets, income statement, and reconciliation of net worth. The next step is to categorize the various funds flows as operating funds flows, discretionary funds flows, and financing funds flows. In addition, each category of funds flows is further subdivided into inflows and outflows. In cases where a financial statement item appears to fit in more than one funds flow category, the loan officer must make a judgment based on the nature of the transaction. Once such a decision is made, however, the loan officer should be consistent in its application.

Since cash is the common denominator in all funds flows, the format of the funds flow statement presented in this chapter is reconciled to cash. That is, when all sources have been netted against all uses, the net aggregate funds flow equals the actual change in the company's cash balance for the period. For this reason, this type of funds flow statement is sometimes called a *cash flow statement.*

A funds flow statement for the Garcia-Duran Design Company for the year ended December 31, 1988, is presented as Exhibit 5.5. (The

1987 figures, which are included for comparison, will be discussed later.) The statement shows the inflows and outflows of operating funds flows, discretionary funds flows, and financing funds flows subtotaled separately, then combined for a net inflow or outflow for each activity. The results for each category of funds flow are then summarized. Each funds flow category will be examined in turn.

Operating Funds Flows

The first category of funds flows includes those funds flows involved in or resulting from the daily operations of the business—activities such as purchasing inventory, manufacturing, selling products or providing services, and collecting receivables. Bank notes or other interest-bearing debt is not included here since these types of debt are included in financing funds flows. Accounts that generate operating funds flows are marketable securities, accounts receivable, notes receivable, inventory, accounts payable, accruals, current-year income taxes, any deferred taxes, net profit after tax, and depreciation. Note that *operating funds flows* differs from *funds flows from operations*, a term frequently found in financial statements prepared by accountants. The latter term refers only to funds flows generated through the income statement and as such constitutes only a part of operating funds flows.

Discretionary Funds Flows

The second category of funds flows includes flows of funds that relate to the acquisition or sale of fixed assets and other investments and the payment of dividends. These funds flows are considered discretionary because a company's management may choose not to make them—for example, the company may postpone or cancel fixed asset purchases and investments or reduce or eliminate dividends. Balance sheet accounts that are categorized as discretionary funds flows include any changes in gross fixed assets (*not* including depreciation), due from officers or affiliates, investments in affiliates, deferred charges or pre-paid expenses, and cash dividends paid.

Financing Funds Flows

This category includes those flows of funds that directly relate to the external financing of the business whether involving debt instruments or equity contributions. Balance sheet accounts that create financing

Funds Flow Statement

Garcia-Duran Design Company
Funds Flow Statement
for the Years Ended December 31, 1987 and 1988
(in thousands of dollars)

	1987	1988
Operating Funds Flows		
Operating inflows		
Net profit after tax	38	27
Depreciation	12	10
Increase in reserve for deferred taxes	6	18
Increase in accounts payable	42	53
Increase in accruals	4	12
Total operating inflows	102	120
Operating outflows		
Increase in accounts receivable	66	163
Increase in inventory	101	125
Decrease in current-year income taxes	1	3
Total operating outflows	168	291
Net operating outflows	66	171
Discretionary Funds Flows		
Discretionary inflows		
Decrease in fixed assets	—	1
Decrease in other assets	1	—
Total discretionary inflows	1	1
Discretionary outflows		
Increase in fixed assets	26	—
Cash dividends paid	21	21
Increase in investments in affiliates	—	6
Increase in other assets	—	1
Total discretionary outflows	47	28
Net discretionary outflows	46	27
Financing Funds Flows		
Financing inflows		
Increase in notes payable to banks	94	180
Total financing inflows	94	180
Financing outflows		
Decrease in long-term debt	1	1
Total financing outflows	1	1
Net financing inflows	93	179
Summary		
Net operating outflows	(66)	(171)
Net discretionary outflows	(46)	(27)
Net financing inflows	93	179
Net decrease in cash	(19)	(19)

funds flow include notes payable to banks, commercial paper outstanding, notes payable to others, current maturities of long-term debt, secured and unsecured long-term debt, subordinated debt, preferred and common capital stock, paid-in surplus, and treasury stock.

Summary of Funds Flows

Because this kind of funds flow statement is reconciled to cash, the difference between all inflows (sources) and outflows (uses) of funds identifies the amount of cash available to support all these activities.

▌▌▌▌ Funds Flow Analysis

The funds flow statement is a very important analytical tool because it enables the loan officer to identify, quantify, and evaluate what sources of funds the company has, what uses the company makes of those funds, and what implications those actions have for the company's present condition and future viability—and thus its acceptability as a borrower.

In evaluating the funds flow statement, the loan officer should address three primary questions:

- Do the company's operations generate adequate funds? Cash generated internally from the operating funds flows is in the long run the primary source of the company's ability to fund growth and repay debt.

- Are the company's discretionary uses of funds appropriate? Discretionary decisions directly affect the adequacy of the company's operating flows because funds used for discretionary purposes are unavailable for funding growth or debt repayment.

- Are the company's financing flows properly structured? Financing flows are partially dictated by operating and discretionary funds flows. Therefore, the loan officer needs to examine these flows to determine if their structures can support the company in terms of timing, magnitude, and future cash demands.

ADEQUACY OF OPERATING FUNDS FLOWS

The first step in funds flow analysis is to analyze operating funds flows. This entails comparing the magnitude of the cash generated from the company's profitable operation (net income plus depreciation plus any other noncash charges) to the funding needs associated with that operation (such as increased accounts receivable and inventory). The key areas for the lender to analyze in operations are quality of earnings, management of current assets, and management of current liabilities.

Quality of Earnings

The loan officer should assess the consistency and reliability of the company's reported profits since their usefulness as a measure of cash flow depends upon their derivation as well as the accounting methods used to report them. For example, if a company's profits in a given year include a gain from the sale and leaseback of its own physical facilities, that portion of its earning stream will not be duplicated in future years. Changing the method of inventory valuation (from LIFO to FIFO, or vice versa) can also distort the relationship between reported profits and actual operating cash flow.

Management of Current Assets

If the funds flow statement reveals that current assets have grown (a use of funds), the loan officer should investigate whether this growth is in proportion to the growth of the revenue stream or whether it suggests a managerial problem or perhaps simply a change in strategy. If, on the other hand, the company's current assets have decreased for the period (a source of funds), the loan officer must determine whether that decrease reflects a decrease in the level of revenues or a conscious management decision to change the way the company manages that asset category. In the latter case, the loan officer needs to ask whether the company can sustain that change. If not, the funding represents a temporary measure that will have to be reversed in the future and will thus create an additional need for funds.

Management of Current Liabilities

If the funds flow statement shows that accounts payable or other accruals have grown (a source of funds), the loan officer must determine whether that growth is in response to increased sales or whether the company has been slow in paying its trade debt because of cash constraints. The latter situation may suggest that the company will face a need for funds in the near future. If payables are shrinking (a use of funds), the loan officer must determine whether this is in response to a decrease in sales or reflects a reversal of previous trade credit problems.

If a company's current debt service changes dramatically, the loan officer must investigate whether this reflects a change in management's financing philosophy or a difficulty with its creditors.

APPROPRIATENESS OF DISCRETIONARY FUNDS FLOWS

Discretionary funds flow is the second area of funds flow analyzed. The company's dividend policy is one important area to look at since payment of dividends diminishes the amount of cash flow available to repay loans and fund growth. Thus the loan officer needs to compare dividends to the magnitude of the company's operating flows and to the debt and growth requirements that could otherwise have been funded.

A decrease in fixed assets or other noncurrent assets represents a source of funds. The loan officer must determine whether this represents the elimination of surplus or unnecessary assets or the disposition of assets that are critical to the operation of the company. Although elimination of surplus or unnecessary assets is appropriate, it typically represents only a one-time or occasional source of funds. On the other hand, the disposition of critical assets may be very damaging in terms of diminishing the company's ability to operate, and thus may hinder the company's ability to create funds from operations, to fund growth, and to repay debt. If fixed assets increase (a use of funds), the lender needs to determine the source of funds used to pay for the purchase. Discretionary funds flows may also reflect such financial maneuvers as the aforementioned sale and leaseback of a major facility. Although this is a legitimate maneuver on the company's part, the loan officer should appreciate that it is a one-time source of funds and that it creates a future funds requirement in the form of lease payments.

PROPER STRUCTURING OF FINANCING FUNDS FLOWS

Financing flows is the last part of the funds flow analysis. An increase in the company's capital accounts (reflecting the sale of additional stock) is welcome because it diminishes the company's financial leverage and thus the risk involved in lending. Unfortunately, the introduction of capital other than through the retention of profit is an infrequent occurrence with smaller companies.

The categorization of funds flows used here highlights the importance of notes payable to banks by including this account as a financing flow rather than an operating flow despite its short-term nature. This serves to highlight one of the most prevalent problems with the financing structure of many companies—the funding of long-term or "permanent" increases in working capital or fixed asset requirements with short-term debt. The loan officer, when confronted with this situation, must ask what change in the method of operation, level of fixed assets, or financing will result in this short-term financing being repaid by its maturity date.

Revolving debt is a good method of financing that is especially appropriate for growing companies. From an analytical standpoint, the primary consideration is whether the timing of revolving-debt conversion to term payout coincides with the timing of the company's operating cycle and therefore its repayment ability.

With long-term debt, the loan officer must consider whether the amortization requirement matches the company's ability to generate cash from its operating cycle. In this regard, the loan officer needs to be aware not only of immediate amortization requirements, but also any future changes in that schedule.

▌▎▌▎▌▎▌▎ Analysis of the Garcia-Duran Funds Flow Statement

The funds flow statement for 1988 (Exhibit 5.5) shows that Garcia-Duran generated cash flow from its operations in the form of profit of $27,000 and noncash charges ($10,000 in depreciation). The loan officer should question the adequacy of that cash flow, however, since the 1987 and 1988 income statements (shown in Exhibit 5.4) reveal that the company made approximately 29 percent less income on 30 percent more revenue in 1988. Other sources of operating funds for Garcia-Duran included increases in deferred taxes, accounts payable, and accruals—all of which appear consistent with the company's revenue growth.

The loan officer should next observe that the total operating inflows of $120,000 were outstripped by operating outflows of $291,000, comprised primarily of increases in accounts receivable and inventory. Again, this would seem to be consistent with the company's growth. Nevertheless, negative operating flow often reflects pricing, product, or operations control problems. Thus the loan officer will want to do a further analysis before making a loan commitment.

Up to this point, Garcia-Duran's ability to generate profits from operations has been outstripped by the growth in working capital associated with an increase in revenues. The problem is compounded by declining profit margins experienced along with that growth.

As to discretionary funds flows, the primary movement in this category was $21,000 in cash dividends paid. Outflows were further increased by a $6,000 increase in investments in an affiliate and only very slightly offset by a $1,000 decrease in fixed assets. Thus the $171,000 in operating funds shortfall was further exacerbated by the fact that nearly three-fourths of the company's $37,000 in operating cash flows (from profits and depreciation) went either to the owners or to an affiliated company. Garcia-Duran, then, requires at this point $198,000 ($171,000 from net operating outflows plus $27,000 from net discretionary outflows) through financing or reduction in cash.

The financing funds flow section reveals that most of the $198,000 funding requirement was funded through short-term borrowing of $180,000. The loan officer would want to determine the structure and purpose of this debt. The only other change, a $1,000 reduction in long-term debt, was normal. Since the financing inflow was inadequate to fund all operating and discretionary outflows, the company also reduced its cash balance by $19,000 (as shown in the funds flow summary).

The loan officer at this point should have four concerns:

• The company's profitability has declined during its growth period, which has decreased its capacity to fund its operations.

• The working capital increases associated with the company's growth are substantial in relation to the amount of profit created.

• A large portion of the cash flow from operations was diverted either to the owners or to affiliated companies.

- The operating and discretionary shortfalls, which appear to be permanent or long-term in nature, were funded with short-term debt and a reduction in cash balances. The loan officer should be concerned about the company's likely inability to reduce that short-term debt within a short period. Thus, the loan officer must look at the company's ability to amortize such debt in the event it is restructured.

COMPARATIVE FUNDS FLOW ANALYSIS

Tentative conclusions such as these can frequently be verified or contradicted by analyzing funds flows over more than one year. Thus the lender will next look at the funds flow figures for Garcia-Duran Design Company for the preceding year (1987), as shown in Exhibit 5.5.

It is immediately apparent that net operating outflows and discretionary outflows exceeded inflows during 1987 as well as during 1988 and that the resulting funding requirements were met primarily by increased bank debt. As a company grows, its operating activities increase and consequently its operating accounts for purchasing, manufacturing, selling, and collecting also grow. Thus in a profitable, growing company, a lender would expect to see positive net income, depreciation, and an increase in deferred tax liability (as well as increases in accounts receivable, inventories, and accounts payable). During 1987, Garcia-Duran's operating accounts increased as expected. Its total operating inflows of $102,000 were generated primarily by funds flows from operations (net income, depreciation, and deferred taxes) and increased accounts payable. The $168,000 in operating outflows resulted substantially from the increase in accounts receivable and inventory. The net result of operating activities was an outflow of $66,000.

The funds flow statement for 1987 also shows net discretionary outflows of $46,000—including $21,000 in cash dividends paid and a $26,000 increase in fixed assets. Again, the lender might question this level of dividends and would also investigate what assets were acquired.

Financing inflows in the form of short-term bank debt totaled $94,000 during 1987, compared with a $1,000 outflow (reflecting a decrease in long-term debt).

The statement summary shows that the $66,000 in net operating outflows and the $46,000 in discretionary outflows were offset by a $93,000 net financing inflow and a $19,000 net decrease in cash. This again raises the question of whether long-term needs are being met by short-term sources of funds. Because accounts receivable, inventory, and accounts payable increased along with sales, the lender would probably conclude that the increases in these operating accounts represented long-term financing needs. Thus if the Garcia-Duran Company has not already addressed the issue of an imbalance of temporary versus permanent funding, the funds flow analysis suggests it should do so.

As shown by its balance sheet (Exhibit 5.2), Garcia-Duran has borrowed $410,000 in short-term loans which it has used to fund operating assets to support a rapid increase in sales. Assuming this rapid growth in sales continues and assuming the company's profitability doesn't improve greatly, Garcia-Duran's need for debt will continue to increase. Since the funds used to support operating assets exceed the funds provided by ongoing operations, the question arises as to how and when the bank is to be repaid.

The loan officer will also want to take a closer look at the company's use of its operating funds—for example, whether its accounts receivable and inventory relative to sales could be reduced. The lender might also conclude that the payment of dividends at this point should be reduced or eliminated since operating earnings are proving insufficient to support both the growth of the company and the payment of dividends. Finally, the loan officer should question whether long-term debt or an equity contribution would be a more appropriate alternative to the financing inflows provided by short-term bank debt. The loan officer must also decide how best to structure the increasing debt.

▪▪▪▪ Pitfalls of Funds Flow Analysis

As is true of any analytical tool, funds flow analysis will not provide a final answer to a loan decision, but rather should prompt the loan officer to ask appropriate questions. In many cases, the "obvious" reason for a given trend in funds flows is not the correct or only reason for the trend. Most funds flows, if analyzed in a vacuum, might offer several plausible explanations from which the loan officer could choose.

When analyzing a growing, profitable company, many loan officers immediately assume the company is healthy (which, in most cases, is true). Yet rapid growth, even when it is profitable, can lead to insolvency because the company's requirements for working capital may exceed its internal funding capability—and the need for outside financing may outstrip the company's borrowing capacity.

Numerous other situations can lead the loan officer to false conclusions when analyzing a funds flow statement. Thus the loan officer must gather sufficient information to draw correct conclusions with the aid of other analytical tools.

Facts to Note:

There are many formats for funds flow statements other than that described in this chapter. Three other formats that are commonly used are shown as Exhibits 5.6, 5.7, and 5.8.

The two types of funds flow statements that are most frequently used by accountants as part of a complete set of financial statements using GAAP are shown as Exhibits 5.6 and 5.7. Their chief drawback is that they are not so well suited for use in interpretive financial analysis. A third format (shown as Exhibit 5.8) is very similar to that used in the text, except that it doesn't separately categorize inflows and outflows of funds. It should be readily apparent that each of these funds flow statements presents basically the same information, but in slightly varying formats. To emphasize this, the funds flow information for Garcia-Duran Design Company already presented in Exhibit 5.5 is shown again in Exhibits 5.6, 5.7, and 5.8.

The first traditional method, shown in Exhibit 5.6, is sometimes called a *working capital reconciliation statement*. It begins with funds flows from operations, then balances all sources and uses of funds arising from the noncurrent portion of the balance sheet (applications of working capital), which results in a net change (in this case, an increase) in working capital. The bottom section of the statement lists each of the components comprising increases or decreases in the company's current or working capital accounts. The net change in working capital is then added to the working capital at the beginning of the period to determine the amount of working capital available at the end of the period.

The second traditional method of preparing a funds flow statement (here called a *sources and applications of funds* statement) is shown in Exhibit 5.7. It begins by listing sources of funds flows provided by operations, as in the method just examined. It next lists all sources of funds and all uses, or applications, of funds (except for the change in cash), regardless of their classification as current or noncurrent. The statement then balances directly to cash without the interim step of balancing to working capital.

Exhibit 5.8 shows yet another format for presenting funds flows. The statement categorizes funds flows as operating, discretionary, and financing—the same method used in the text—but does not separately tabulate inflows and outflows. Positive numbers are used to indicate sources of funds while negative numbers indicate uses of funds. This format facilitates comparative and trend analysis, and for this reason is becoming more widely used by loan officers than the method described in the text.

∎∎∎∎ Summary

The funds flow statement is an important analytical tool that enables the loan officer to determine how a company obtains and uses its economic resources. By providing a structured format showing the inflows and outflows of funds associated with the operating, discretionary, and financing activities of a company, the loan officer can answer such questions as these:

- Is the company using its funds wisely?
- How is the company's growth or lack of growth affecting its operating funds needs?
- How fast can the company grow from internally generated funds?
- How much outside funding is needed?
- How is the company financing its activities?
- Are permanent uses of funds being supplied by permanent sources or by temporary sources?
- What funding needs can be anticipated?

EXHIBIT 5.6 ■■■■■■■■■■■■■■■■■■■■■■■■■■■■■■■■■■■■■■

Working Capital Reconciliation Statement

Garcia-Duran Design Company
Working Capital Reconciliation Statement
for the Year Ended December 31, 1988
(in thousands of dollars)

Sources of Working Capital
From operations:
Net income	27
Charges against income not requiring the outlay of working capital:	
Depreciation	10
Increase in deferred taxes	18
Total from operations	55
Decrease in fixed assets	1
	56

Applications of Working Capital
Increase in other assets	1
Decrease in long-term debt	1
Cash dividends paid	21
	23
Increase in Working Capital	33

Components of Increase (Decrease) in Working Capital
Cash	(19)
Accounts receivable	163
Inventory	125
Notes payable	(180)
Accounts payable	(53)
Accruals	(12)
Current-year income taxes	3
~~Investments in affiliates~~	~~6~~
Increase (decrease) in working capital	~~33~~ 27
Working capital at beginning of period	469
Working capital at end of period	~~502~~ 496

Sources and Applications of Funds Statement

Garcia-Duran Design Company
Sources and Applications of Funds
for the Year Ended December 31, 1988
(in thousands of dollars)

Sources of Funds
From operations:
Net income	27
Charges against income not requiring the outlay of working capital:	
Depreciation	10
Increase in deferred taxes	18
Total from operations	55
Decrease in fixed assets	1
Increase in notes payable	180
Increase in accounts payable	53
Increase in accruals	12
	301

Applications of Funds
Increase in accounts receivable	163
Increase in inventory	125
Increase in other assets	1
Increase in investments in affiliates	6
Decrease in current-year income taxes	3
Decrease in long-term debt	1
Cash dividends paid	21
	320
Less: Net decrease in cash	19
Total	301

Comparative Funds Flow Statement

Garcia-Duran Design Company
Comparative Funds Flow Statement
for the Years Ended December 31, 1987 and 1988
(in thousands of dollars)

	1987	1988
Operating Funds		
Net income	38	27
Add: Depreciation/amortization	12	10
Change in deferred tax liability	6	18
Change in accounts receivable	(66)	(163)
Change in notes receivable	—	—
Change in inventory	(101)	(125)
Change in other current assets	—	—
Change in accounts payable	42	53
Change in deferred/prepaid items	—	—
Change in accruals	4	12
Change in income tax—current	(1)	(3)
Change in other current liabilities	—	—
Net operating flow	(66)	(171)
Discretionary Funds		
Change in other noncurrent assets	1	(1)
Add to fixed assets	(26)	1
Change in affiliated investments	—	(6)
Change in other investments	—	—
Change in intangibles	—	—
Dividends paid	(21)	(21)
Decrease in capital accounts	—	—
Net discretionary flow	(46)	(27)
Financing Funds		
Change in notes payable to banks	94	180
Change in notes payable to others	—	—
Change in commercial paper	—	—
Change in commercial long-term debt	—	—
Change in long-term debt	(1)	(1)
Change in other reserves	—	—
Increase in capital accounts	—	—
Net financing flow	93	179
Change in cash/marketable securities	(19)	(19)
Summary		
Net operating flow	(66)	(171)
Net discretionary flow	(46)	(27)
Net financing flow	93	179
Change in cash/marketable securities	(19)	(19)

■ ■

The funds flow statement is a period statement that generally covers a period of a year. It ties together two balance sheets, which are point-in-time statements reflecting the company's financial status at the beginning and end of the year. Besides the changes in balance sheet accounts (each of which reflects either a source or a use of funds), additional funds flow information (net profit, depreciation, and dividends paid) is derived from the income statement or the reconciliation of net worth. In constructing a funds flow statement, an important underlying concept is that all sources of funds must equal all uses of funds.

A lender's analysis of a company's funds flow statement revolves around an assessment of the adequacy of the company's operating funds flows, the appropriateness of its discretionary funds flows, and the proper structuring of its financing funds flows. Tentative conclusions can often be verified or contradicted by doing a comparative analysis using the prior year's funds flow statement.

Various types of funds flow statements with differing names are in common use. The advantage of the funds flow statement presented in the text is that it clearly identifies the inflows and outflows of funds and categorizes them according to how they actually occur in the business— that is, a company takes actions in the course of doing business, some of which are required for operations (operating funds flows) and some of which are discretionary (discretionary funds flows), and then finances the actions taken (financing funds flows). This easily understood format is gaining in popularity among publicly held companies.

A major drawback of financial analysis based on the use of a funds flow statement is that it is easy to reach unjustified and erroneous conclusions. Since almost any flow of funds can be subject to widely varying interpretations, it is important that any conclusions be substantiated. Thus funds flow statements should always be used in the context of a comprehensive financial analysis, never as the sole tool of analysis.

Questions

1. Explain how changes in asset, liability, and equity accounts result in sources and uses of funds.

2. Why do sources and uses of funds always equal each other?

3. What sources of information does a loan officer use in constructing a funds flow statement?

4. Describe the steps involved in constructing a funds flow statement.

5. Is a funds flow statement a period or point-in-time statement?

6. Explain what accounts are represented in each of the three categories of funds flow—operating, discretionary, and financing.

7. What questions should the analysis of a funds flow statement answer?

8. Why should a funds flow statement be used only in conjunction with other financial analysis tools?

Exercises

E-1

Prepare a presentation of net changes in balance sheet accounts using the following balance sheets of the B. Wiley Manufacturing Company, Inc. (Use the format illustrated in Exhibit 5.2.)

B. Wiley Manufacturing Company, Inc.
Balance Sheet
(in thousands of dollars)

	12/31/87	*12/31/88*
Assets		
Cash	$ 432	$ 360
Accounts receivable	1,696	2,520
Inventory	3,776	4,968
Total current assets	$ 5,904	$ 7,848
Fixed assets (net)	4,296	4,324
Prepaid expense	130	160
Total noncurrent assets	$ 4,426	$ 4,484
Total assets	$10,330	$12,332
Liabilities		
Notes payable	$ 800	$ 1,815
Accounts payable	776	1,112
Accruals	200	312
Current maturities of long-term debt	400	400
Current-year income taxes	376	608
Total current liabilities	$ 2,552	$ 4,247
Long-term liabilities	$ 3,600	$ 3,200
Total long-term liabilities	3,600	3,200
Total liabilities	$ 6,152	$ 7,447

	12/31/87	12/31/88
Net Worth		
Common stock	$ 1,200	$ 1,200
Paid-in surplus	840	840
Retained earnings	2,138	2,845
Total net worth	$ 4,178	$ 4,885
Total liabilities and net worth	$10,330	$12,332

E-2

Using the information from the statement generated in the preceding exercise and the information following, prepare a funds flow statement for the B. Wiley Manufacturing Company for the year ended December 31, 1988. (Use the format shown in Exhibit 5.5.) From the 1988 income statement:

- Net income for the year was $827,000.

- Depreciation expenses were $304,000.

From the 1988 reconciliation of net worth:

- Cash dividends paid were $120,000.

E-3

What analytical issues are raised by the funds flow statement for the B. Wiley Manufacturing Company?

E-4

Given the following financial statement and additional information for Roland Industries, prepare a funds flow statement (again using the format shown in Exhibit 5.5) for the year ended December 31, 1988.

Roland Industries
Balance Sheet
(in thousands of dollars)

	12/31/87	12/31/88
Assets		
Cash	$ 399	$ 587
Accounts receivable (net)	1,603	2,354
Inventory	1,249	1,808
Total current assets	$ 3,251	$ 4,749
Fixed assets (net)	4,998	5,121
Deferred charges/prepaid expense	248	327
Total noncurrent assets	$ 5,246	$ 5,448
Total assets	$ 8,497	$10,197
Liabilities		
Accounts payable	$ 1,587	$ 1,906
Accruals	320	387
Current maturities of long-term debt	120	130
Total current liabilities	$ 2,027	$ 2,423
Long-term debt (secured)	$ 506	$ 581
Total long-term liabilities	506	581
Total liabilities	$ 2,533	$ 3,004
Reserve—deferred income taxes	$ 389	$ 422
Net Worth		
Common stock	$ 800	$ 800
Paid-in surplus	200	200
Retained earnings	4,575	5,771
Total net worth	$ 5,575	$ 6,771
Total liabilities and net worth	$ 8,497	$10,197

Additional information for the year ended December 31, 1988:

Net income	$1,584
Depreciation	433
Cash dividends	388

E-5

What analytical issues are raised by the funds flow statement for Roland Industries?

E-6

The Preisendorfer Company incurred a net loss during 1988 totaling
$143,500. Its depreciation expense for the year amounted to $73,000;
its goodwill amortization was $8,000; and it issued 15,000 shares of
$1 per common stock in satisfaction of $300,000 in long-term debt.
Illustrate how these transactions would be reported in the company's
funds flow statement.

6 Ratios

Learning Objectives

After studying this chapter, you should be able to

- calculate key financial ratios
- explain what the ratios mean and how they are used in financial analysis
- identify the five ratio analysis groups—liquidity, leverage, coverage, profitability, and activity—and the various ratios that fit into each category
- use financial ratios to compare a company's performance with that of the industry
- explain why ratios must be used with caution

▌▌▌▌▌▌▌▌ Introduction

Ratios are among the most well-known and widely used financial analysis tools. Ratios allow the loan officer to study the relationships among various components of a given set of financial statements by putting information in a manageable form. Because ratios serve as comparative tools, the loan officer can measure a company's performance over time and compare it with that of its competitors. The loan officer can also compare the company's performance to various standards, or benchmarks, of performance.

Ratios are perhaps the most overrated and most widely misused of financial analysis tools as well. Although easily calculated, ratios can be very misleading. They should be used as a measuring device that leads the loan officer to ask instructive questions and as building blocks in the construction of a company's total financial picture. They should never be used as the primary basis for a lending decision.

The figures used in calculating ratios come from the income statement, the balance sheet, and the funds flow statement. Thus ratio analysis is really an extension of the analytical techniques discussed in the preceding chapters. Moreover, the ability to calculate and use key ratios provides the framework for the more advanced analytical techniques presented in Chapter 9.

This chapter explains the arithmetic computation and meaning of five key categories of financial ratios—liquidity, leverage, coverage, profitability, and activity. It also discusses how ratios are selected and used to spot significant trends over time and to compare a company's performance in key areas with that of other companies in its industry.

▌▌▌▌▌▌▌▌ Uses and Limitations of Ratios

Ratios show the relative size of things. Ratios in financial analysis help the loan officer measure relationships or proportions between various accounts included in a company's financial statements. For example, a ratio will clearly show that the relationship between $10 of assets and $20 of liabilities is the same as the relationship between $50,000 of assets and $100,000 of liabilities. Thus ratios enable the loan officer to compare various measures of a company's performance over time, as well as to compare companies of different sizes.

Since a ratio can be calculated using any two numbers, the loan officer must recognize that the analytical significance of a ratio depends upon there being a meaningful relationship between the accounts being compared. For example, because the relationship between a company's debt and its net worth has meaning, the debt-to-worth ratio is significant. The ratio of inventory to deferred taxes, on the other hand, is not significant because no meaningful relationship exists between the two accounts.

The quality of the numbers used to calculate a ratio also affects the significance of a ratio. Meaningful ratio analysis depends not only on the accuracy of the computations used in deriving a financial statement, but also on the comparability of the numbers in terms of the underlying accounting methods of the companies being compared. For example, any intercompany comparisons of ratios involving assets must take into consideration the many different valuation methods that may be used. For example, the valuation of inventory can differ dramatically depending on whether the company employs the first-in, first-out (FIFO) or the last-in, first-out (LIFO) method. The valuation of accounts receivable depends on the company's policy for determining the reserve for bad debts. The valuation of fixed assets will be affected by whether the company uses straight-line depreciation or the accelerated cost recovery system (ACRS). In addition, some balance sheets may include significantly undervalued fixed assets, such as land that has been held for a considerable length of time or a heavily depreciated plant.

The loan officer must also recognize that any management action or policy choice that influences the valuation of a balance sheet item also affects the income statement. Using the examples just cited, a lower valuation of inventory resulting from the use of LIFO in times of rising prices, the establishment of a larger bad debt reserve, and the use of ACRS to more rapidly write off depreciable assets all have the additional effects of reducing a company's net profit. This, in turn, affects any ratio involving net profit, such as the return on assets or return on sales.

When performing a trend analysis comparing ratios for a single company over time, the particular accounting policies used in preparing the statements are less important as long as they are consistently applied. However, when making industrywide comparisons, the loan officer should try to find companies that use the same accounting procedures and apply them consistently. Even if this cannot be done, industry comparisons have some validity since ratios are not intended to be absolute indicators, but rather relative indicators that may point up areas for further study or inquiry.

Useful sources of industry information include the Robert Morris Associates (RMA) *Annual Statement Studies* and the Dun & Bradstreet *Key Business Ratios*. Care must be taken when using such sources, however, since generally the industry figures available for comparison will be a year behind the statements available for the company being analyzed. With the business environment subject to large and rapid economic swings, it may be difficult to draw meaningful comparisons using year-old data.

Another drawback to using industry comparisons is that some diversified companies consolidate their various lines of business into a single financial statement, making accurate comparisons very difficult. However, the loan officer may not know that a particular company's financial statements are consolidated.

This text stresses throughout that no single financial technique yields a complete financial picture of a company. This is especially true of ratios. They are relative measures that have significance only in relation to other reference points or benchmarks. Ratio analysis is usually most useful in the following situations:

- when it relies on the intuition and the previous personal experience of the loan officer
- when ratios are used to compare a company's past financial performance with its current performance
- when ratios are used to analyze projected financial statements supplied to the loan officer
- when ratios are used as the basis for industry comparisons, such as to compare a company's performance with a specific group of companies in the same industry

Selection and Interpretation of Ratios

For analytical purposes, ratios can generally be grouped into five categories, each representing an important aspect of a company's financial well-being. These categories are liquidity, leverage, coverage, profitability, and activity. Many banks use computer programs to generate certain key ratios that are most often used in financial analysis. In practice, a loan officer will not normally calculate every ratio, but may select one or two ratios from each category to begin an analysis and then select additional ratios as deemed appropriate to help interpret and complete the analytical picture. An experienced loan officer may use additional ratios not included in this chapter, some of which are presented in Chapter 9.

In the following sections, each of the five categories of ratios are discussed in turn. In each case, the calculation of ratios is based on financial statements for the Carroll Company, a discount retailer. Exhibit 6.1 is a common-sized comparative (4-year) income statement for the company, while Exhibit 6.2 shows the company's balance sheet results for the same 4 years.

LIQUIDITY RATIOS

Liquidity measures a company's ability to meet its short-term obligations as they come due. Because maturing obligations must generally be paid in cash, liquidity also represents the availability of cash or the company's ability to generate cash by converting its assets into cash without a significant loss in value. The level of liquidity required to meet short-term obligations is directly related to the risk and fluctuation involved in a company's short-term stream of funds flows. For example, a manufacturer that cannot predict with reasonable accuracy its level of sales for the next quarter needs more liquidity to ensure it will be able to meet its obligations than a utility company that can accurately forecast the demand for power and thus has a steady and predictable level of operating cash inflow. A company's need for financial flexibility also affects its desirable level of liquidity. For example, a company that wants to be able to rapidly stockpile inventory when customers make occasional large purchases, or the company that wants to increase advertising outlays in response to competitive demands needs added liquidity. The amount of prearranged outside funding available to a company on demand may also affect its need for liquidity.

A company is illiquid if it cannot meet its current financial obligations. This may be a temporary, self-correcting problem, or it may be a symptom of more serious and permanent problems in a company's

Income Statement

Carroll Company
Income Statement
(in thousands of dollars)

	FYE 1/31/85	%	FYE 1/31/86	%	FYE 1/31/87	%	FYE 1/31/88	%
Net sales	11,696	100	12,731	100	14,204	100	16,527	100
Cost of goods sold	8,566	73	9,283	73	10,417	73	12,360	75
Gross profit/revenues	3,130	27	3,448	27	3,787	27	4,167	25
Total operating expenses	2,503	21	2,839	22	3,326	24	3,810	23
Operating profit	627	6	609	5	461	3	357	2
Other income	151	1	190	1	208	1	246	1
Interest expense	142	1	171	1	227	1	276	1
Profit before tax	636	6	628	5	442	3	327	2
Income taxes	292	3	270	2	181	1	107	1
Net profit after tax	344	3	358	3	261	2	220	1
Notes:								
Dividends	88		103		113		117	
Depreciation	146		166		198		230	

■ ■

Balance Sheet

Carroll Company
Balance Sheet
(in thousands of dollars)

	1/31/85	%	1/31/86	%	1/31/87	%	1/31/88	%
Assets								
Cash and marketable securities	241	5	300	5	213	3	115	2
Accounts receivable—net	43	1	76	1	80	1	90	1
Inventory	2,376	49	2,746	49	2,846	47	3,135	47
Current assets	2,660	55	3,122	55	3,139	51	3,340	50
Fixed assets—net	1,942	40	2,234	40	2,601	43	2,876	43
Other assets	235	5	286	5	362	6	457	7
Noncurrent assets	2,177	45	2,520	45	2,963	49	3,333	50
Total assets	4,837	100	5,642	100	6,102	100	6,673	100
Liabilities and Net Worth								
Notes payable to banks	—	—	186	3	—	—	168	3
Accounts payable—trade	936	20	1,058	19	1,060	17	1,253	19
Accruals	405	8	485	9	550	9	499	7
Current maturities—long-term debt*	48	1	53	1	59	1	64	1
Current debt	1,389	29	1,782	32	1,669	27	1,984	30
Long-term debt—secured	1,503	31	1,632	29	2,037	34	2,167	32
Total debt	2,892	60	3,414	61	3,706	61	4,151	62
Reserve—deferred income taxes	29	—	43	1	51	1	64	1
Capital stock—common	122	3	123	2	124	2	124	2
Paid-in surplus	230	5	243	4	254	4	264	4
Retained earnings	1,564	32	1,819	32	1,967	32	2,070	31
Net worth	1,916	40	2,185	38	2,345	38	2,458	37
Total liabilities and net worth	4,837	100	5,642	100	6,102	100	6,673	100

*Includes current capitalized lease obligations.

operation. Illiquidity typically results from a combination of several situations.

First, the company may have its funds tied up in illiquid assets—that is, assets that the company cannot quickly convert to cash. A company, for example, that invests its money in a new factory cannot readily liquidate the factory to obtain needed cash if the factory itself does not generate sufficient cash. Second, the company may have funded its operation improperly. For example, the business may have taken on too much debt given its level of equity capitalization and its ability to generate cash. Or the schedule for repaying its financial obligations may not match the timing of its cash generation. Third, the company may be losing money in its operation. A business that is spending more money than it takes in cannot generate sufficient cash to meet its obligations. Finally, the company's current financial obligations may have grown faster than its ability to generate cash. This situation often occurs when the company is experiencing growth.

Depending on the reasons for and the magnitude of a company's illiquidity, the results can range from simple inconvenience to impending disaster. Illiquidity might merely result in having to forgo discounts offered by creditors for exceptionally prompt payment. Or it might result in a need to borrow money from its bank. On a more serious note, illiquidity may damage a company's credit rating. Or the company may have to pass up additional business because of its inability to handle its existing financial obligations. Most seriously, the company may have to liquidate its operating assets, which can impair its future ability to generate cash through operations. This, of course, puts the business into a downward spin of ever-increasing illiquidity until the company ultimately fails to operate profitably or survive.

Loan officers often think of liquidity ratios as liquidation ratios because they show the margin of current assets to current liabilities that should result from a liquidation or total elimination of the company's accounts. Two common liquidity ratios are the *current ratio* and the *quick ratio*.

Current Ratio

The current ratio—so called because it compares a company's current assets to its current liabilities—measures a company's ability to pay its currently maturing obligations on a timely basis. In other words, it shows the amount of protection provided by a company's current assets relative to its current liabilities. A ratio of 2 to 1 (or 2:1, or simply 2) of current assets to current liabilities has historically been the accepted standard for the current ratio. However, the need for a high liquidity cushion and thus a high current ratio varies among industries and also depends on such factors as the composition and quality of the company's current assets.

Generally, the higher the current ratio, the more comfortable is the cushion against the effects of reduced inventory values, uncollected receivables, and unanticipated cash needs. However, a large current ratio may signify idle cash, too much inventory, or a slow collection of accounts receivable. Thus the loan officer must be able to correctly interpret the current ratio.

The current ratio is calculated using the following formula:

$$\text{Current ratio} = \frac{\text{Current assets}}{\text{Current liabilities}}.$$

A look at the 1988 figures on the Carroll Company's balance sheet (Exhibit 6.2) shows the company's current assets at $3,340 and its current liabilities (or debt) at $1,984. (Dollar amounts in this chapter are in thousands of dollars to correspond with the amounts in the exhibits.) Using the formula, the Carroll Company's current ratio can be calculated as follows:

$$\text{Current ratio} = \frac{3,340}{1,984} = 1.68:1.$$

The Carroll Company's current ratio of 1.68:1 means that, for every dollar of current debt, the Carroll Company has $1.68 of current assets. Thus the value of the Carroll Company's current assets could shrink as much as 40 percent (.68/1.68) without impairing the company's ability to pay its creditors through the liquidation of its current assets. Although the current ratio is a valid tool for measuring liquidity, it is not an absolute measure of debt-paying ability since the company will not, in its normal operations, ever fully liquidate its current assets. Moreover, the current ratio does not measure the quality of the current assets, but only their availability.

Quick Ratio

The quick ratio (also called the *acid test ratio*) is a more stringent measure of liquidity than the current ratio because the quick ratio includes only the most liquid current assets—those that can be quickly converted to cash at amounts close to their book value. The company's inventory and other less liquid current assets are eliminated from current assets for this calculation, leaving only cash, marketable securities, and accounts receivable—those assets that a company can quickly convert to cash to pay pressing obligations if necessary. The quick ratio is calculated using the following formula:

$$\text{Quick ratio} = \frac{\text{Cash + Marketable securities + Accounts receivable}}{\text{Current liabilities}}.$$

The Carroll Company's 1988 balance sheet in Exhibit 6.2 shows the company's cash and marketable securities at $115, its accounts receivable at $90, and its current liabilities (the same figure used in the current ratio) at $1,984. Using the formula, the Carroll Company's quick ratio can be calculated as follows:

$$\text{Quick ratio} = \frac{115 + 90}{1,984} = 0.10:1.$$

Historically, a quick ratio of 1:1 has been accepted as an indication of good liquidity. Thus the Carroll Company's quick ratio of 0.10:1, which means the company has only 10 cents of very liquid assets available for each $1 of current debt, is very low by the standard for most industries. However, retailers typically have low quick ratios because they have very low accounts receivable, and most cash is quickly reinvested in inventory.

LEVERAGE RATIOS

Financial leverage measures the relative levels of risk borne by the creditors and the shareholders of a business. Thus leverage ratios show the loan officer how much protection the company's assets provide for a creditor's debt—since assets must be financed either by owners' equity (net worth) or creditors' equity (liabilities or debt). Like liquidity ratios, they show the margin of protection provided by a certain group of assets relative to a corresponding group of liabilities. The higher the proportion of borrowed funds to owner-contributed funds, the greater the risk to lenders. Not only are highly leveraged firms more vulnerable to an economic downturn, creditors also stand to lose more than the shareholders should liquidation occur. Two leverage ratios that are useful in financial analysis are the *debt-to-worth ratio* and the *debt-to-capitalization ratio.*

Debt-to-Worth Ratio

The debt-to-worth (or debt-to-equity) ratio provides an indication of how well the shareholders' investment in the company protects a creditor's debt. It also measures how much the shareholders have at risk versus how much the creditors have at risk and, thus, the strength of the company's capital structure.

Like the current ratio, the debt-to-worth ratio measures a company's ability to liquidate its assets in order to satisfy debt. This ratio enables the loan officer to gauge how much a company can reduce the valuation of its assets before its creditors sustain a loss. Typical debt-to-worth ratios vary greatly for different industries. The debt-to-worth ratio is calculated using the following formula:

$$\text{Debt-to-worth ratio} = \frac{\text{Total liabilities}}{\text{Net worth}}.$$

In calculating the debt-to-worth ratio, the company's long-term deferred income tax liability, if any, should not be included as a liability because, as explained in Chapter 4, the reserve for deferred income taxes can normally be deferred indefinitely.

The Carroll Company's balance sheet (Exhibit 6.2) shows its total debt (as of year-end 1988) at $4,151. Since the company's reserve for deferred taxes is not included in the company's total liabilities, no adjustment is required. The company's net worth at the end of 1988 was $2,458. Thus, the Carroll Company's debt-to-worth ratio is calculated as follows:

$$\text{Debt-to-worth ratio} = \frac{4,151}{2,458} = 1.69{:}1.$$

The Carroll Company's debt-to-worth ratio of 1.69:1 indicates that creditors have 1.69 times as much value entrusted to the company as the shareholders, as measured by the book value of the assets. The relative value of the shareholders' and creditors' risk could be different from what the debt-to-worth ratio shows if the market, or liquidation, value of the assets differs significantly from their book value.

Debt-to-Capitalization Ratio

Less frequently used is the debt-to-capitalization ratio, which is based on an assessment of the permanent capital of a company—that is, its long-term debt and net worth. This ratio shows what portion of the company's permanent capital is financed with debt as opposed to shareholders' investment. The ratio is useful because the company's operating cash flow resulting from profitable operations generally pays for the company's term debt and lease obligations. A company's short-term debt is typically seasonal or of short duration and is paid by a seasonal decrease in business activity, which results in a lowering of working capital requirements. This ratio suggests to what extent the company is relying on long-term debt and lease obligations for financing assets and the resulting need of profitable operations to support this leverage. The debt-to-capitalization ratio is calculated using the following formula:

$$\text{Debt-to-capitalization ratio} = \frac{\text{Long-term debt}}{\text{Long-term debt} + \text{Net worth}}.$$

If a company has capitalized lease obligations shown on its balance sheet that are not already included as part of its long-term debt, these obligations should be added to long-term debt both in the numerator and denominator of this equation. The Carroll Company's 1988 balance sheet shows long-term debt at $2,167 (a figure that includes capitalized lease obligations) and net worth at $2,458. Thus, the company's debt-to-capitalization ratio is calculated as follows:

$$\text{Debt-to-capitalization ratio} = \frac{2,167}{2,167 + 2,458} = \frac{2,167}{4,625} = 0.47:1.$$

The Carroll Company's debt-to-capitalization ratio of 0.47:1 indicates that the company's long-term creditors supply just under half of its permanent capital. This ratio is primarily used for comparison of companies in the same industry.

COVERAGE RATIOS

Coverage ratios are the next category of ratios commonly used in financial analysis. They measure the extent to which a company's current debt obligations are met or exceeded by the flow of funds from the company's operations. Obviously a company's ability to cover principal and interest payments is a key indicator of financial health that is of crucial concern to lenders. While a detailed analysis of funds flow entails the preparation of a funds flow statement (as discussed in detail in Chapter 5), coverage ratios are calculated using a simplistic measure of funds flow consisting basically of net profit plus any noncash charges such as depreciation. In contrast to liquidity and leverage ratios, both of which measure the lender's margin of comfort in the event of liquidation, coverage ratios indicate the margin of comfort while regarding the company as a going concern. *Cash flow-to-current maturities, times interest earned,* and *dividend payout* are common coverage ratios.

Cash Flow-to-Current Maturities Ratio

The cash flow-to-current maturities (CF-to-CM) ratio shows what proportion of a company's cash flow (after deducting dividends) will be needed to pay the principal and interest due on term debt in the coming year. This ratio serves as a fairly reliable indicator of a company's future performance provided profitability and cash flow are expected to remain the same or increase. The lower the ratio, the smaller the margin of safety. Theoretically, if a company's cash flow-to-current maturities ratio falls below 1:1, it is not generating enough cash to repay its current obligations. The CF-to-CM ratio is calculated as follows:

$$\text{CF-to-CM ratio} = \frac{\text{Profit after tax} + \text{Depreciation} - \text{Dividends paid.}}{\text{Current maturities of long-term debt}}$$

The Carroll Company's income statement (Fxhibit 6.1) shows that after-tax profits, depreciation, and dividends paid for 1988 are $220, $230, and $117, respectively. No noncash expense other than depreciation is shown.

Exhibit 6.2, the Carroll Company's balance sheet, shows current maturities of long-term debt for 1988 at $64. The lender should add the current amount of any noncancelable (or capitalized) lease obligations to current maturities; however, the Carroll Company's balance sheet indicates that the current maturities figure already includes these obligations. Therefore, the company's 1988 CF-to-CM ratio is calculated as follows:

$$\text{CF-to-CM ratio} = \frac{220 + 230 - 117}{64} = 5.20{:}1.$$

The company's CF-to-CM ratio of more than 5:1 indicates that cash flow could decrease by more than 80 percent while still allowing the business to pay its current maturities. This ratio can be misleading, however, because cash flow is calculated simplistically. Its major weakness is that it does not address the cash flow required to fund the increased operating assets associated with an increase in sales. Nor does it take into consideration the timing of a company's cash flow, which could affect a company's ability to repay debt as it comes due. An analysis using a funds flow statement is one measure of a company's cash flow coverage. A cash budget indicates the timing of a company's ability to pay debt as it comes due. Nevertheless, the CF-to-CM ratio is a good general measure to use, especially when doing a trend analysis of a company's earnings over several years.

Times Interest Earned Ratio

The times interest earned ratio, another measure of coverage, shows what proportion of a company's earnings is needed to pay interest on its debt. Although this ratio suffers from the same drawbacks as the cash flow-to-current maturities ratio, it provides a valuable picture of the extent to which earnings are penalized to pay the financing costs of the company and the potential impact of an increase in interest rates on the company's cash flow. A ratio of greater than 1 is almost mandatory since a lower ratio would indicate a company's earnings are insufficient to cover the interest on its debt. This ratio is calculated as follows:

$$\text{Times interest earned ratio} = \frac{\text{Profit before tax} + \text{Interest expense}}{\text{Interest expense}}.$$

The Carroll Company's income statement (Exhibit 6.1) shows profits before tax for 1988 at $327 and interest expense at $276. Thus, the 1988 times interest earned ratio for the Carroll Company is calculated as follows:

$$\text{Times interest earned ratio} = \frac{327 + 276}{276} = 2.18{:}1.$$

With a times interest earned ratio of 2.18:1, the Carroll Company's interest expense could more than double before the company would be unable to pay its interest when due given the company's current profitability level. This conclusion assumes that the company has all its cash flow available for interest payments, and thus fails to consider any cash flow for funding the company's operating assets or the principal portion of debt maturities.

Dividend Payout Ratio

The dividend payout ratio shows what percentage of profit after tax a company pays to shareholders in the form of dividends—funds that thereby become unavailable for other uses such as to support asset growth and to fund current maturities of long-term debt. The ratio can help explain trends in equity growth and leverage. The dividend payout ratio is calculated as follows:

$$\text{Dividend payout ratio} = \frac{\text{Cash dividends paid}}{\text{Profit after tax}} \times 100.$$

Exhibit 6.1 shows that the Carroll Company paid $117 in cash dividends and earned $220 in profit after tax for 1988. Consequently, the 1988 dividend payout ratio is calculated as follows:

$$\text{Dividend payout ratio} = \frac{117}{220} \times 100 = 53\%.$$

A dividend payout ratio of 53 percent indicates that the company pays slightly more than half its earnings to shareholders in the form of dividends. Such a high dividend ratio could mean the company is retaining too little profit to fund growth or repay debt. The Carroll Company's high dividend payout ratio is addressed in more detail in the analysis section of this chapter.

PROFITABILITY RATIOS

Profitability is another very important measure of a company's financial well-being because it generally determines a company's ability to grow, as well as its ability to repay debt. The analysis of a company's profitability relates the company's profits to various measures such as the level of sales, assets, and equity. Taken together, they give the loan officer a good indication of a company's ability to grow, remain solvent, and repay debt.

As discussed in Chapter 3, the common-sizing of an income statement (in which each account is shown as a percentage of sales) produces several useful ratios, including gross profit margin, which was discussed in relation to income statement analysis. Not discussed in any detail was the after-tax profit margin—also called return on sales—perhaps the most frequently used measure of profitability. However, since the true measure of profitability is the efficient use of assets and the return on the shareholders' equity, the amount of assets required to support a given level of sales and the amount of equity required to support that level of assets are also important measures of the overall profitability of the company.

Consider, for example, Company X and Company Y. On the same level of sales, Company X makes $5,000 profit while Company Y makes $10,000 profit. It would appear on the surface that Company Y is more profitable. Suppose, however, that Company Y required $50,000 in assets to support its sales, while Company X required only $15,000 in assets to support the same level of sales. Company X, then, made more profits per dollar of assets employed than Company Y. The two companies might also require different levels of shareholders' investment to support a given level of assets. Thus, the loan officer must consider several variables when assessing a company's profitability.

Return on Sales Ratio

The return on sales ratio (or net profit margin) simply measures the extent to which a company's revenues exceed all of its expenses—that is, how much profit the company earns on each dollar of sales. There is no benchmark figure that a lender looks for since return on sales will vary greatly with the industry. However, a company with highly volatile sales should have a higher return on sales than a company with predictable profits over the years. In addition, the level of assets and equity required to generate a specified sales level should also be taken into consideration in determining a satisfactory return on sales. The return on sales ratio is calculated as follows:

$$\text{Return on sales ratio} = \frac{\text{Net profit}}{\text{Sales}} \times 100.$$

Exhibit 6.1, the Carroll Company's income statement, shows net profit at $220 and sales at $16,527 for 1988. Thus, the Carroll Company's 1988 return on sales ratio is calculated as follows:

$$\text{Return on sales ratio} = \frac{220}{16,527} \times 100 = 1.33\%.$$

This return on sales ratio shows that the company earned $1.33 for each $100 of sales. Thus this shows the percentage of each sales dollar (1.33 cent) that remains after accounting for all expenses. However, any dividends paid to shareholders reduces the amount that can be applied to equity. The return on sales ratio is useful in comparing companies within the same industry and in analyzing the trend in the relationship between a company's profits and sales over several years. The ratio also indicates how much cost of goods and operating expenses can change without adversely affecting profits. In this case, if the Carroll Company's operating expenses (such as rent and salaries) were to increase only slightly, the company would become unprofitable. The company, therefore, must pass on any increases in product costs and efficiently control expenses.

Return on Assets Ratio

The return on assets (ROA) ratio measures the profitability of a company in terms of how efficiently it uses its assets. Although this ratio can be calculated in several ways, it is basically a comparison of net profit to total assets. A more precise calculation results when the numerator is fine-tuned by adding interest expense to net profit and then subtracting the tax benefit of interest expense (as explained in the next paragraph). Calculated in this way, the ratio eliminates the effect on profit of how a company is financed. Average total assets is the preferred denominator, although, for simplicity's sake, many loan officers use ending assets rather than average assets. While somewhat less accurate, this practice is generally accepted. The return on assets ratio is calculated, then, as follows:

$$\text{Return on assets ratio} \ = \ \frac{\left(\begin{array}{l}\text{Net profit } + \text{ Interest expense } - \\ \text{Tax benefit of interest expense}\end{array}\right)}{\text{Average total assets}} \ \times \ 100.$$

Carroll Company's income statement (Exhibit 6.1) shows net profit at $220 and interest expense at $276 for 1988. The tax benefit of interest expense equals the interest expense multiplied by the company's tax rate. The tax rate may be found by dividing income taxes (as shown on the income statement) by profit before tax, which in this case comes to 33 percent (107 ÷ 327). The company's balance sheet (Exhibit 6.2) provides the information needed to calculate average total assets. The total assets as of the end of the 1988 fiscal year are listed as $6,673 compared to the previous year-end assets of $6,102. Average total assets is obtained by summing both amounts and dividing by 2. Thus, the Carroll Company's 1988 return on assets ratio is calculated as follows:

$$\text{ROA ratio} \ = \ \frac{220 + 276 - (0.33 \times 276)}{(6{,}102 + 6{,}673) \div 2} \times 100 \ = \ 6.34\%.$$

Carroll Company's return on assets is 6.34 percent, or about 6 cents on every dollar of sales—a number that is meaningful only when it is compared to the ROA of previous years or of other companies in the industry. When applying this ratio, the loan officer must remember that the ratio may be misleading if the company has significant fixed assets, such as land, that are undervalued on the balance sheet. In addition, because the income information is generated from a period statement and the asset information from a point-in-time statement, imbalances may occur due to timing differences. For example, if a manufacturing company spent much of the year building a new manufacturing facility only to begin production at the end of the year, the facility's impact as an asset in the denominator of the ratio will be far greater than its profit-generating impact in the numerator.

Return on Equity Ratio

Another measure of profitability is the return on equity (ROE) ratio, which measures the efficiency with which a company uses its stock-holders' equity (without, however, taking into account the riskiness of the company's capital structure). Again, the loan officer may substitute ending net worth for average net worth in the calculation with only a modest impairment of the ratio's accuracy. The return on equity ratio is calculated as follows:

$$\text{Return on equity ratio} = \frac{\text{Net profit}}{\text{Average net worth}} \times 100.$$

The Carroll Company's 1988 income statement shows a net profit of $220, while the balance sheet lists the company's net worth for fiscal year-end 1987 and 1988 as $2,345 and $2,458, respectively. The sum of these two figures are averaged to obtain the denominator for the equation. The company's 1988 return on equity ratio is calculated as follows:

$$\text{ROE ratio} = \frac{220}{(2,345 + 2,458) \div 2} \times 100 = 9.16\%.$$

The Carroll Company's return on equity ratio is 9.16 percent. Depending on what alternative investments are available, such a low return may not provide a good, short-run incentive for investors to invest their capital in Carroll Company's stock. However, a one-year return on equity of 9.16 percent may not be indicative of return on equity in future years. If management is making efficient use of the company's assets (that is, the company has an adequate return on assets), a low return on equity ratio may result from excessive equity relative to debt which, from a shareholder's point of view, suggests inefficient use of equity or insufficient financial leverage. A high return on equity ratio, on the other hand, could indicate undercapitalization, which is usually associated with high financial leverage. This is another instance where the loan officer might draw erroneous conclusions by looking at a ratio outside of a comparative context.

ACTIVITY RATIOS

Activity ratios give the loan officer some further insights into how efficiently a company uses its assets. Generally, these ratios compare the company's sales to total assets and the three major trading accounts—accounts receivable, inventory, and accounts payable. The ratios measure how frequently the company turns over these accounts—that is, how long it takes for accounts receivable to be collected, inventory to be sold, and accounts payable to be paid.

Asset Turnover Ratio

The asset turnover ratio measures how efficiently a company uses its assets by showing how many dollars of sales are generated by each dollar of assets. When comparing the asset turnover ratios of various companies, the loan officer must remember that the ratio is calculated using the book value of assets (which may not reflect the true value of assets). For example, a fully depreciated loom in a textile mill may produce just as many yards of cloth of the same quality as a new loom. Yet its effect will be to increase the company's asset turnover ratio by decreasing the book value of assets used in the calculation. This means that the asset turnover ratio for companies with older equipment will tend to be higher than for companies with newer equipment. The asset turnover ratio is calculated using the following formula:

$$\text{Asset turnover ratio} = \frac{\text{Sales}}{\text{Average assets}}.$$

The Carroll Company's income statement, Exhibit 6.1, shows sales of $16,527 for 1988. Its assets as of fiscal year-end 1987 and 1988 list as $6,102 and $6,673 on the balance sheet, Exhibit 6.2. These asset figures may be averaged or ending assets may be substituted for average assets. Thus, the Carroll Company's asset turnover ratio for 1988 is calculated as follows:

$$\text{Asset turnover ratio} = \frac{16,527}{(6,102 + 6,673) \div 2} = 2.59 \text{ times.}$$

The asset turnover ratio shows that the Carroll Company generates $2.59 of revenues for every $1.00 of assets employed. Again, this ratio is used primarily to compare a company to its industry peers.

Accounts Receivable Turnover Ratio

The relationship between accounts receivable and sales can be expressed in either of two ways. The first method gives the number of times during the year that the average accounts receivable is collected. The receivables turnover ratio is calculated as follows:

$$\text{Receivables turnover ratio} = \frac{\text{Credit sales}}{\text{Average accounts receivable}}.$$

The second method gives the average number of days that uncollected sales are outstanding in the company's accounts receivables. The average collection period is calculated as follows:

$$\text{Average collection period} = \frac{365}{\text{Receivables turnover ratio}}$$

$$= \frac{\text{Average accounts receivable}}{\text{Credit sales}} \times 365.$$

The little extra work of converting a receivables turnover ratio into days will be more than repaid by the added meaning that expressing the relationship in this way provides. For example, a slowing in a company's average collection period from 37 days to 44 days is much easier to grasp than a decline in receivables turnover from 9.9 to 8.3 times per year. The conversion to days also makes it easier to compare a company's actual accounts receivable turnover with the credit terms it offers.

The average collection period shows the average number of days it takes for a company to collect on credit sales to its customers. Since this will vary greatly for different types of companies, it is important to make comparisons with similar companies or to look at trends over time. Ideally this ratio is calculated using an annualized number derived from the credit sales which gave rise to the level of receivables shown on the balance sheet. For example, if the average collection period is approximately 60 days, the loan officer would annualize the most recent

2 months of sales divided by the current level of receivables to determine the collection period.

Because such detailed information is rarely available, the ratio is generally calculated using the average of the beginning and ending receivables and the aggregate sales level for the entire period. In addition, because the loan officer often cannot distinguish between the company's credit sales and cash sales and because cash sales are often insignificant amounts, total sales are typically used. The resulting ratio provides a reasonable approximation of the company's average collection period.

If any significant deviation in the collection period shows up from the trend or comparative analysis, the loan officer should discuss it with a company representative. The loan officer should also compare the company's average collection period to the collection terms allowed by the company to determine whether its collection of receivables is in line with its credit policy.

Again, the average collection period is calculated using the following formula:

$$\text{Average collection period} = \frac{\text{Average accounts receivable}}{\text{Sales}} \times 365.$$

The Carroll Company's balance sheet shows accounts receivables for fiscal year-end 1987 and 1988 at $80 and $90, respectively. The average of these two figures is taken, or ending accounts receivable can be substituted. Since credit sales are not shown separately, the company's total sales for 1988 ($16,527) are used. The resulting calculation is as follows:

$$\text{Average collection period} = \frac{(80 + 90) \div 2}{16,527} \times 365 = 1.88 \text{ days.}$$

The Carroll Company's average collection period is slightly less than 2 days, indicating almost no receivables, as would be expected for a retailer accepting payment in cash, checks, or bank credit cards. This ratio has more meaning for a company with significant credit sales or with an ability to isolate credit from cash sales.

Inventory Turnover Ratio

The inventory turnover, or *days inventory*, ratio shows how often the inventory is turned or sold to generate the current sales volume. The days inventory measures the company's purchasing, selling, and manufacturing efficiency, but is meaningful only in relation to the company's past performance and to the performance of similar companies in the same industry. Cost of goods sold is used instead of sales in this formula since it shows the cost to the company of inventory sold during the year (although, for a manufacturer, cost of goods sold also includes overhead and manufacturing costs). The days inventory is calculated using the following formula:

$$\text{Days inventory} = \frac{\text{Average inventory}}{\text{Cost of goods sold}} \times 365.$$

The Carroll Company's balance sheet (Exhibit 6.2) shows inventory for fiscal year-end 1987 and 1988 at $2,846 and $3,135. The two inventory figures are averaged (or ending inventory may be substituted for average inventory). The resulting figure is divided by the cost of goods sold for 1988, shown on the income statement as $12,360. Thus, Carroll Company's days inventory is calculated as follows:

$$\text{Days inventory} = \frac{(2,846 + 3,135) \div 2}{12,360} \times 365 = 88.31 \text{ days.}$$

The Carroll Company's days inventory during 1988 was about 88 days. This means that if sales were to continue at the current level, the company could theoretically liquidate its entire inventory in 88 days. However, this calculation assumes a going concern with a fully stocked inventory, not a liquidation situation. Moreover, because detailed inventory information is rarely available and because a company may stock various types of inventory at widely varying levels, this ratio is only an approximation. In addition, the accuracy of the calculation is affected by many differences in the numbers that make up both the numerator and denominator. For example, the use of LIFO or FIFO in valuing inventory also affects the result and may mean that days inventory may not be comparable among companies. Nevertheless, the ratio does allow for general company comparisons and the detection of general trends. A change in this ratio, while not conclusive in itself, may help the loan officer ask questions that will lead to a better understanding of the company. For example, a trend of increasing days may indicate obsolescence of inventory. Although the ratio itself does not tell the lender if any inventory is obsolete or the mix of the inventory, it may signal the lender to ask these questions.

Accounts Payable Turnover Ratio

The accounts payable turnover, or *days payable*, ratio, measures how promptly the company pays its trade accounts. This ratio will vary greatly for different industries since standard credit terms vary greatly. The loan officer should be alert to any significant changes in this ratio since a significant decrease could simply mean the company is taking advantage of discounts offered for early payment, or it could be an indication that suppliers are withdrawing trade credit. On the other hand, a significant lengthening of the payables turn could reflect the fact that suppliers have granted the company additional trade credit or longer terms, or it could reflect cash flow problems that are delaying payments to suppliers.

This ratio is also subject to significant inaccuracies because, while it should relate purchases to payables, purchase figures are frequently unavailable. Consequently, the cost of goods sold is substituted for purchases even though, for a manufacturer, this will include certain overhead accounts as well as direct labor. For this reason, the ratio is best used as an approximation in comparing similar companies or in trend analysis. The days payable ratio is calculated using the following formula:

$$\text{Days payable ratio} = \frac{\text{Average accounts payable}}{\text{Purchases (or Cost of goods sold)}} \times 365.$$

Accounts payable as of fiscal year-end 1987 and 1988, taken from the Carroll Company's balance sheet shown in Exhibit 6.2, list as $1,060 and $1,253, respectively. Either the average of these two payable figures is used, or ending accounts payable may be substituted. Since purchases are unavailable for Carroll Company, the cost of goods sold for fiscal year 1988 ($12,360) is taken from the income statement (Exhibit 6.1). Thus, the company's days payable ratio is calculated as follows:

$$\text{Days payable ratio} = \frac{(1,060 + 1,253) \div 2}{12,360} \times 365 = 34.15 \text{ days.}$$

The days payable ratio shows that Carroll Company pays its creditors, on the average, in 34 days. This should be quite accurate since as a retailer the Carroll Company's cost of goods sold should equal its purchases unless the company is increasing the inventory level. If greater accuracy is desired, especially in the case of a manufacturer, the loan officer can request an aging of payables from management.

▮▮▮▮▮ Interpretive Ratio Analysis

After the five major categories of ratios—liquidity, leverage, coverage, profitability, and activity—have been calculated, the loan officer can begin the interpretive analysis. In this case, the ratios calculated for the Carroll Company will be compared over time (trend analysis) and to ratios calculated for the Strickland Corporation and the Moritz Company, two of the Carroll Company's competitors in the discount retail industry (comparative analysis). The Strickland Corporation's financial statements for 1987 and 1988 are shown in Exhibits 6.3 and 6.4, while the Moritz Company's financial statements for the same 2 years are shown in Exhibits 6.5 and 6.6.

Each of the five ratio categories will be examined using both comparative analysis and trend analysis. Thus the Carroll Company's liquidity ratios as of January 31, 1988, will first be compared to the liquidity ratios of its two competitors as of the same date. Then the Carroll Company's liquidity ratios as of fiscal year-end 1986, 1987, and 1988 will be compared. This same order of analysis will be followed for the leverage, coverage, profitability, and activity ratios. All the ratios will be compared, but those that appear to be significant to the analysis of the Carroll Company will be emphasized.

Income Statement

Strickland Corporation
Income Statement
(in thousands of dollars)

	FYE 1/31/87	%	FYE 1/31/88	%
Net sales	1,649	100	2,450	100
Cost of goods sold	1,208	73	1,787	73
Gross profit/revenues	441	27	663	27
Total operating expenses	332	20	495	20
Operating profit	109	7	168	7
Other income	7	0	12	0
Interest expense	17	1	31	1
Profit before tax	99	6	149	6
Income taxes	43	3	66	3
Net profit after tax	56	3	83	3
Notes:				
Dividends	6		9	
Depreciation	18		26	

■ ■

LIQUIDITY ANALYSIS

Comparative Analysis

The 1988 current ratios for the Carroll Company and its two competitors are as follows:

	Current Ratio
Strickland Corporation (1988)	1.52:1
Carroll Company (1988)	1.68:1
Moritz Company (1988)	2.02:1

These figures are derived from the companies' balance sheets shown in Exhibits 6.2, 6.4, and 6.6. The fact that all three current ratios are in the same general range, with the Carroll Company in the middle, suggests that the Carroll Company is able to pay its currently maturing obligations on a timely basis (at least as compared with its competitors). However, the loan officer will find it useful to remember the relative differences between the three companies' current ratios while analyzing the other ratios.

The three companies' 1988 quick ratios are as follows:

	Quick Ratio
Strickland Corporation (1988)	0.08:1
Carroll Company (1988)	0.10:1
Moritz Company (1988)	0.16:1

An experienced loan officer would recognize that all of these quick ratios are low by most standards. However, this ratio is not very significant for retailers since inventory (which is included in the current ratio, but not in the quick ratio) comprises the primary type of current asset for all three companies. Moreover, their level of receivables is very small because discount retailers primarily deal in cash or bank credit cards. The loan officer could conclude that the Carroll Company's low quick ratio appears to be in line with that of other companies in the industry. A low quick ratio is far less risky for a retailer than for a manufacturer since a retailer's inventory can quickly be converted to cash.

Balance Sheet

Strickland Corporation
Balance Sheet
(in thousands of dollars)

	1/31/87	%	1/31/88	%
Assets				
Cash and marketable securities	18	3	9	1
Accounts receivable—net	13	2	17	2
Inventory	280	47	491	52
Current assets	311	52	517	55
Fixed assets—net	246	42	333	35
Other assets	35	6	88	10
Noncurrent assets	281	48	421	45
Total assets	592	100	938	100
Liabilities and Net Worth				
Notes payable to banks	15	3	56	6
Accounts payable—trade	97	16	189	20
Accruals	59	10	86	9
Current maturities—long-term debt*	7	1	10	1
Current debt	178	30	341	36
Long-term debt—secured	165	28	259	28
Total debt	343	58	600	64
Reserve—deferred income taxes	1	0	7	1
Capital stock—preferred	0	0	7	1
—common	3	1	3	—
Paid-in surplus	67	11	69	7
Retained earnings	178	30	252	27
Net worth	248	42	331	35
Total liabilities and net worth	592	100	938	100

*Includes current capitalized lease obligations.

■ ■

Trend Analysis

Carroll Company

Year	Current Ratio	Quick Ratio
1986	1.75:1	0.20:1
1987	1.88:1	0.18:1
1988	1.68:1	0.10:1

The Carroll Company's current ratio increased from 1.75:1 in January 1986 to 1.88:1 in 1987 and then dropped to 1.68:1 in 1988—all of which are in line with the industry. However, an examination of the Carroll Company's balance sheets shows that long-term debt increased by about $400,000 during fiscal 1987. This reduced the company's need for short-term borrowings to support its asset base, thus improving its current ratio for 1987. If the company had had no additional long-term debt, the current ratio for both 1987 and 1988 would have been lower.

From fiscal year-end 1986 to 1988, the Carroll Company's quick ratio dropped from 0.20:1 to 0.10:1, reflecting a lowered cash balance and higher debt. This could be the result of a more aggressive cash management program, a cash flow problem, or a temporary decrease in cash. Since the dollar amount of the very liquid assets included in this ratio is not a significant portion of the balance sheet, the loan officer cannot trace the flow of funds in the balance sheet. Nevertheless, given the similar ratios of Carroll Company's competitors, the loan officer can safely assume that the drop in its quick ratio does not indicate a cash flow problem, particularly in light of the company's size and its probable ready access to public debt markets.

LEVERAGE ANALYSIS

Comparative Analysis

The Carroll Company's debt-to-worth ratio of 1.69:1 is stronger than that of its competitors:

	Debt-to-Worth Ratio
Carroll Company (1988)	1.69:1
Strickland Corporation (1988)	1.81:1
Moritz Company (1988)	2.19:1

Income Statement

Moritz Company
Income Statement
(in thousands of dollars)

	FYE 1/31/87	%	FYE 1/31/88	%
Net sales	1,594	100	1,797	100
Cost of goods sold	1,209	76	1,362	76
Gross profit/revenues	385	24	435	24
Total operating expenses	328	20	366	20
Operating profit	57	4	69	4
Interest expense	28	2	32	2
Profit before tax	29	2	37	2
Income taxes	11	1	15	1
Net profit after tax	18	1	22	1
Notes:				
Dividends	2		2	
Depreciation	22		24	

■ ■

As discussed earlier, the Carroll Company's debt-to-worth ratio of 1.69:1 means that the company's creditors have 1.69 times as much value entrusted to the company as the shareholders have. This is considered a strong position in the retail industry and would be unusually low for a manufacturing company. The Moritz Company's debt-to-worth ratio of 2.19:1 means that it has the highest risk posture of the three companies. Further analysis may show that the added interest expense resulting from its higher financial leverage penalizes the Moritz Company's profits.

The debt-to-capitalization ratios for the three companies are as follows:

	Debt-to-Capitalization Ratio
Strickland Corporation (1988)	0.44:1
Carroll Company (1988)	0.47:1
Moritz Company (1988)	0.55:1

As would be expected from the debt-to-worth ratios, the Moritz Company's debt-to-capitalization ratio, at 0.55:1, is higher than its competitors' ratios. This means that its long-term creditors have a relatively greater stake in the company than the shareholders have. The Strickland Corporation's ratio of 0.44:1 is stronger than the 0.47:1 ratio for the Carroll Company, a departure from the relative position of their debt-to-worth ratios. A review of both companies' balance sheets would show that the Carroll Company has structured more long-term debt on its balance sheet than the Strickland Corporation has.

The debt-to-capitalization ratio may be misleading if a company has the use of a long-term debt facility, such as a revolving credit line, that extends over several years. This enables a company to borrow and repay under the credit facility as if it were a short-term line of credit. Thus, the company gains the flexibility of short-term access to funds while its balance sheet reflects the funds as long-term debt.

Trend Analysis

Calculations of the debt-to-worth and debt-to-capitalization ratios for the Carroll Company for the past 3 years yield the following results:

Balance Sheet

Moritz Company
Balance Sheet
(in thousands of dollars)

	1/31/87	%	1/31/88	%
Assets				
Cash and marketable securities	37	7	22	3
Accounts receivable—net	7	1	8	1
Inventory	296	53	357	56
Current assets	340	61	387	60
Fixed assets—net	201	35	231	36
Intangibles	5	1	5	1
Other assets	15	3	20	3
Noncurrent assets	221	39	256	40
Total assets	561	100	643	100
Liabilities and Net Worth				
Accounts payable—trade	73	13	100	16
Accruals	67	12	84	13
Current maturities—long-term debt*	9	2	8	1
Current debt	149	27	192	30
Long-term debt—secured	233	41	245	38
Total debt	382	68	437	68
Reserve—deferred income taxes	5	1	7	1
Capital stock—common	5	1	5	1
Paid-in surplus	19	3	24	4
Retained earnings	150	27	170	26
Net worth	174	31	199	31
Total liabilities and net worth	561	100	643	100

*Includes current capitalized lease obligations.

Carroll Company

Year	Debt-to-Worth Ratio	Debt-to-Capitalization Ratio
1986	1.56:1	0.43:1
1987	1.58:1	0.47:1
1988	1.69:1	0.47:1

The increasing debt-to-worth ratio suggests that the Carroll Company's retained earnings are insufficient to fund its balance sheet growth in the same proportions as it had in former years. Although this situation could result from a conscious managerial decision to more aggressively use the company's leverage, a review of Carroll Company's after-tax profits for fiscal years 1986–1988 ($358,000, $261,000, and $220,000) and its dividend policy (a dividend payout ratio of 29 percent, 43 percent, and 53 percent) would appear to support a conclusion of insufficient retained earnings.

To stabilize its debt-to-worth ratio, the Carroll Company could slow its asset growth relative to its equity growth or increase its equity more rapidly relative to its asset growth. The company could control its asset growth either through more efficient use of assets or through slower growth in revenues and number of business locations, thus reducing the need for operating assets. On the other hand, the company could increase its equity growth through higher earnings, lower dividends, or additional equity contributions.

The growth in the Carroll Company's debt-to-capitalization ratio from 0.43:1 to 0.47:1 is not large enough to be considered significant. Nevertheless, the growth does show that the company's funded permanent debt has grown faster than its equity.

COVERAGE ANALYSIS

Comparative Analysis

The times interest earned ratio, cash flow-to-current maturities ratio, and the dividend payout ratio (expressed as a percentage) are as follows for the three competitors:

	Times Interest Earned Ratio	CF-to-CM Ratio	Dividend Payout Ratio
Carroll Company (1988)	2.18:1	5.20:1	53%
Strickland Corporation (1988)	5.81:1	10.00:1	11%
Moritz Company (1988)	2.16:1	5.50:1	9%

An examination of the times interest earned ratio for the three companies shows the Strickland Corporation to be in the strongest position. This may indicate that the company is less highly leveraged than the others and thus carries a low level of interest-bearing debt or that the company's operating performance is so strong it more than overcomes its interest burden. The earlier analysis of debt-to-worth ratios showed the Strickland Corporation to be more heavily leveraged than the Carroll Company, but less leveraged than the Moritz Company.

Based on both the times interest earned and the debt-to-worth ratios, the loan officer might conclude that the Strickland Corporation significantly outperforms its competition and that the Carroll Company lags in the industry. However, the loan officer should exercise caution in reaching such a conclusion since other factors, such as the cost of debt, can also affect the ratio results.

A look at the cash flow-to-current maturities ratio shows the Strickland Corporation again leading the other two companies by a large margin. However, since current maturities of various debt issues may fluctuate and the level of current maturities may change from year to year, this ratio may not be directly comparable from one company to another. With a cash flow-to-current maturities in excess of 5.0, all three companies rate well in this area.

The Carroll Company's dividend payout ratio of 53 percent is very high relative to its competitors. This high payout appears to be impeding its equity growth during a time when the analysis indicates that equity growth is most needed. The relatively low payout ratios for the other two businesses significantly help these companies generate equity growth internally.

Trend Analysis

For the last 3 years, the Carroll Company has experienced a deterioration in each of its coverage ratios:

Carroll Company

	Times Interest Earned Ratio	CF-to-CM Ratio	Dividend Payout Ratio
1986	4.67:1	7.94:1	29%
1987	2.95:1	5.86:1	43%
1988	2.18:1	5.20:1	53%

While the company's 1988 times interest earned ratio of 2.18:1 and its 1988 cash flow-to-current maturities ratio of 5.20:1 remain in the acceptable range, the deterioration should prompt the loan officer to further explore this area.

Of additional concern is the dividend payout ratio, which has increased from 29 percent to 53 percent. While the cash dividends paid by the Carroll Company increased from $103,000 in 1986 to $117,000 in 1988, as shown in Exhibit 6.1, the company's after-tax profit declined during this same period from $358,000 to $220,000. In order to support their stock price and provide a stable and dependable dividend stream to their investors, publicly held companies sometimes make decisions based on their shareholders' short-term satisfaction that, in the long run, may not serve the best interest of the company. A loan officer should be concerned if too large a proportion of a company's earnings is diverted to the payment of dividends when a real need exists for building equity.

PROFITABILITY ANALYSIS

Comparative Analysis

As might have been anticipated from the analysis of coverage ratios, the Strickland Corporation has much stronger profitability ratios than the Carroll and Moritz companies:

	Return on Sales Ratio	Return on Assets Ratio	Return on Equity Ratio
Carroll Company (1988)	1.33%	6.34%	9.16%
Strickland Corporation (1988)	3.39%	13.12%	28.67%
Moritz Company (1988)	1.22%	6.84%	11.80%

The Strickland Corporation's high return on sales shows that it receives more than twice as much profit for each dollar of sales as the Carroll and Moritz companies. Its high return on assets indicates that it uses its assets more efficiently to produce profits. In terms of shareholders' return, the Strickland Corporation's return on equity ratio is also excellent, far surpassing that of the other two companies. The Carroll Company is comparable to the Moritz Company, which could be an indication of similar products and prices.

Trend Analysis

A review of the Carroll Company's profitability ratios shows a continuing decline in its operating performance:

Carroll Company

	Return on Sales Ratio	Return on Assets Ratio	Return on Equity Ratio
1986	2.81%	8.69%	17.46%
1987	1.84%	6.73%	11.53%
1988	1.33%	6.34%	9.16%

In 2 years, the Carroll Company's profitability declined from 2.81 percent to 1.33 percent, its return on assets declined from 8.69 percent to 6.34 percent, and its return on equity declined from 17.46 percent to 9.16 percent. All three return indicators are at the low end of the industry and should prompt the loan officer to conduct an in-depth review to determine the reason for their decline. The low return on sales may signify poor pricing of the company's products, lack of expense control, or both. The low return on assets is again from a poor sales to assets ratio (reflected in the activity ratios) and the low return on sales. A review of the Carroll Company's management policies is definitely in order.

ACTIVITY ANALYSIS

Comparative Analysis

The activity ratios for the three companies for fiscal year 1988 are as follows:

	Asset Turnover Ratio	Average Collection Period	Days Inventory	Days Payable Ratio
Carroll Company (1988)	2.59 times	2 days	88 days	34 days
Strickland Corporation (1988)	3.20 times	2 days	79 days	29 days
Moritz Company (1988)	2.99 times	2 days	87 days	23 days

The turnover ratios support the previous conclusion that the Strickland Corporation operates more efficiently than its competitors. The loan officer could examine the primary trading accounts—inventory and accounts payable—to further evaluate this conclusion. The average collection period (or accounts receivable turnover) can be ignored since accounts receivable is not a significant factor in these retailers' financial statements.

Besides having faster total asset turnover than its competitors, the Strickland Corporation also has the fastest turnover of inventory (79 days compared to the Carroll Company's 88 days). Although the evidence of previous analysis may lead the loan officer to conclude that the Strickland Corporation manages its inventory better than the other two companies, the loan officer should remain open to the possibility that the Moritz and Carroll companies purposely maintain a broader inventory resulting in higher margins or greater customer loyalty. However, the profitability ratios do not support this thesis since the Strickland Corporation commands greater profitability while maintaining a faster inventory turn.

The Moritz Company appears to pay its creditors more rapidly than do the other two companies. Its calculated payables turnover is 23 days (compared to the Carroll Company's 34 days). However, unless this ratio is extremely high or extremely low, the loan officer will find it nearly impossible to draw a reliable conclusion from it.

Trend Analysis

The Carroll Company's turnover ratios for 1986, 1987, and 1988 were as follows:

Carroll Company

	Asset Turnover Ratio	Average Collection Period	Days Inventory	Days Payables Ratio
1986	2.43 times	2 days	101 days	39 days
1987	2.42 times	2 days	98 days	37 days
1988	2.59 times	2 days	88 days	34 days

Over this period, the Carroll Company made marginal improvements in its asset turnover ratio—from 2.43 to 2.59. This apparently resulted from a marked improvement in its inventory turnover (which went from 101 days to 88 days) although the Carroll Company still has the slowest inventory turnover of the three companies compared. The Carroll Company's payables turnover also improved (from 39 days to 34 days), possibly the result of a recovery from a cash squeeze in 1986. However, another plausible conclusion would be that the Carroll Company implemented a policy change concerning its payments to suppliers. Because the company is turning its inventory more quickly, it is less likely to have obsolescent inventory. The company could have begun to turn its inventory more quickly because it lowered its prices, which would be reflected in a decline in the profit ratios.

RATIO ANALYSIS CONCLUSIONS

The loan officer's foregoing comparative and trend analysis may result in the following conclusions about the Carroll Company:

- Its financial condition as exhibited by its liquidity and leverage ratios remains strong.

- Its operating performance in terms of coverage, profitability, and asset use is weak when compared to the industry as a whole; moreover, its downward trend in these areas is negatively impacting its financial condition as exhibited by its liquidity and leverage ratios.

Summary

While it is easy to calculate an impressive array of ratios, they are not meaningful in and of themselves and can lead to erroneous conclusions if they are not analyzed in a broad context, rather than in isolation. Ratio analysis is only one part of the total financial analysis of a company and does not in itself lead to any definite lending decisions.

Ratios do, however, assist in converting a company's financial information into a meaningful analytical format. Ratios are particularly useful in facilitating comparisons of companies of varying size, particularly among companies in the same industry. They also facilitate trend analysis, which entails looking at a company's ratios over a period of 2 or more years.

The most widely used ratios help in analyzing a company's liquidity, leverage, coverage, profitability, and activity. The liquidity ratios—the current ratio and the quick ratio—measure a company's financial strength in liquidation based on the assumption that all assets will be sold and all liabilities will be paid. However, these ratios also have significant implications for the analysis of going concerns since they show a company's ability to meet its current obligations and sustain operations by using cash or converting current assets to cash. The leverage ratios—the debt-to-worth and debt-to-capitalization ratios—measure the degree of risk shouldered by a company's owners versus its creditors. The coverage ratios—times interest earned, cash flow-to-current maturities, and dividend payment ratios—measure the ability of a company to meet its current debt obligations through the flow of funds from its operations. Profitability ratios—return on sales, return on assets, and return on equity—look at the relationship between net profit and sales, assets, and equity, respectively. Activity ratios measure management's ability to efficiently use the company's assets. The principal activity ratios compare income statement accounts (sales or cost of goods sold) to balance sheet accounts to determine asset turnover, accounts receivable turnover, inventory turnover, and accounts payable turnover. These turnover ratios are often expressed in days—as in the average accounts receivable collection period, days inventory, and days payable.

It is important to keep in mind that because financial statements may reflect different accounting methods, corporate structures, and management policies, ratio comparison is rarely exact. Therefore, the loan officer should view any findings as general indicators of performance rather than as absolute predictors.

Questions

1. Name the five categories into which ratios are grouped for analytical purposes. Explain the significance of each.

2. What does *relative nature,* or *proportionality*, of ratios mean?

3. What determines whether a particular ratio is analytically significant?

4. List several valid benchmarks or reference points that are useful in ratio analysis.

5. Why should industry comparisons be used with caution?

6. Explain the difference between the two liquidity ratios—the current ratio and the quick ratio.

7. Why is a company's financial leverage, as evidenced by its debt-to-worth ratio, important to a lender?

8. What are the three major coverage ratios used in financial analysis?

9. What are the profitability ratios that measure the efficiency with which a company uses its assets and its equity?

10. What two ways can the turnover in accounts receivable, inventory, and accounts payable be expressed?

Exercises

E-1

The following case involves the calculation and interpretation of ratios. Read the case and answer the questions.

The Banner Company and the Neon Company are two manufacturers producing nearly identical products. In spite of their apparent similarities, the management and operations of the two companies differ considerably. The Banner Company was founded in 1960 by Jeff Duke. Still president of the company, Mr. Duke has become unwilling in recent years to replace the company's original machinery with modern, more efficient equipment. He has also refused to engage in what he terms "foolhardy marketing adventures" to increase sales. He feels that the Banner Company can continue to maintain an adequate sales volume and remain profitable because of the reputation it has built during the last quarter-century of operations.

In contrast, the Neon Company is a young company, formed 7 years ago by a recent MBA graduate, Jane Clifford. Acting on the basis of predictions that product demand would increase substantially in the next year, Ms. Clifford recently purchased the latest, most efficient equipment in order to achieve the highest production possible at the least cost. To do this, Ms. Clifford borrowed as much as she felt her company could safely handle. The Neon Company's marketing strategy has also been far more aggressive than that of the Banner Company. Neon's products have been promoted through extensive advertising campaigns managed by a well-known advertising agency.

Recently, the chief executive officer (CEO) of your bank, which handles the deposit and loan accounts of both the Banner and the Neon companies, was asked to conduct an annual credit review of the two companies. The CEO became somewhat perplexed by the performance of both companies as compared with industry averages. The CEO has asked you, a commercial loan officer, to examine the data in detail. You are to answer the following questions to help explain the current positions of both companies and the trends in their past performances that have led to their current positions.

a. From the data provided, calculate the following ratios for the industry and for both companies for the past 5 years:

- current ratio
- debt-to-worth ratio
- cash flow-to-current maturities ratio
- return on sales ratio
- asset turnover ratio (use end-of-year figures)

b. Comment on the trends revealed by the ratios. What do they reveal about the relative success of the two companies?

c. How much confidence can you place in the industry figures, given the information on the number of companies reporting?

d. Which company is stronger financially? Why?

e. Which company would you prefer to retain as a customer of your bank? Why?

Banner Company
Comparative Balance Sheet
As of December 31, 1984–1988

	1984	1985	1986	1987	1988
Assets					
Cash	$ 31,200	$ 46,300	$ 51,500	$ 54,800	$ 55,500
Accounts receivable	156,000	149,200	128,700	136,800	126,100
Inventory	124,800	112,300	105,800	82,000	70,400
Total current assets	$ 312,000	$ 307,800	$ 286,000	$ 273,600	$ 252,000
Fixed assets (net)	288,000	262,200	234,000	206,400	198,000
Total assets	$ 600,000	$ 570,000	$ 520,000	$ 480,000	$ 450,000
Liabilities and Net Worth					
Accounts payable	$ 114,500	$ 104,600	$ 94,300	$ 79,000	$ 64,000
Notes payable	15,500	18,500	6,700	10,000	12,000
Current maturities of long-term debt	5,000	5,000	5,000	5,000	5,000
Total current liabilities	$ 135,000	$ 128,100	$ 106,000	$ 94,000	$ 81,000
Long-term debt	65,000	60,000	55,000	50,000	45,000
Total debt	200,000	188,100	161,000	144,000	126,000
Net worth	400,000	381,900	359,000	336,000	324,000
Total liabilities and net worth	$ 600,000	$ 570,000	$ 520,000	$ 480,000	$ 450,000
Net sales	$1,584,000	$1,470,600	$1,456,000	$1,396,800	$1,260,000
Net income	$ 33,100	$ 30,900	$ 27,700	$ 25,100	$ 22,700
Depreciation	$ 31,000	$ 29,800	$ 28,200	$ 27,600	$ 26,500
Dividends	$ 55,000	$ 49,000	$ 50,600	$ 48,100	$ 34,700

Neon Company
Comparative Balance Sheet
As of December 31, 1984–1988

	1984	1985	1986	1987	1988
Assets					
Cash	$ 4,500	$ 5,100	$ 3,900	$ 4,600	$ 6,000
Accounts receivable	90,000	100,800	117,600	137,700	159,000
Inventory	55,500	62,100	74,500	87,200	100,000
Total current assets	$ 150,000	$ 168,000	$ 196,000	$ 229,500	$ 265,000
Fixed assets (net)	150,000	182,000	204,000	220,500	235,000
Total assets	$ 300,000	$ 350,000	$ 400,000	$ 450,000	$ 500,000
Liabilities and Net Worth					
Accounts payable	$ 50,000	$ 58,500	$ 71,000	$ 84,000	$ 96,500
Notes payable	15,000	15,500	27,000	39,000	45,500
Current maturities of long-term debt	7,000	10,000	11,000	12,000	14,000
Total current liabilities	$ 72,000	$ 84,000	$ 109,000	$ 135,000	$ 156,000
Long-term debt	42,000	59,000	63,000	72,000	84,000
Total debt	114,000	143,000	172,000	207,000	240,000
Net worth	186,000	207,000	228,000	243,000	260,000
Total liabilities and net worth	$ 300,000	$ 350,000	$ 400,000	$ 450,000	$ 500,000
Net sales	$ 696,000	$ 751,500	$ 844,000	$ 972,500	$1,075,000
Net income	$ 16,000	$ 18,000	$ 21,000	$ 29,000	$ 33,000
Depreciation	$ 30,000	$ 36,000	$ 41,000	$ 44,000	$ 47,000
Dividends	$ 0	$ 0	$ 0	$ 14,000	$ 16,000

Comparative Balance Sheet for the Industry
As of December 31, 1984–1987

	1984	1985	1986	1987
Assets				
Cash	$ 20,100	$ 20,100	$ 21,500	$ 22,400
Accounts receivable	220,800	219,700	235,900	246,400
Inventory	160,600	159,800	171,600	179,200
Total current assets	$ 401,500	$ 399,600	$ 429,000	$ 448,000
Fixed assets (net)	328,500	340,400	351,000	352,000
Total assets	$ 730,000	$ 740,000	$ 780,000	$ 800,000
Liabilities and Net Worth				
Accounts payable	$ 132,000	$ 145,600	$ 136,500	$ 163,200
Notes payable	28,000	21,400	40,500	22,800
Current maturities of long-term debt	16,000	15,000	18,000	18,000
Total current liabilities	$ 176,000	$ 182,000	$ 195,000	$ 204,000
Long-term debt	95,000	90,000	110,000	110,000
Total debt	271,000	272,000	305,000	314,000
Net worth	459,000	468,000	475,000	486,000
Total liabilities and net worth	$ 730,000	$ 740,000	$ 780,000	$ 800,000
Net sales	$1,882,000	$1,963,000	$1,983,000	$2,200,000
Net income	$ 41,400	$ 45,100	$ 47,600	$ 53,000
Depreciation	$ 65,000	$ 68,000	$ 86,000	$ 90,000
Dividends	$ 37,400	$ 36,100	$ 40,600	$ 42,000
Number of firms				
Total reporting	30	39	36	31
With year-end—				
December 31	25	35	32	20
June 30	4	3	3	8
October 31	1	1	1	3

E-2

Although companies in the same industry may have widely disparate
operational and financial policies, the nature or structure of an
industry has an important influence on companies' funding needs,
the methods of meeting those needs, and the financial results of most
companies within the industry. The following statement presents
common-sized balance sheets (that is, the figures reflect percentages
of total assets or total liabilities and equity) and selected financial
ratios for five companies that are fairly representative of five
different industries. Match up each set of financial information with
one of the five industries listed. Be prepared to explain your choices
based upon the balance sheet structures and ratios that are
characteristic of each of the following industries:

- basic chemical manufacturer
- electric utility
- supermarket chain
- fast-food franchise
- bank

Balance Sheet Percentages and Selected Ratios for Five Companies

	A	B	C	D	E
Balance Sheet Percentages					
Cash and marketable securities	5.9	17.3	22.8	3.3	1.4
Accounts receivable	2.1	3.1	72.3	18.3	2.1
Inventory	—	38.2	—	18.9	0.7
Other current assets	7.4	1.9	1.6	1.5	1.8
Fixed assets (net)	84.6	38.9	0.8	53.4	86.0
Other assets	—	0.6	2.5	4.6	8.0
Total assets	100.0	100.0	100.0	100.0	100.0
Notes payable	—	0.2	18.4	1.9	0.2
Accounts payable	3.4	22.6	60.5	10.6	4.7
Accrued taxes	1.0	1.7	2.2	2.2	1.9
Other current liabilities	1.1	12.4	3.5	5.8	5.4
Long-term debt	45.4	9.8	9.1	26.9	31.9
Other liabilities	11.4	2.7	2.5	8.7	5.0
Preferred stock	8.4	—	0.3	1.0	—
Capital stock and capital surplus	24.8	3.0	1.1	19.5	3.6
Retained earnings and surplus reserves .	4.5	47.6	2.4	23.4	47.3
Total liabilities and net worth	100.0	100.0	100.0	100.0	100.0
Selected Ratios					
Current ratio (x:1)	2.80	1.64	N/A	2.05	0.49
Quick ratio (x:1)	1.45	0.55	N/A	1.05	0.29
Days inventory (days)	0	26	0	106	12
Average collection period (days)	23	2	N/A	70	11
Asset turnover (times)	0.34	6.70	0.14	0.96	0.66
Return on sales (%)	10.5	1.5	2.9	5.9	13.8
Return on assets (%)	3.6	10.2	0.4	4.4	9.1
Return on equity (%)	9.6	20.3	11.6	13.3	19.3

7 The Pro Forma Statement

Learning Objectives

After studying this chapter, you should be able to

- identify the primary uses of the pro forma statement as a financial analysis tool
- construct and analyze pro forma income statements and balance sheets
- identify the benefits and shortcomings of pro forma statement analysis
- explain the importance of properly interpreting pro forma projections

▎▎▎▎▎▎▎▎ Introduction

Most companies prepare pro forma financial statements as part of their routine financial planning. Pro forma income statements and balance sheets represent management's best guess as to how the company will perform in the coming year or years taking into consideration the expected economic, competitive, and regulatory environments in which the company will operate. Lenders typically require commercial loan applicants to supply pro forma financial statements to the lender showing the company's projected financial results over the term of the loan. Some lenders also request copies of pro forma statements for past years so that the loan officer can compare management's past predictions with the company's actual results.

For loan officers, an important part of financial analysis lies in predicting a company's future financial results based on its past performance and present condition as evidenced by its past financial statements, funds flow statements, and ratio analysis. Pro forma statement analysis enables loan officers to also take into consideration the financial consequences of management's plans and strategies—and to assess their effect on the company's borrowing needs, repayment capacity, and general creditworthiness. Often, however, management's predictions about a company's likely performance in the future are overly optimistic from the lender's standpoint. In that case, the loan officer may revise the company's pro forma statements using more conservative assumptions.

Even at their best, pro forma statements have their shortcomings. No one can predict the future with certainty, and many unforeseen factors can dramatically affect a company's projected financial plans. Thus a loan officer should not rely too heavily on pro forma statement analysis as the basis for a loan decision.

▎▎▎▎▎▎▎▎ Framework for Analysis

The basic framework for pro forma statement analysis involves attention to the company's past performance and dependability and to the external and internal factors that affect the company's operation. The loan officer should also make use of the many available sources of information about a company and the industry in which it operates to ensure that a company's financial projections are not only technically correct, but based on reasonable assumptions.

BASIC CONSIDERATIONS

When approaching the task of analyzing a company's pro forma statements, the loan officer should keep several basic lending considerations in mind. These considerations include the assessment of the company's past performance, the consistency of its past results, an emphasis on conservative assumptions, and attention to the time intervals represented by the pro forma statements.

Past Performance

A thorough understanding of the company, the industry, and the market help the loan officer judge the reliability of a company's financial projections. Much of this information will already have been derived from analyzing the company's balance sheets and income statements, as well as industry trends and ratios. At this point in the analysis, the loan officer should have a solid grasp of the company's operations and its past and current performance. Besides having analyzed the financial documents submitted by the company, a loan officer may have personally visited the company to meet the principals and to see the company in action, or may have consulted with outside sources such as competitors, suppliers, customers, and trade associations. Only with this depth of background knowledge can the loan officer expect to assess the company's future confidently and accurately.

Dependability of Performance

Pro forma analysis is generally most dependable for companies that have established consistent performance trends that closely track those of the industry. Doing a meaningful pro forma analysis for new companies with no established record or for companies with inconsistent performance records is exceedingly difficult. When looking at young companies, the loan officer should evaluate management's past performance in other ventures and err on the safe side by using very conservative assumptions.

Conservatism

Management typically is overly optimistic when making forecasts about the future of a company. The loan officer must balance this tendency by slanting projections toward the conservative side even if the company has experienced favorable results for several years. This gives the bank a greater cushion against the inevitable unpredictability of the future.

Time Intervals

The loan officer should be sure that the time interval represented by the company's pro forma statements suits the purpose and matches the repayment period for the proposed loan. For example, in projecting seasonal borrowing needs, the company should construct its pro forma statements with monthly or quarterly intervals to capture the various points in the operating cycle that reflect its seasonal needs. Such interim statements should also include enough intervals to depict the company's complete operating cycle. The projections will then depict the company's borrowing needs both at the bottom of the cycle, when they are presumably low, as well as at the peak of the cycle, when they should be highest.

Projections to support long-term financing requests should extend far enough into the future to assure the loan officer that current trends indicate the company's ability to repay the debt. These projections should be consistent with trends established over the same period of time in the past.

EXTERNAL AND INTERNAL FACTORS

Both external and internal factors affect a company's operations and thus the analysis of its pro forma statements. The loan officer needs to keep in mind how these various factors may change over time and thereby influence the company's future performance in unexpected ways.

External Factors

Although a company's management cannot control the external factors that make up the company's operating environment, it must anticipate and plan for them if the company is to reach its financial objectives. In making or analyzing projections, the company and the loan officer should take into consideration the following major external factors:

- the economy—predictions as to general business conditions, interest rates, and anticipated economic fluctuations

- the industry—its growth or stagnancy, ease of entry, its degree of competitiveness and number of competitors, and the company's position in the industry (whether it is a leader or a marginal producer)

- the market—its degree of diversification (number of buyers), restrictiveness (do a few large buyers control the market and price?), the basis of competition (price, quality, technology), competition from complementary products, and sociological trends (for example, consumer preferences and demographics)

- government regulations—prospects for regulatory changes (for example, deregulation) and future vulnerability to imports or protection by import restrictions

- labor—future availability and cost of labor; if nonunionized, prospects for unionization; if unionized, likelihood of strikes and anticipated costs of new contract negotiations

Internal Factors

Internal factors include the human, financial, and physical resources available to the company. Company management can control these factors and use them to maximize its operational performance and to provide future direction. The following are major internal factors that the loan officer should consider:

- management—experience, past performance, ability to make accurate projections and to perform according to projections, ability to achieve objectives and to grow with the company

- physical plant—capacity, condition, efficiency compared to that of competitors, and technological sophistication

- financial controls—accounts receivable systems (approval and collection), inventory and purchasing systems, accounts payable systems, expense controls, and budgetary provisions

- marketing strategy—company's niche, marketing plan and market territory, adequacy of financial and human resources to support the plan, and distribution system

- other internal factors—quality and adequacy of financial and other managerial reports that are a basis for decisionmaking

The essence of good management is the ability to contemplate an uncertain future, to plan for that future, and to marshal the company's resources to fulfill its objectives. This requires a thorough knowledge of both the external and internal factors that affect a company and the capabilities and limitations they impose. Pro forma analysis enables the company's management and the bank's loan officer to anticipate together the financial consequences of the company's plans and strategies.

INFORMATION SOURCES

A loan officer does not rely totally on the company's pro forma statements, but will generally want to introduce more conservative assumptions and sometimes even worst-case scenarios. Then the company's results and the loan officer's results can be compared. However, the basis of both sets of projections and of the resulting analysis is basically the company's past financial results. The loan officer should have on hand the following information to ensure a comprehensive and credible pro forma analysis:

- management's pro forma income statements and balance sheets

- income statements and balance sheets for the past 3 to 5 years

- company projections for past periods

- the company's formal business plan

- management's organizational diagram

- the company's debt schedule

- information about competitors (especially those who bank with the lender)

- industry trends and projections
- Robert Morris Associates' Annual Statement Studies
- current economic forecasts relative to the industry
- past economic data for comparisons with performance

These items provide the underlying information necessary for engaging in pro forma analysis. This information should help the loan officer understand the company's past performance, its financial structure, and its managerial philosophy, strategy, and positioning within the industry, as well as provide the basis for reasonable expectations as to the company's future performance. With this background, the loan officer can better evaluate the assumptions that are critical to any pro forma analysis.

■ ■ ■ ■ Pro Forma Analysis: Setting the Stage

The Pearson Company is a fictitious business that will be used throughout this chapter to illustrate the pro forma analysis process. The Pearson Company specializes in the production of automotive and farm machinery, but also has a secondary line of products in the oil-drilling industry. The company has been in operation for about 10 years.

The company has requested bank financing for a new ball-bearing casting mold that costs $600,000. The Pearson Company plans to pay $100,000 down and finance the balance over 5 years (the depreciable life of the casting mold). The company has requested a loan with a 5-year level amortization of principal plus interest.

REQUIRED INFORMATION

Management has provided the bank with 3 years of operating statements, past pro forma statements to compare against actual results, and a pro forma income statement and balance sheet for the current year. Normally, the loan officer would expect to review pro forma statements showing projections for a minimum of 2 to 3 years when a loan with a

3- to 5-year term is being requested. However, for instructional purposes, this chapter is centered around a 1-year projection.

The bank has provided various services to the Pearson Company for the past 3 years. As part of their commercial relationship, the Pearson Company provides the bank with copies of its quarterly and annual financial statements. Because of these past dealings, the loan officer has a good feel for the company's strengths and weaknesses and knows a number of its officers. The company's borrowings have traditionally been term loans for the purchase of equipment; however, it has one permanent working capital loan outstanding.

To supplement the company's financial statements, the loan officer has also obtained industry information from the company's trade institute.

External Factors

The economy is currently strong, and all economic indicators project stability for the next 2 to 3 years. Monetary growth and inflation also appear stable for the immediate future.

Industry predictions are that the value of ball- and roller-bearing shipments will increase by 5 percent in the current year to $3.95 billion in order to satisfy the expanding demand from the aircraft and automotive industries. Demand for these products by the construction, mining and oil, and farm machinery industries is also growing. The producer price index for bearings climbed 19 percent in 1987, following a 14.5 percent jump in 1986. Figures for 1988 are not yet available. The bearing industry, after keeping price increases to a minimum during the previous several years, substantially increased prices in 1986 and 1987 to catch up with accumulated labor and material cost increases. Price increases in 1989 are not expected to exceed 9 or 10 percent because domestic companies continue to face stiff price competition from imports.

Imports of ball bearings have increased significantly each year since 1984. They continue to penetrate the high-volume, price-competitive U.S. market. Import revenues from ball and roller bearings increased to $550 billion in 1987. They were expected to reach $633 billion in 1988, or 16 percent of U.S. consumption. Government regulations have little direct effect on the bearing industry, and no import protections are expected in the foreseeable future.

The Pearson Company employs unionized workers, but the union has made only reasonable demands in the past, and no work days have been lost due to union negotiations. Moreover, a contract settlement was reached in 1988, and no new negotiations are expected for the next 3 years.

Internal Factors

The Pearson Company's management team strongly desires to lead the industry. For the last 3 years, the company has performed well. Now, the team wants to direct a growth-oriented company with top-of-the-line products. Management's primary weakness lies in its lack of a chief financial officer; the controller recently left the company and has not been replaced.

The Pearson Company has excellent facilities—its plant capacity is considerably greater than is required by the company's current sales level. Much of the equipment is relatively new and state-of-the-art.

An examination of the company's internal controls shows them to be good, but still subject to improvement. Although the Pearson Company has not had a major receivable remain unpaid in 3 years, many of its customers do not pay on the 30-day terms quoted.

While the company's management intends to take an aggressive position in the market, it is unwilling to erode profit margins to achieve an increased market share. Management believes in hiring top-notch sales-people and compensating them well; unproductive employees are readily let go.

PAST PERFORMANCE

Before examining the Pearson Company's projections for 1989, the loan officer should review the company's previous 3 years of financial information. A company's past performance is an important indicator of the predictability of the future. Thus the company's past history enables the loan officer to judge the reasonableness of the assumptions used to construct the projected statements. Exhibits 7.1 and 7.2 show the Pearson Company's common-sized income statements and balance sheets for the past 3 years, including the industry standard (based on the most recent figures available).

Income Statement

Pearson Company
Income Statement
for the Years Ended December 31, 1986–1988
(in thousands of dollars)

	YE 12/31/86	%	YE 12/31/87	%	YE 12/31/88	%	I.S.
Net sales	4,000	100	4,800	100	5,500	100	100
Cost of goods sold	2,800	70	3,312	69	3,850	70	70
Gross profit/revenues	1,200	30	1,488	31	1,650	30	30
Officers' salaries	120	3	144	3	165	3	—
Selling expenses	160	4	192	4	220	4	—
General and administrative expenses	440	11	672	14	660	12	—
Total operating expenses	720	18	1,008	21	1,045	19	19
Operating profit	480	12	480	10	605	11	11
Interest expense	120	3	144	3	110	2	2
Profit before tax	360	9	336	7	495	9	9
Income taxes	144	4	134	3	192	3	—
Net profit after tax	216	5	202	4	303	6	—
Reconciliation of net worth:							
Net worth—beginning	884		1,100		1,302		
Add: Net profit	216		202		303		
Retained earnings—increase	216		202		303		
Net worth—increase	216		202		303		
Net worth—ending	1,100		1,302		1,605		
Depreciation	80		80		120		
Cash flow-to-current maturities	2.5		1.6		2.0		3.8
Times interest earned	4.0		3.3		5.5		4.1

■ ■

Past Income Statements

The Pearson Company has had 2 successive years of sales increases—20 percent in 1987 and 15 percent in 1988—compared to an industry growth of only 16 percent in 1987 and projected growth of 5 percent in 1988 (actual figures not yet available). Thus the Pearson Company is growing faster than the market. The loan officer will want to determine how the company accomplished this—by selling more ball bearings or simply by raising prices.

The income statement (Exhibit 7.1) also shows that the company's gross margin is both dependable and predictable—holding steady in the 30 percent range. Although total operating expenses have fluctuated a few points over the years, operating profits have consistently measured a very respectable 10 to 12 percent of sales. General and administrative expenses have ranged from 11 to 14 percent of sales. And although a major new company entered the market during the past 18 months, Pearson's profitability is holding well. It appears to have an established niche in the marketplace.

Past Balance Sheets

An analysis of past years' balance sheets should help the loan officer create expectations for the company's future financing needs. The Pearson Company's balance sheet, shown in Exhibit 7.2, shows the company's financial position to be stable. Its liquidity measures—current and quick ratios of 2.4 and 1.1, respectively—are well within industry guidelines as is its debt-to-worth ratio at 0.84.

The company sells on 30-day terms but lags in its collection efforts—receivables are collected on the average in 61 days. However, the company's inventory turnover, at 107 days, equates to 3.4 times a year, right on industry averages.

THE COMPANY'S PRO FORMA PROJECTIONS

Having reviewed the company's past performance, the loan officer must now focus on the pro forma statements prepared by the company's management. The loan officer should first compare the pro forma statements to the previous years' statements to identify any obvious discrep-

Balance Sheet

Pearson Company
Balance Sheet
As of December 31, 1986–1988
(in thousands of dollars)

	12/31/86	%	12/31/87	%	12/31/88	%	I.S.
Assets							
Cash	25	1	87	3	85	3	3
Marketable securities	125	6	130	5	5		
Accounts receivable—net	548	25	727	28	916	31	28
Inventory	652	30	946	36	1,132	38	39
Other current assets	—	—	—	—	—	—	1
Current assets	1,350	62	1,890	72	2,138	72	71
Fixed assets—net	822	38	742	28	822	28	24
Noncurrent assets	822	38	742	28	822	28	29
Total assets	2,172	100	2,632	100	2,960	100	100
Liabilities and Net Worth							
Accounts payable—trade	400	18	500	19	559	19	16
Accruals	39	2	60	2	62	2	8
Current maturities—long-term debt	120	5	170	6	210	7	3
Current-year income taxes	33	2	40	2	54	2	—
Other current liabilities	—	—	—	—	—	—	4
Current debt	592	27	770	29	885	30	42
Long-term debt—secured	480	22	560	21	470	16	15
Other long-term debt	—	—	—	—	—	—	1
Total long-term debt	480	22	560	21	470	16	16
Total debt	1,072	49	1,330	50	1,355	46	58
Capital stock—common	50	2	50	2	50	1	—
Retained earnings	1,050	49	1,252	48	1,555	53	—
Net worth	1,100	51	1,302	50	1,605	54	42
Total liabilities and net worth	2,172	100	2,632	100	2,960	100	100
Working capital	758		1,120		1,253		
Ratios:							
Quick/current	1.2/2.3		1.2/2.4		1.1/2.4		0.9/2.0
Debt-to-worth	0.97		1.02		0.84		1.3
Sales-to-receivables (days)	7.3 (50)		6.6 (55)		6.0 (61)		6.1
Cost of goods-to-inventory (days)	4.3 (85)		3.5 (104)		3.4 (107)		3.4
Purchases-to-payables (days)	4.9 (75)		4.6 (79)		4.8 (76)		—

ancies that should be examined. Exhibits 7.3 and 7.4 show the company's projected income statement and balance sheet. (The bank's projections can be ignored for the time being.) The loan officer's review of these statements results in the following observations.

The company's pro forma income statement (Exhibit 7.3) shows projected operating profits at 14 percent of sales. This is two points higher than the company's actual experience at any time in the last 3 years and three points higher than the most recent fiscal year-end. It reflects a projected reduction in the company's general and administrative expenses and in officers' salaries. Management also has projected pretax profits at 12 percent of sales, three points higher than at any time in the past 3 years.

Turning to the company's pro forma balance sheet (Exhibit 7.4), management is projecting that inventory will turn over 22 days faster than during the past year. The statement also projects more rapid collections of accounts receivable (from 61 days to 50 days) and more prompt payments to trade creditors (from 76 days to 57 days).

The loan officer should ask the company's management to justify these projections and then may want to alter the company's pro forma statements taking into consideration these explanations and the other information gathered during the preparation stage, as discussed previously.

THE BANK'S PRO FORMA PROJECTIONS

The loan officer is now prepared to compose the bank's own pro forma statements for the Pearson Company. This entails making assumptions about each number on the company's pro forma statements. The loan officer should ask: "Does this entry appear reasonable?" Each entry, from the cornerstone sales estimate on the income statement to the final total on the balance sheet, must have some logical basis.

The loan officer's reconstruction of the Pearson Company's pro forma income statement and balance sheet are shown, along with the company's projections, in Exhibits 7.3 and 7.4. The following discussion compares the company's projections and the loan officer's projections for each account of the pro forma income statement and balance sheet.

Pro Forma Income Statements

Pearson Company
Pro Forma Income Statements
for the Year Ending December 31, 1989
(in thousands of dollars)

	Company-Prepared Pro Forma		Bank-Prepared Pro Forma	
	YE 12/31/89	%	YE 12/31/89	%
Net sales	6,325	100	5,500	100
Cost of goods sold	4,428	70	3,850	70
Gross profit/revenues	1,897	30	1,650	30
Officers' salaries	127	2	165	3
Selling expenses	253	4	220	4
General and administrative expenses	633	10	770	14
Total operating expenses	1,013	16	1,155	21
Operating profit	884	14	495	9
Interest expense	123	2	144	3
Profit before tax	761	12	351	6
Income taxes	259	4	119	2
Net profit after tax	502	8	232	4
Ratios:				
Net profit-to-worth	25.66		12.63	
Net profit-to-total assets	14.61		6.91	
Cash flow-to-current maturities	1.9		1.5	
Times interest earned	7.2		3.4	
Reconciliation of net worth:				
Net worth—beginning	1,605		1,605	
Add: Net profit	502		232	
Less: Dividends—common	151		—	
Retained earnings—increase	351		232	
Net worth—increase	1,956		1,837	
Net worth—ending	1,956		1,837	
Depreciation	240		240	

■ ■

Pro Forma Balance Sheets

Pearson Company
Pro Forma Balance Sheets
As of December 31, 1989
(in thousands of dollars)

	Company-Prepared Pro Forma		Bank-Prepared Pro Forma	
	12/31/89	%	12/31/89	%
Assets				
Cash	125	4	125	4
Marketable securities	234	4		
Accounts receivable—net	866	25	917	27
Inventory	1,030	30	1,132	34
Current assets	2,255	66	2,174	65
Fixed assets—net	1,182	34	1,182	35
Noncurrent assets	1,187	34	1,182	35
Total assets	3,437	100	3,356	100
Liabilities and Net Worth				
Notes payable to banks	—	—	149	4
Accounts payable—trade	475	14	421	13
Accruals	69	2	67	2
Current maturities—long-term debt	310	9	310	9
Current-year income taxes	67	2	12	0
Current debt	921	27	959	29
Long-term debt—secured	560	16	560	17
Total debt	1,481	43	1,519	45
Capital stock—common	50	1	50	2
Retained earnings	1,906	55	1,787	53
Net worth	1,956	57	1,837	55
Total liabilities and net worth	3,437	100	3,356	100
Working capital	1,334		1,215	
Ratios:				
Quick/current	1.3/2.5		1.1/2.3	
Debt-to-worth	0.76		0.83	
Sales-to-receivables (days)	7.3 (50)		6.0 (61)	
Cost of goods-to-inventory (days)	4.3 (85)		3.4 (107)	
Purchases-to-payables (days)	6.4 (57)		6.4 (57)	

■ ■

▌▌▌▌▌▌▌ The Pro Forma Income Statement

SALES

The sales projection is the cornerstone for the entire pro forma income statement and also affects key accounts on the pro forma balance sheet. An unrealistic sales figure causes the rest of the projections to be of questionable value since the pro forma income statement accounts are usually calculated as a percentage of sales. The sales projection also affects many balance sheet accounts such as accounts receivable and inventory. The basis for the estimate of sales can vary. Sales can be projected on the basis of a very precise, detailed sales budget, or as a percentage increase over the previous year's figures.

The company's projections. The Pearson Company's management has projected a 15 percent sales increase for 1989. Thus, based on 1988 sales of $5,500,000, sales of $6,325,000 are predicted for 1989.

The bank's projections. The loan officer can see from the company's past pro forma statements (not shown here) that its past sales projections have been unrealistically high. For example, management projected a 30 percent increase in sales for 1987 and a 25 percent increase for 1988 while actual sales increases were 20 percent and 15 percent, respectively. Moreover, although Pearson's sales growth in recent years has exceeded that of the industry, industry growth is expected to remain steady at 5 percent annually. The loan officer is also aware that a major new competitor has recently entered the market. Preferring to err on the conservative side, the loan officer considers the possibility of flat sales, which could force the company to reduce its prices and increase its selling expenses.

Assuming no sales growth, then, the loan officer projects $5,500,000 as the sales figure for 1989 rather than the $6,325,000 projected by the company. The loan officer justifies the lower sales projection on the basis of management's overly optimistic sales projections in the past and the increased competition in the marketplace.

COST OF GOODS SOLD

The cost of goods sold usually ranks second in importance on the pro forma income statement behind sales. As was discussed in Chapter 3, the cost of goods sold for a manufacturer consists of the cost of raw materials, labor, and overhead (including depreciation) related to the production of inventory. It is usually calculated as a percentage of projected sales, taking into consideration both the company's past and anticipated performance. The loan officer should remember that when a company must trim its selling prices to remain competitive, the cost of goods sold as a percentage of sales increases.

The loan officer should check that management's projected cost of goods sold is consistent with previous years' figures. If it appears inconsistent, the loan officer should find out why. For example, the company may be planning to take a higher markup, to switch to lower-quality products, or to begin buying products at a discount.

The company's projections. The Pearson Company's cost of goods sold has held constant at just about 70 percent of sales for the past 3 years. Management projects cost of goods sold at 70 percent of projected sales for the following year as well. Its calculation is as follows:

$$\$6,325,000 \times 0.70 = \$4,428,000.$$

The bank's projections. The loan officer believes the company's projected cost of goods sold as a percentage of its sales is realistic since it is consistent with past performance. In addition, the company's estimate is consistent with industry averages. Thus, the loan officer applies the same percentage to the level of sales projected by the bank:

$$\$5,500,000 \times 0.70 = \$3,850,000.$$

OPERATING EXPENSES

A company's operating expenses include selling expenses, general and administrative expenses, and officers' salaries. These expenses differ from those included in the cost of goods sold in that they represent expenses not directly related to the purchase or production of goods or services. A company normally projects its operating expenses as a percentage of projected sales or as a percentage change from the previous year's operating expenses.

Officers' Salaries

The company's projections. The Pearson Company has a policy that its officers' salaries may not exceed 3 percent of sales. Because the company's controller recently left the company and management does not plan to immediately fill the position, the company projects that its officers' salaries will drop from 3 percent to 2 percent of sales. The company's calculation of officers' salaries is as follows:

$$\$6,325,000 \times 0.02 = \$127,000.$$

The bank's projections. The loan officer thinks it more prudent to project officers' salaries at 3 percent of gross sales as prior years indicate. The bank feels the company cannot operate much longer without a controller due to the size and complexity of its operation. The loan officer also believes that company management will reach the same conclusion in the near future. Thus the bank calculates officers' salaries as follows:

$$\$5,500,000 \times 0.03 = \$165,000.$$

Selling Expenses

Selling expenses include the cost of advertising, market research, sales training, promotion, and commissions. These are expenses that management controls—that is, management can vary these expenses at its discretion as warranted by changing conditions in the marketplace. For instance, when a company introduces a new product or if it encounters increased competition in the industry, management might increase its sales commissions or promotional outlays.

The company's projections. In the past, management has consistently held selling expenses to approximately 4 percent of sales and plans to do so again in the coming year. Thus, the company projects its selling expenses as follows:

$$\$6,325,000 \times 0.04 = \$253,000.$$

The bank's projections. The loan officer thinks that with a new competitor entering the market, the company might need to increase its advertising budget or pay higher commissions to remain competitive. Nevertheless, the bank accepts the company's projection of selling expenses as 4 percent of sales because this cost has been so well controlled at this level over the last 3 years. Thus, the bank projects the Pearson Company's selling expenses as follows:

$$\$5,500,000 \times 0.04 = \$220,000.$$

General and Administrative Expenses

General and administrative (G&A) expenses include rent, utilities, real estate, taxes, depreciation (of assets not used in production—such as administrative offices and equipment), telephones, staff salaries and benefits, travel, entertainment, and subscriptions. These items can usually be calculated as a percentage of sales based on past history if the company anticipates no dramatic changes. However, calculation as a percentage increase over prior years is usually preferable if there is a large component of fixed costs. Most companies include a detailed listing of their general and administrative expenses in their financial statements. When analyzing loan requests from companies with marginal repayment ability or high risk, the loan officer must evaluate the assumptions behind each figure in this category. Management controls the company's general and administrative expenses; however, if past trends show that their predictability in the past was poor, then more margin is needed for error.

The company's projections. Although the Pearson Company's general and administrative expenses have ranged from 11 to 14 percent of sales over the past 3 years, management anticipates reducing this category of expenses to 10 percent of sales for the coming year. Specifically, they foresee lower spending for professional services, having recently decided to change attorneys and accountants because of their excessive fees. The company also anticipates more telephone sales and, hence, reduced travel expenses. The company has not, however, provided the bank with a general and administrative budget to substantiate its intentions. Management's projection for G&A expenses is calculated as follows:

$$\$6,325,000 \times 0.10 = \$633,000.$$

The bank's projections. Because no detailed budget is available, the loan officer takes a conservative posture and uses the company's highest general and administrative expense percentage to date—that is, 14 percent (for 1987). Thus, the loan officer calculates the general and administrative expenses for the company as follows:

$$\$5,500,000 \times 0.14 = \$770,000.$$

OPERATING PROFIT

After subtracting operating expenses from gross revenues, the company's operating profit remains. Management's projected sales and expense figures result in a very optimistic operating profit of 14 percent, or $884,000; the bank's more conservative projections result in a projected operating profit of 9 percent of sales, or $495,000. The industry average is about 11 percent.

OTHER INCOME AND EXPENSE

Income statements often include other income and other expense items not resulting from the company's normal business operations. Although these accounts are normally quite small, the loan officer should understand what specific items are included and whether they are recurring or nonrecurring. These accounts are not usually predictable as a percentage of a company's sales. The Pearson Company has not had such other sources of income in the past and does not anticipate any in the coming year. Its only nonoperating expense is interest.

Interest Expense

Interest expense is often listed separately on the income statement. This is usually a relatively predictable expense since a range of interest rates can be assumed for term debt and short-term (seasonal) borrowings.

The interest expense is estimated on the basis of the average amount of term and seasonal debt outstanding during the year. In the case of the

Pearson Company, management projects no seasonal needs. An examination of the company's schedules of existing and projected long-term debt, shown in Exhibits 7.5 and 7.6, indicates the average outstanding debt for 1989 projected at $1,025,000. This is calculated by adding together the amount of outstanding debt as of December 31, 1988 ($680,000 plus $500,000 for the proposed loan, or a total of $1,180,000) and the projected amount of outstanding debt as of December 31, 1989 ($870,000) and dividing by two ($2,050,000 ÷ 2 = $1,025,000).

The company's projections. The Pearson Company projects interest expense at $123,000, up from $110,000 for 1988, although the company has applied for a loan that would increase its long-term debt by $500,000 and would be repayable over 5 years. Management predicts that the prime rate will average 10 percent in 1989 and that it will pay two points over prime for the new loan (as it does for its current loans). Although the prime rate is currently 12 percent, management expects Congress to take action to reduce the federal deficit, which it believes will in turn result in lower interest rates. The company's calculation of interest expense, based on an average outstanding debt of $1,025,000, is as follows:

$$\$1,025,000 \times 0.12 = \$123,000.$$

The bank's projections. Companies are often overly optimistic that interest rates will decline, and thus project interest expense that is unrealistically low. Certainly very few companies accurately projected their annual interest costs in the 20 percent range on pro forma statements composed in 1979 and 1980! A conservative approach would be to assume that interest rates will remain level or possibly rise one to two points during the year. The volatility of interest rates makes it especially prudent for banks to assume a conservative stance when performing a pro forma analysis. Thus, the loan officer projects the company's interest expense based on a prime rate of 12 percent. Since the company's loans are priced at prime plus 2 percent, the following calculation results:

$$\$1,025,000 \times 0.14 = \$144,000.$$

Schedule of Existing Debt

Pearson Company
Schedule of Existing Debt
As of December 31, 1988

Loan #	Origination Date	Original Amount	Outstanding	Rate	Terms	Current Maturity	Long-Term
1	12/15/86	$600,000	$360,000	Prime + 2%	60 monthly payments @ $10,000 + Interest	$120,000	$240,000
2	12/15/87	250,000	200,000	Prime + 2%	60 monthly payments @ $4,167 + Interest	50,000	150,000
3	01/7/88	160,000	120,000	Prime + 2%	48 monthly payments @ $3,333 + Interest	40,000	80,000
Total			$680,000			$210,000	$470,000
Projected loan	01/2/89	$500,000	$500,000	Prime + 2%	60 monthly payments @ $8,333 + Interest	$100,000	$400,000

Schedule of Projected Debt

Pearson Company
Schedule of Projected Debt
As of December 31, 1989

Loan #	Origination Date	Original Amount	Outstanding	Rate	Terms	Current Maturity	Long-Term
1	12/15/86	$600,000	$240,000	Prime + 2%	60 monthly payments @ $10,000 + Interest	$120,000	$120,000
2	12/15/87	250,000	150,000	Prime + 2%	60 monthly payments @ $4,167 + Interest	50,000	100,000
3	1/7/88	160,000	80,000	Prime + 2%	48 monthly payments @ $3,333 + Interest	40,000	40,000
4 (Projected)	1/2/89	500,000	400,000	Prime + 2%	*60 monthly payments @ $8,333 + Interest	100,000	300,000
Total			$870,000			$310,000	$560,000

*1st payment—Jan. 31, 1989

INCOME TAXES

Income taxes are normally projected using current IRS income tax tables. Exhibit 7.7 shows that, using the current corporate tax schedule, the Pearson Company's tax can be figured at a flat rate of 34 percent of taxable income. Both the company and the loan officer use this figure.

The company's projections. The Pearson Company, which has projected its taxable income at $761,000, calculates its tax as follows:

$$\$761,000 \times 0.34 = \$259,000.$$

The bank's projections. Since the bank's loan officer has projected the Pearson Company's taxable income at only $351,000, the following calculation results:

$$\$351,000 \times 0.34 = \$119,000.$$

NET PROFIT AFTER TAX

This account is calculated as profit before tax minus income taxes. Based on the assumptions and calculations discussed previously, the company projects after-tax income of $502,000 for 1989 compared to the bank's projection of $232,000 and compared to the company's actual 1988 after-tax profit of $303,000.

■■■■■ The Pro Forma Balance Sheet

After analyzing and reworking the Pearson Company's pro forma income statement, the loan officer turns to the pro forma balance sheet (Exhibit 7.4) that was submitted with the loan application. The assumptions made and conclusions reached in projecting the various income statement accounts also affect many entries on the pro forma balance sheet. Therefore, the assumptions used in composing (or critiquing) the

Corporate Tax Rates

On taxable income of:	The tax is:
0 to $50,000	15%
$50,000 to $75,000	25%
$75,000 and up	34%*

*A 5% surtax is imposed on taxable income between $100,000 and $335,000. The effect of the surtax is to tax every extra dollar of earnings in the $100,000–$335,000 range at 39%. Thus a corporation with taxable income of more than $335,000 will, in effect, pay a flat tax rate of 34% on *all* taxable income.

pro forma balance sheet must be consistent with those made for the income statement.

The cash account in the assets section and the notes payable to banks account in the liabilities section of the balance sheet are the *plug figures* used in constructing the pro forma balance sheet—that is, they are used to balance the statement after all the other accounts have been calculated. If, after calculating the pro forma balance sheet, assets exceed total liabilities and net worth (stockholders' equity), any difference can simply be added to notes payable to banks. If, on the other hand, total liabilities and net worth exceed assets, the difference can be added to the cash account to balance the statement. Plug figures are discussed in greater detail later in this chapter.

ASSETS

Cash and Marketable Securities

A company's cash balance can be assumed to be the minimum cash needed at the end of the financial period or the minimum cash required as compensating balances in the borrower's loan agreement. Cash may also represent the minimum amount needed by the company to function normally. For purposes of pro forma analysis, the balance sheet accounts for cash and marketable securities are usually combined.

The company's projections. The Pearson Company projects a strong accumulation of cash and marketable securities in 1989. The company forecasts its minimum cash needs at $125,000 per month, but anticipates building cash and marketable securities to $359,000 by year-end. Management attributes this projected cash accumulation to improved management of its inventory and receivables. The $234,000 in marketable securities was derived by the company after all the other balance sheet accounts had been calculated. Then the difference between the year-end 1989 total liabilities and net worth ($3,437,000) and total assets up to that point ($3,203,000) was plugged into the marketable securities account.

The bank's projections. The loan officer agrees with the Pearson Company's assessment of its minimum cash needs as $125,000 per month, but does not foresee any accumulation in marketable securities. However, this will not be known until the remainder of the balance sheet accounts are projected.

Accounts Receivable

Accounts receivable reflect the amount owed to the company by its customers at the end of the period covered by the pro forma income statement. To assess a company's projected accounts receivable, the loan officer should look at the company's past performance with respect to receivables turns—that is, its sales-to-receivables ratio, or average collection period.

The loan officer should also clearly understand management's sales and collection policies. Credit terms should be compared to actual collection periods to determine the effectiveness of a company's collection policies. A company's sales posture can also affect accounts receivable. For example, management may try to increase sales by offering longer credit terms, by offering credit terms for products formerly sold only for cash, or by lowering prices.

The loan officer should also look at the accounts receivable calculation in light of trends from previous statements. For example, the Pearson Company's year-end 1988 balance sheet (Exhibit 7.2) indicates receivables turning 6.0 times per year, or collected every 61 days. The loan officer should note the turns and the level of sales when calculating accounts receivable. From year-end 1986 to year-end 1988, while sales increased from $4,000,000 to $5,500,000, the average collection period slowed by 11 days—from 50 days to 61 days.

If the loan officer has several months of accounts receivable agings for the most recent fiscal or interim statement dates, the agings should be used as an aid in evaluating the company's pro forma balance sheet. As discussed in Chapter 4, the agings reveal the actual age of receivables, rather than the average collection period. Sometimes the turn analysis alone may be misleading and fail to reveal problems with uncollectible receivables or disputed bills. By comparing several months, the loan officer can also determine new accounts and better predict collection times of existing accounts. This is especially helpful if a company has a concentration of sales to one company. The aging of accounts should be used to evaluate management's assumptions for future receivables since the aging reflects management's actual practices and success with respect to the collection of receivables.

The company's projections. The Pearson Company rarely has receivables outstanding over 75 days and has not charged off a major receivable in 3 years. Management believes that in 1989 the company will collect its receivables every 50 days, or 11 days faster than in 1988. This assumption is based on a stricter collection policy recently initiated by management, which the company hopes will help reduce its average collection period. Thus, the company calculates its projected accounts receivables as follows:

$$\frac{365 \text{ days}}{50 \text{ days}} = 7.3 \text{ (Receivables turnover)}$$

$$\frac{\$6,325,000 \text{ (Projected sales)}}{7.3 \text{ (Receivables turnover)}} = \$866,000 \text{ (Projected receivables)}.$$

The bank's projections. The bank's loan officer decides to use a more conservative average collection period in light of the increased competition in the market which could put some pressure on the company's receivable turns. Moreover, if management follows its aggressive sales strategy, the company may need to offer more liberal sales terms to its customers. Normally, the bank could expect to see an industry average receivables turn of 6.4 times per year. However, the Pearson Company's receivables turn has slowed over the past 3 years from 7.3 to 6.0 (an average collection period of 61 days). Therefore, with the anticipated and continued pressure on the company's accounts receivable turns, the loan officer projects receivable turns at the same rate as in 1988. Thus the bank calculates the company's projected receivables as follows:

$$\frac{365 \text{ days}}{61 \text{ days}} = 6.0 \text{ (Receivables turnover)}$$

$$\frac{\$5,500,000 \text{ (Projected sales)}}{6.0 \text{ (Receivables turnover)}} = \$917,000 \text{ (Projected receivables)}.$$

The bank projects $51,000 more in receivables by year-end 1989 than the company projects ($917,000 − $866,000 = $51,000), despite the lower projected sales figure being used by the bank. The bank's figure is nearly identical to the company's actual accounts receivable as of year-end 1988 ($916,000).

Inventory

The inventory account on a pro forma balance sheet is usually calculated on the basis of the company's inventory turnover ratio (called *cost of goods to inventory* on the Pearson Company's balance sheet). In addition to past performance, inventory predictions should take into account any anticipated changes in the company's sales and purchasing policies.

The company's projections. Although the company's inventory turnover ratio was 3.4, or 107 days inventory for 1988, management believes that inventory will turn at 4.3 times per year, or once every 85 days, in 1989. This projection is based on improved inventory control resulting from replacing its old manual inventory system with a computerized system. This was also the company's inventory turnover experience in 1986. Thus, the company calculates its inventory projection as follows:

$$\frac{365 \text{ days}}{85 \text{ days}} = 4.3 \text{ (Inventory turnover)}$$

$$\frac{\$4,428,000 \text{ (Projected cost of goods sold)}}{4.3 \text{ (Inventory turnover)}} = \$1,030,000 \text{ (Projected inventory)}.$$

The bank's projections. Although the Pearson Company schedules its production of bearings on a relatively level basis throughout the year, the loan officer believes the company will have to maintain the same inventory level as in the past if it is to provide the service necessary to accomplish its sales objectives. Thus the loan officer assumes that the company's inventory will turn at about the same rate as during the past year. The loan officer calculates the bank's inventory projection as follows:

$$\frac{365 \text{ days}}{107 \text{ days}} = 3.4 \text{ (Inventory turnover)}$$

$$\frac{\$3,850,000 \text{ (Projected cost of goods sold)}}{3.4 \text{ (Inventory turnover)}} = \$1,132,000 \text{ (Projected inventory)}.$$

The company's assumptions concerning its future sales strategy and service policies apparently affect inventory turns dramatically. The company's projected inventory turn requires $102,000 less in inventory investment than the bank's estimate (which reflects the company's actual experience in 1988).

Fixed Assets

Many companies routinely prepare a capital expense budget, which lists planned projects and their costs and anticipated sources of funding. If no such budget exists, management should provide a schedule of fixed assets and depreciation to the bank, or this information may be included in the notes to its financial statements. The fixed asset schedule should include the purchase date, useful life, cost, method of depreciation, and depreciation taken to date for each principal asset. Any projected increases in fixed assets (that is, anticipated purchases) should also be shown.

The loan officer can also use the company's past net sales-to-net fixed asset ratio as a rough measure for projecting fixed assets. This calculation divides net sales by net fixed assets (that is, the book value of assets net of accumulated depreciation). Thus it assumes that net fixed assets will increase at about the same rate as net sales. However, fully depreciated assets can distort this ratio since the book value of such assets will be zero. Since companies typically must replace their fully depreciated assets (which are carried at zero) at a much higher cost, the loan officer must have an idea of the age and useful life of the company's fixed assets in order to determine its replacement needs. A plant having considerable excess capacity also distorts the ratio because the company can increase sales without a corresponding increase in fixed assets. Thus the capacity of the company's existing plant and equipment relative to projected production and space needs must be taken into consideration.

Some companies may show no fixed assets on their balance sheet (or a very small amount relative to sales). In this case, the company may lease its equipment, or the principals of the company may own the fixed assets and rent them to the company.

The company's and the bank's projections. The Pearson Company's forecast for its fixed assets account appears to be consistent with its projected sales growth since management feels that its present fixed assets can support sales of $7,000,000 to $7,500,000. The schedule of depreciation and fixed assets furnished by the company (not shown) appears reasonable to the loan officer. Consequently, the bank accepts management's projections, calculated as follows:

Net fixed assets as of 12/31/88	$ 822,000
Less: Depreciation on existing equipment for 1988	− 120,000
	$ 702,000
Plus: Cost of casting machine (to be purchased early in 1989)	+ 600,000
	$1,302,000
Less: Depreciation on new machine—alternate ACRS—5-year (a half-year of depreciation the first and last years—$600,000 × ⅕ × 200% × ½)	− 120,000
Net fixed assets as of 12/31/89	$1,182,000

Other Assets

Although the Pearson Company has no other assets, when preparing a pro forma statement the lender would consider the company's projections and historical data for any other assets shown, just as is done with the preceding categories of assets.

LIABILITIES AND NET WORTH

Having completed the analysis of the asset side of the company's pro forma balance sheet, the loan officer would logically move next to the first item on the liability side of the balance sheet—notes payable to banks. However, as mentioned previously, notes payable to banks serves as a plug figure in balancing pro forma statements. Thus, the loan officer should analyze the remainder of the pro forma balance sheet accounts before calculating this figure.

Accounts Payable

The amount of accounts payable is a function of the amount and terms of trade credit extended by suppliers and the company's actual payment practices. Chapter 6 discussed how to calculate a company's accounts payable turnover ratio, or days payable. The loan officer can confirm the validity of the company's days payable by using a company-provided listing and aging of accounts payable, similar to the aging of accounts receivable used in verifying a company's average collection period.

The Pearson Company provides, at the bank's request, a listing of purchased raw materials (not shown), which shows 1988 purchases totaling $2,695,000 and projected purchases of $3,040,000 for 1989 (a 13 percent increase).

The company's projections. Management projects purchases of $3,040,000 for 1989. The company has for the past 3 years paid its trade creditors on a 75- to 79-day basis. However, in 1989, management expects to pay its suppliers more promptly in order to take advantage of more early-payment discounts. Projecting payment on a 57-day basis, it calculates projected payables as follows:

$$\frac{365 \text{ days}}{57 \text{ days}} = 6.4 \text{ (Payable turns)}$$

$$\frac{\$3,040,000 \text{ (Projected purchases).}}{6.4 \text{ (Payable turns)}} = \$475,000 \text{ (Projected payables).}$$

The Pearson Company projects $475,000 in outstanding payables at the end of 1989 based on its assumptions about its future payment policies.

The bank's projections. Consistent with the bank's projection of flat sales, the loan officer projects 1989 purchases at $2,695,000—the same level as 1988 purchases (a figure supplied by the company in its yearly schedule of purchases). The bank also projects a days payable ratio of 57 days, down from 76 days, but for different reasons than company management. Whereas company suppliers have previously allowed late payments, the loan officer believes the demand for raw materials has reached the point where suppliers will require that payments be made within normal 60-day terms, effective January 1, 1989. Thus, the bank projects accounts payable as follows:

$$\frac{365 \text{ days}}{57 \text{ days}} = 6.4 \text{ (Payable turns)}$$

$$\frac{\$2,695,000 \text{ (Projected purchases)}}{6.4 \text{ (Payable turns)}} = \$421,000 \text{ (Projected payables).}$$

Accruals

Accruals are expenses that are recognized as having been incurred on the income statement, but which remain unpaid as of the statement date. Wages and bonuses are examples of typical accrued expenses. Accruals typically make up an insignificant part of the company's total liabilities and can be estimated as a percentage of assets based on past trends, or actual amounts can be projected based on management budgets.

The company's projections. The Pearson Company projects accruals as 2 percent of total projected assets, since accruals have totaled approximately 2 percent of assets for the past 3 years. Thus, the company's projection is calculated as follows:

$$\$3,437,000 \times 0.02 = \$69,000.$$

The bank's projections. The loan officer also anticipates no change in the company's level of accruals; thus, accruals are calculated as 2 percent of total projected assets:

$$\$3,356,000 \times 0.02 = \$67,000.$$

Current Maturities of Long-Term Debt

Current maturities represent the amounts of long-term debt due in the next 12 months. This figure can be calculated based on the schedule of debt included in the footnotes to a company's financial statements. Any current maturities resulting from the proposed loan should also be included.

The company's and the bank's projections. Current maturities of the Pearson Company's three existing loans total $210,000 per year. The proposed additional debt ($500,000 repayable over 5 years) adds an additional $100,000 per year to the current maturities. Thus, projected current maturities as of year-end 1989 total $310,000 (as shown in Exhibit 7.6).

Current-Year Income Taxes

Typically, this liability represents taxes due from the just-completed fiscal year but not yet paid or deferred as of the statement date. This liability usually does not equal the tax expense shown on the income statement because most corporations pay quarterly taxes based on their estimated earnings. Thus, current-year income taxes are the remaining amount (after estimated payments) due when the company files its corporate tax return. Note that, in their projections, neither the company nor the bank assumes any deferred taxes.

The company's projections. Under current tax law, the Pearson Company can pay taxes on a quarterly basis either totaling at least 90 percent of its estimated tax liability for the year ($259,000 × .90 = $233,000) or equal to its previous year's tax expense ($192,000). It chooses the latter option. Thus the Pearson Company projects the following current-year income taxes as of year-end 1989:

Current-year taxes as of 12/31/1988	$ 54,000
Projected income tax for 1989	259,000
	$313,000
Less: Payment of current-year taxes	54,000
Payments of estimated taxes (paid quarterly)	192,000
	$246,000
Current-year taxes as of 12/31/1989	$ 67,000

The bank's projections. The bank projects the company paying estimated taxes of $107,000 during 1989, which is 90 percent of the company's expected tax liability for 1989 using the bank's income projections ($119,000 × .90 = $107,000), rather than the previous year's tax expense of $192,000. Thus, the bank's loan officer projects the following current-year income taxes as of year-end 1989:

Current-year taxes as of 12/31/1988	$ 54,000
Projected income tax for 1989	119,000
	$173,000
Less: Payment of current-year taxes	54,000
Payments of estimated taxes (paid quarterly)	107,000
	$161,000
Current-year taxes as of 12/31/1989	$ 12,000

Long-Term Debt

Long-term debt represents that portion of the debt schedule with maturities in excess of one year. Both the Pearson Company and the bank use the same calculation for long-term debt. On the schedule of projected debt, shown in Exhibit 7.6, all four loans (including the proposed loan) have maturities that extend beyond the current year. The total amount of long-term debt not due until after the end of 1989 is $560,000.

Net Worth

The net worth section of the balance sheet is easily projected. Capital stock figures (for preferred and common stock) can be picked up from previous balance sheets unless additions or deletions to the stock were made in the current year. The Pearson Company's common stock value remains unchanged at $50,000. The retained earnings account ($1,555,000 as of December 31, 1988) is increased by the amount of projected after-tax profits from the pro forma income statement less projected dividends.

The company's projections. Management projects the company's net worth as of the end of 1989 as follows:

Capital stock	$ 50,000
Retained earnings as of 12/31/1988	1,555,000
Net profit after tax (projected)	502,000
Less: Projected dividend payments	151,000
Retained earnings as of 12/31/1989	1,906,000
Net worth as of 12/31/1989	$1,956,000

The bank's projections. The bank projects the company's net worth as follows:

Capital stock	$ 50,000
Retained earnings as of 12/31/1988	1,555,000
Net profit after tax (projected)	232,000
Less: Projected dividend payments	—
Retained earnings as of 12/31/1989	1,787,000
Net worth as of 12/31/1989	$1,837,000

The "Plug" Accounts

As discussed previously, the notes payable account is traditionally one of two balancing or plug figures on the balance sheet—the other being the cash account. Thus if assets exceed liabilities and net worth on the pro forma balance sheet, the difference is added to the notes payable to banks in order to balance the statement. If, on the other hand, liabilities and net worth exceed assets, the difference is added to cash in order to balance the statement.

Discretion must be exercised when balancing amounts into notes payables because, while this procedure accurately balances the balance sheet, the financing need may be a long-term rather than short-term need. For example, the financing of current assets may reflect a permanent credit need if the debt is to fund accounts receivable and inventory that are required to support a permanent higher base level of sales. Or the assets requiring financing may be fixed assets, which would appropriately require long-term debt. In these cases, then, long-term debt is a more appropriate account to balance than notes payable to banks. If long-term debt is used as the plug account, the loan officer should also make allowance for a portion of the new debt to be carried as current maturities. In addition, when a pro forma statement is prepared at the low point in the company's operating cycle, any need for seasonal debt to finance a seasonal buildup in receivables and inventory will not be apparent.

The company's projections. In constructing the company's pro forma balance sheet, management initially wound up with liabilities plus net worth totaling more than assets. As a result, management balanced its pro forma balance sheet by including $234,000 in its marketable securities account so that projected assets total $3,437,000—the same as projected total liabilities and net worth.

The bank's projections. In the bank's version of the company's pro forma balance sheet, total liabilities and net worth total $149,000 less than the $3,356,000 in projected total assets up to this point. Thus, the loan officer plugs $149,000 into the notes payable to banks account so that assets equal liabilities plus net worth. This indicates that, with flat sales (as projected by the bank), the company will have to borrow $149,000 at the time of the projected balance sheet in addition to the $500,000 loan already requested for the new equipment.

The loan officer must now decide what assets the bank will actually finance, how to structure the debt, and whether this reflects a long-term, permanent, or short-term borrowing need. The company appears to need the additional debt to support the higher level of inventory and receivables that the bank projects the Pearson Company will need to support the company's base level of sales in an increasingly competitive environment.

∎∎∎∎∎∎∎ Interpreting the Pro Forma Analysis

The Pearson Company and the bank's loan officer have composed two very different sets of pro forma financial statements, as seen in Exhibits 7.3 and 7.4. The bank's projections, which are purposely conservative, show the company needing considerably more funds than it has asked for. Some of the more significant changes made by the loan officer to the Pearson Company's pro forma statements include the following:

- The bank projects $825,000 less in sales revenues than the company.

- The bank projects $137,000 more in general and administrative expenses than the company.

- The bank projects significantly less cash flow—$472,000 (net profit after tax of $232,000, plus depreciation of $240,000) compared to the company's projection of $742,000 ($502,000 net profit after tax and $240,000 depreciation).

- The bank projects slower inventory and receivables turnovers than management projects; if the loan officer's assumptions are correct, the company will have a greater investment in current assets despite a lower projected sales level.

- The bank projects an additional $149,000 financing need to support these increased assets (accounts receivable and inventory).

- The bank's projections include no dividend payment, whereas the company's projections show a $151,000 dividend payment. If the dividend is paid, the company will need $300,000 in additional financing (rather than $149,000), according to the bank's projections.

Substantial differences in the assumptions made about the Pearson Company by its own management and by the loan officer lead to significantly different projected financial results. The bank may also reach far less optimistic conclusions than management as to a company's financial needs, its ability to repay the proposed loan, and its overall creditworthiness. This emphasizes how important it is for a loan officer to thoroughly understand all the facets of the borrowing company in order to arrive at realistic assumptions and accurate projections.

▌▌▌▌ Pitfalls of Pro Forma Analysis

The advantages of pro forma analysis have been presented at some length. However, pro forma statements also have certain inherent shortcomings—including uncertainties they fail to address (such as the possibility of economic recession or natural disasters), their inability to identify interim financing needs, and the fact that they may be based on unreliable information or erroneous assumptions.

Pro forma statements attempt to estimate a company's financial future in an uncertain environment. These uncertainties include the economy, competition, government regulations, technological change, and management's ability to perform effectively. The further into the future the projection extends, the greater the uncertainty—hence, the more conservative the loan officer's decisions must be.

Another shortcoming of pro forma analysis is that it can cause the loan officer to overlook the company's interim financing needs. Because the pro forma balance sheet reflects the company's financial state at a given point in time (usually the fiscal year-end), it does not reveal any funding needs that might arise between fiscal year-end balance sheet dates. These hidden funding needs typically involve the need for seasonal asset buildups in preparation for heavy sales periods. The use of projected monthly cash budgets to identify interim cash requirements is discussed in Chapter 8.

▌▌▌▌ Summary

Pro forma analysis must be based on accurate knowledge of the company's past performance as well as of the many external and internal factors that affect the company's operations. It is particularly difficult to make accurate projections for new companies and for companies that have had erratic operating results in the past.

Pro forma analysis enables the loan officer to reach conclusions about the probable financing needs and repayment ability of a company.

However, the pro forma results can only be as good as the underlying assumptions on which the projections are based. Therefore, the loan officer must closely examine the validity of the company's assumptions, making adjustments to the company's pro forma statements as deemed necessary. In general, the loan officer will favor more conservative assumptions than company management.

The single most important element of pro forma financial statements is the sales projection. Without a reasonable sales figure, the entire pro forma process is of questionable value. A change in sales can affect projected profits, accounts receivable, inventory, accounts payable, and the perceived borrowing needs of the company. Thus even a small miscalculation in this key assumption can dramatically affect many areas of the pro forma analysis. Therefore, the lender should understand how a 1 percent change in the net margin or a one-day change in inventory turnover will affect the various statements and the cash flow of the company.

In constructing a pro forma balance sheet, assets are made to equal liabilities and net worth by using a plug figure—either for cash and marketable securities (on the assets side) or notes payable to banks (on the liabilities side). This latter may be misleading, however, since the company may actually need long-term rather than short-term financing.

Pro forma analysis has a number of limitations including the fact that it fails to reveal seasonal financing needs. In addition, because the future is full of unpredictabilities, all pro forma projections should be tempered with appropriate conservatism. Even so, the loan officer should not rely too heavily on pro forma statements as the basis for a loan decision.

Questions

1. What is pro forma analysis, and what are its benefits?
2. What steps of financial analysis normally precede pro forma analysis?
3. What is the single most important number on the pro forma income statement, and why?

4. Explain the function of "plug accounts" in creating a pro forma balance sheet. What accounts are usually used as the plug accounts?

5. Explain the shortcomings of pro forma financial analysis.

6. Explain the importance of the lender using conservative assumptions when evaluating pro forma statements.

Exercises

E-1

A company that is applying to your bank for a loan has submitted financial statements for its fiscal year ended December 31, 1988. On the basis of the financial statements and the other information about the company that follows, prepare a pro forma income statement and a pro forma balance sheet for the year ending December 31, 1989.

Income Statement for the Year Ended December 31, 1988

Net sales (36,000 units)	$4,680,000
Cost of goods manufactured and sold (36,000 units)	3,744,000
Gross profit on sales	$ 936,000
Selling expenses	468,000
General and administrative expenses	254,800
Operating profit	213,200
Other expenses	5,200
Net profit before taxes	$ 208,000
Income taxes	83,200
Net profit after taxes	$ 124,800

Balance Sheet as of December 31, 1988

Assets		Liabilities and Net Worth	
Cash	$ 78,000	Bank notes payable	$ 520,000
Accounts receivable	650,000	Accounts payable	208,000
Inventory	780,000	Total current liabilities	$ 728,000
Total current assets	$1,508,000	Mortgage on plant	260,000
Net fixed assets	1,066,000	Capital stock	1,300,000
Due from officers	130,000	Retained earnings	416,000
Total assets	$2,704,000	Total liabilities and net worth	$2,704,000

During the next 12 months, management anticipates the following:

- The unit sales of the company's product can be increased 25 percent by reducing the unit price 10 percent and increasing selling expenses 10 percent over the amount spent in 1988. All sales are credit sales.

- The unit cost of production can be reduced 10 percent as a result of increased production, and all units produced will be sold.

- Inventory will remain approximately the same in total dollar amount.

- The turnover of receivables will be improved, and uncollected receivables at the close of the year should represent sales for no more than 45 days (a sales-to-receivables ratio of about 8.10).

- General and administrative expenses and other expenses will remain unchanged.

- The income tax rate will remain unchanged, and accrued income taxes, if any, should be assumed to be paid in cash before the year-end.

- Depreciation charges will run about $52,000, and no capital expenditures will be necessary on fixed assets.

- The dividend rate will remain unchanged at $78,000 per year (6 percent of capital stock).

- The receivables due from officers will be reduced by $26,000—the amount of the dividend payments they receive.

- Accounts payable at year-end 1989 should not exceed payables as of December 31, 1988.

- The company will make a $52,000 payment on its mortgage debt during 1989.

- All cash in excess of $78,000 at the end of 1989 will be used to reduce bank notes payable.

8 Cash Budgets

Learning Objectives

After studying this chapter, you should be able to

- describe the primary uses of cash budgets
- construct a cash budget
- do an interpretive analysis of a cash budget as part of a comprehensive financial analysis
- explain why cash budgets are useful in determining seasonal and other interim funding needs

▌▌▌▌▌▌▌ Introduction

Cash budgets are another tool that help a loan officer forecast a company's future financing needs. It supplements the pro forma analysis by bridging the gap between statement dates (usually fiscal year-ends). By projecting a company's schedule of receipts and disbursements on a monthly basis, the cause, timing, and magnitude of a company's peak borrowing needs can be identified. Because a cash budget provides an estimation of a company's cash position and funding requirement each month, it is particularly useful in determining the credit needs of companies with seasonal variations in operations.

Normally a company will supply a cash budget as part of its loan application package since most companies use cash budgets as a part of their own internal financial planning process. However, in some cases, a loan officer may have to construct a cash budget, as well as analyze it.

Because a cash budget is based on past and pro forma financial statements, as well as on other more detailed cash flow information, the loan officer may want to rework a company-provided cash budget to see how the lender's more conservative pro forma assumptions affect the company's monthly cash flow. This may enable the lender to uncover financing needs not foreseen by the company.

A cash budget looks at a company's inflows and outflows on a cash basis, rather than on an accrual basis. This means that while a company's income statement recognizes a sale at the time it is transacted, a cash budget recognizes a sale when payment is received. Similarly, while an income statement recognizes expenses at the time a purchase is transacted, the cash budget recognizes expenses when they are actually paid. Thus the turnover in a company's accounts receivable and accounts payable are important considerations in the construction of a cash budget, as is the timing of other expenses, such as when interest and principal payments on a loan actually come due.

▌▌▌▌▌▌▌ Cash-Basis Accounting

As discussed in Chapter 2, most companies prepare their financial statements using accrual accounting rather than cash accounting. Thus the income statement recognizes earnings when sales are transacted, not when payment is received. Likewise, expenses are recognized when they are incurred, rather than when payment is made.

Companies use accrual accounting for financial reporting because it matches related revenues and expenses and therefore more accurately portrays the company's earnings. However, the amount of net income reported on a company's accrual-basis income statement does not reflect the amount of cash generated. Hence, the loan officer may have difficulty determining the borrower's ability to consistently generate cash and repay debt on the basis of pro forma financial statements.

The loan officer must be able to take the information derived from accrual-basis financial statements and convert it to cash-basis information. This involves creating a cash budget to take into account the timing of cash flow and the company's actual cash requirements. Thus if a company makes credit sales on 30-day terms, a cash budget recognizes the collection of cash 30 days hence rather than on the day of sale. If an insurance premium is paid annually, it shows up as a cash expense during the month it is actually paid, rather than being expensed evenly throughout the year. If the loan officer understands the differences between accrual and cash accounting, the transition from one to the other is not difficult.

▮▮▮▮ Use of Cash Budgets

Cash budgets forecast a company's cash receipts and disbursements between statement dates, usually monthly. The most common source of cash is the collection of sales revenues, while the most common uses of cash include purchases of inventory, payment of operating expenses and interest, and capital expenditures. In simplest terms, projected receipts and projected disbursements represent a company's projected cash flow—either positive or negative. A negative cash flow or a positive cash flow that is less than the company's minimum cash requirement indicates the company faces at least a temporary funding requirement.

A cash budget includes all of a company's anticipated cash inflows (including loan proceeds, cash sales, and the collection of accounts receivable) and all of its potential cash outflows (purchases, labor, selling expenses, interest and principal on loans, utilities, and other capital expenditures). By evaluating the likely timing and magnitude of these cash inflows and outflows, the loan officer can determine the company's cash needs for daily operations. Thus the cash budget allows a company's management to determine the cash implications of its plans and strategies and enables both management and the loan officer to anticipate the company's financing needs and determine the company's ability to generate sufficient cash to repay a loan.

Since pro forma statements fail to identify a company's interim funding needs, weekly, monthly, or quarterly cash budgets may be needed to bridge the time gap between year-end statements. A toy manufacturer, for example, must be able to forecast its cash needs at the peak inventory season (which is significantly different from its peak sales season) when financing requirements are the greatest. The magnitude and timing of the toy manufacturer's cash needs determine both the amount of the company's loan request and when repayment is possible. By identifying the various components of cash flow, a cash budget also enables management (and the lender) to measure the company's performance on an interim basis. Management can then react quickly if the actual cash flow varies significantly from the expected cash flow. Management's effectiveness in dealing with any such deviations depends upon what time increment is used in preparing a cash budget (usually monthly or weekly) and how often the company's performance is reviewed. Obviously, a company can react to problems more quickly if its cash flow is monitored weekly rather than quarterly or semiannually.

When approving a loan request, the loan officer must have strong confidence in the company's cash budgets. This confidence results directly from how well management has performed against its previous plans and how dependable the company's cash flows have been in the past. If a cash budget is unavailable, a loan officer may need to construct one, especially when analyzing a relatively new or rapidly growing company or one with seasonal sales.

▌▐▐▐▐▐▐▐ ▐ Construction of a Cash Budget

Ideally, the prospective commercial borrower should provide the bank with a detailed cash budget categorized as to cash inflows (receipts) and outflows (disbursements). The loan officer must check the company's assumptions as to the timing and magnitude of a company's projected cash flows based on other available financial information. The analysis that precedes the preparation or interpretation of a cash budget is critical and takes into consideration all the information gathered for the pro forma statement analysis, including income tax information. The assumptions behind the projections are as critical to the cash budget analysis as to the pro forma analysis.

Whether the loan officer must construct a cash budget or simply analyze an existing cash budget, all the aspects of the company's operation that influence incoming and outgoing cash—such as what percentage of a company's sales are credit sales—must be understood. The loan officer must identify the timing and amount of the company's cash sales revenues and the timing and amount of credit sales and the conversion of accounts receivable to cash inflows. The loan officer should also compare the company's receivables turnover to its established credit terms. The loan officer also needs to know its suppliers' credit terms and the company's payment practices with respect to purchased materials. The loan officer must also know the magnitude and timing of the company's direct labor and overhead costs and of its various operating expenses, including its general and administrative expenses and selling expenses. In addition, the lender must be familiar with a company's nonoperating expenses, income tax liability, dividend payment policies, loan repayment schedules, and interest payments.

BASIC FORMAT

The specific format that companies use for their monthly cash budgets varies. A typical format, such as that shown as Exhibit 8.1, includes the following elements:

- cash on hand at the beginning of each month
- cash receipts including cash sales, collections of accounts receivable, and loan proceeds
- total cash available (projected cash on hand plus projected cash receipts)

Sample Cash Budget Form

MONTHLY CASH

NAME OF BUSINESS		ADDRESS										OWNER	
		Pre-Start-up Position		1		2		3		4		5	
YEAR MONTH		Estimate	Actual	Estimate	Actual	Estimate	Actual	Estimate	Actual	Estimate	Actual	Estimate	Actual
1. CASH ON HAND (Beginning of month)													
2. CASH RECEIPTS (a) Cash Sales													
(b) Collections from Credit Accounts													
(c) Loan or Other Cash injection (Specify)													
3. TOTAL CASH RECEIPTS (2a + 2b + 2c = 3)													
4. TOTAL CASH AVAILABLE (Before cash out) (1 + 3)													
5. CASH PAID OUT (a) Purchases (Merchandise)													
(b) Gross Wages (Excludes withdrawals)													
(c) Payroll Expenses (Taxes, etc.)													
(d) Outside Services													
(e) Supplies (Office and operating)													
(f) Repairs and Maintenance													
(g) Advertising													
(h) Car, Delivery, and Travel													
(i) Accounting and Legal													
(j) Rent													
(k) Telephone													
(l) Utilities													
(m) Insurance													
(n) Taxes (Real Estate, etc.)													
(o) Interest													
(p) Other Expenses (Specify each) General & Admin													
Expense													
(q) Miscellaneous (Unspecified)													
(r) Subtotal													
(s) Loan Principal Payment													
(t) Capital Purchases (Specify)													
(u) Other Start-up Costs													
(v) Reserve and/or Escrow (Specify)													
(w) Owner's Withdrawal													
6. TOTAL CASH PAID OUT (Total 5a thru 5w)													
7. CASH POSITION (End of month) (4 minus 6)													
ESSENTIAL OPERATING DATA (Noncash-flow information) A. Sales Volume (Dollars)													
B. Accounts Receivable (End of month)													
C. Bad Debt (End of month)													
D. Inventory on Hand (End of month)													
E. Accounts Payable (End of month)													
F. Depreciation													

SBA FORM 1100 (1-83) REF: SOP 60 10 Previous Editions Are Obsolete

FLOW PROJECTION

Form Approval:
OMB No. 3245-0019
Expires: 3-31-88

TYPE OF BUSINESS				PREPARED BY				DATE		

6		7		8		9		10		11		12		TOTAL Columns 1—12		
Estimate	Actual	Estimate	Actual	Estimate	Actual	Estimate	Actual	Estimate	Actual	Estimate	Actual	Estimate	Actual	Estimate	Actual	
																1.
																2. (a)
																(b)
																(c)
																3.
																4.
																5. (a)
																(b)
																(c)
																(d)
																(e)
																(f)
																(g)
																(h)
																(i)
																(j)
																(k)
																(l)
																(m)
																(n)
																(o)
																(p)
																(q)
																(r)
																(s)
																(t)
																(u)
																(v)
																(w)
																6.
																7.
																A.
																B.
																C.
																D.
																E.
																F.

- cash paid out, including inventory purchases, salaries, direct labor and overhead costs, general and administrative expenses, interest, income taxes, loan principal payments, and capital purchases

- cash position (total cash available minus projected cash outflow)

- minimum ending cash (the amount required for ongoing operations)

- additional funding requirement (the amount needed to bring the company's cash position up to its minimum cash requirement). Negative funding requirements indicate amounts available for repayment of previous funding needs.

- cumulative funding requirement (total cash requirement to date minus any repayments)

PRIMARY ASSUMPTIONS

To illustrate the construction of a cash budget, this chapter continues with the analysis of the Pearson Company begun in Chapter 7. Recall that the loan officer's analysis of the Pearson Company's pro forma financial statements (as reconstructed by the bank) led the loan officer to conclude that the company might need $149,000 worth of permanent working capital in addition to the $500,000 loan requested by the company for the purchase of a casting mold. This was the amount required to balance the pro forma balance sheet, which the loan officer "plugged in" as notes payable to banks, as seen in Exhibit 7.4. The loan officer is also aware that, based on the company's operations for the past several years, the company could face additional interim financing needs as well. Therefore, the loan officer decides to construct a new cash budget coinciding with the loan officer's assumptions used in the pro forma analysis.

Exhibits 8.2 and 8.3 summarize the major accounts from the Pearson Company's 1988 financial statements (shown as Exhibits 7.1 and 7.2 in the previous chapter) and from the loan officer's revised 1989 pro forma financial statements (shown in Exhibits 7.3 and 7.4 in the previous chapter), as well as some additional cost breakdowns supplied by management. These figures provide the basis for the loan officer's construction of the company's 1989 cash budget.

EXHIBIT 8.2 ■■■■■■■■■■■■■■■■■■■■■■■■■■■■■■■■■■■■

Assumptions for the Pearson Company's 1989 Cash Budget
Pro Forma Income Statement Summary

Sales		$5,500,000
All sales are credit sales (on 30-day terms)		
Cost of goods sold		3,850,000
Purchases	$2,695,000	
Direct labor & overhead	1,035,000	
Depreciation	120,000	
Officers' salaries		165,000
($13,000/month + $9,000 bonus in December)		
Selling expenses		220,000
General and administrative expenses		770,000
Interest expense		144,000
Income taxes		119,000
Net profit after tax		$232,000
Dividends		0
Depreciation		$240,000

Note: These figures are taken from the Pearson Company's bank-prepared pro forma income statement (shown as Exhibit 7.3 in the preceding chapter), except for the breakdown of cost of goods sold, which was supplied separately by Pearson Company management.

■■■

Assumptions for the Pearson Company's 1989 Cash Budget Actual and Pro Forma Balance Sheet Summary

Pro Forma (1989) Balance Sheet Summary

Cash and marketable securities (minimum cash requirement)	$ 125,000
Fixed assets (net)	1,182,000
Notes payable	149,000
Accounts payable	421,000
Accruals	67,000
Current maturities—long-term debt	310,000
Current-year income taxes	12,000
Accounts receivable turn	6.0 (61 days)
Inventory turn	3.4 (107 days)
Payables turn	6.4 (57 days)

Actual (1988) Balance Sheet Summary

Cash plus marketable securities	$ 90,000
Accounts receivable	916,000
Accounts payable—trade	559,000
Accruals	62,000
Current-year income taxes	54,000
Accounts receivable turn	6.0 (61 days)
Payables turn	4.8 (76 days)

Note: The pro forma figures are taken from the Pearson Company's bank-prepared pro forma balance sheet (shown as Exhibit 7.4 in the preceding chapter). The remaining figures are from the balance sheet dated 12/31/88 (shown as Exhibit 7.2 in the preceding chapter).

■ ■

■ ■ ■ ■ Components of the Cash Budget

The 1989 monthly cash budget for the Pearson Company, as calculated by the loan officer, is shown in Exhibit 8.4. A discussion of each line of the budget follows.

Cash on Hand

A cash budget begins by showing the amount of cash on hand at the beginning of the year. For cash budget purposes, both cash and marketable securities are considered to be cash. From the Pearson Company's 1988 balance sheet (as summarized in Exhibit 8.3), the cash account at year-end 1988 totaled $90,000 ($85,000 cash and $5,000 of marketable securities). Therefore, the loan officer enters $90,000 as the amount of cash on hand for January 1989. The cash budget shows each subsequent month beginning with $125,000 in cash, the Pearson Company's stated minimum cash balance required for ongoing operations. Any cash in excess of $125,000 at the end of any month is assumed to be used for repayment of the company's short-term debt.

Cash Receipts

The next entry on the cash budget is cash receipts which are normally categorized separately as cash sales, collections from accounts receivable, and loans or other cash injections. Since all of the Pearson Company's sales are credit sales, cash sales are not listed on the cash budget. Since the company's only regular source of cash inflow comes from the collection of accounts receivable, the lender first looks at the company's balance sheet (as summarized in Exhibit 8.3), which shows that its accounts receivable balance at year-end 1988 was $916,000. Since the company's receivables turnover is 61 days, the loan officer concludes that $916,000 in accounts receivable represents 2 months of sales, or $458,000 of collections per month. Thus the loan officer lists $458,000 (expected receipts from November and December 1988 sales) on the cash budget as cash receipts for January and February 1989.

The bank's pro forma income statement (as summarized in Exhibit 8.2) projects the Pearson Company's sales for 1989 at $5,500,000—or $458,000 per month—unchanged from the previous year. The bank's pro forma balance sheet also shows the Pearson Com-

EXHIBIT 8.4 ■■■■■■■■■■■■■■■■■■■■■■■■■■■■■■■■■

Cash Budget

Pearson Company
Cash Budget for the Year Ending December 31, 1989
(in thousands of dollars)

	Jan.	Feb.	Mar.	Apr.	May	June	July	Aug.	Sept.	Oct.	Nov.	Dec.	Total
1. Cash on hand (Beginning of month)	90	125	125	125	125	125	125	125	125	125	125	125	
2. Cash receipts Collections from accounts receivable	458	458	458	458	458	458	458	458	458	458	459	459	5,498
Loan or other cash injection	500	—	—	—	—	—	—	—	—	—	—	—	500
3. Total cash receipts	958	458	458	458	458	458	458	458	458	458	459	459	5,998
4. Total cash available (Before cash out)(1 + 3)	1,048	583	583	583	583	583	583	583	583	583	584	584	
5. Cash paid out Purchases (merchandise)	296	285	225	225	225	225	225	225	225	225	225	225	2,831
Direct labor and overhead	86	86	86	86	86	86	86	86	86	86	86	89	1,035
Officers' salaries	13	13	13	13	13	13	13	13	13	13	13	22	165
Selling expenses	18	18	18	18	18	18	18	18	18	18	18	17	215
General and administrative expenses	54	54	54	54	54	54	54	54	54	54	54	56	650
Interest	12	12	12	12	12	12	12	12	12	12	12	12	144
Income taxes	—	—	54	27	—	27	—	—	27	—	—	26	161
Subtotal	479	468	462	435	408	435	408	408	435	408	408	447	5,201
Loan principal payments	26	26	26	26	26	26	26	26	26	26	25	25	310
Capital purchases (mold)	600	—	—	—	—	—	—	—	—	—	—	—	600
6. Total cash paid out	1,105	494	488	461	434	461	434	434	461	434	433	472	6,111
7. Cash position (4 minus 6)	(57)	89	95	122	149	122	149	149	122	149	151	112	
8. Minimum ending cash ($125,000 or greater)	125	125	125	125	125	125	125	125	125	125	125	125	
9. Additional funding requirement (or repayment) (8 minus 7)	182	36	30	3	(24)	3	(24)	(24)	3	(24)	(26)	13	
10. Cumulative funding requirement	182	218	248	251	227	230	206	182	185	161	135	148	

■■■■■■■■■■■■■■■■■■■■■■■■■■■■■■■■■■■■■■■

pany's receivables continuing to turn 6.0 times per year (every 61 days). This means that January 1989 sales of $458,000 are expected to be collected in March 1989, a pattern of deferred collections that continues for all 12 months. Thus November and December 1989 sales are assumed to be collected the following year and do not show up on the cash budget. The last 2 months of receivables are shown as $459,000 rather than $458,000; this brings the total collections closer to $5,500,000:

$$(\$458,000 \times 8) + (\$459,000 \times 2) = \$5,498,000$$
(Collections from credit accounts).

The $2,000 difference will be collected in the first 2 months of 1990.

The only other cash receipt shown for the company in 1989 is the $500,000 in projected loan proceeds in January. Total cash receipts then equal $958,000 for January ($458,000 in collections and the $500,000 loan), $458,000 each month thereafter through October, and $459,000 per month for November and December (accounts receivable collections only).

Total Cash Available

The total cash available for the company's monthly operations, shown as line 4 of the cash budget, is calculated by adding cash on hand at the beginning of each month (line 1) to the total cash receipts during the month (line 3).

Cash Paid Out

The cash paid out figures are estimated amounts of expenditures based on the expenses calculated for the Pearson Company's pro forma income statement. Cash budget expenditures might also be based on company-provided estimates of its proposed expenses. The cash budget for the Pearson Company itemizes eight categories of expenses: purchases, direct labor and overhead, officers' salaries, general and administrative expenses, interest, income taxes, loan principal payments, and capital purchases. Cash paid out also includes dividends, which are usually paid quarterly. However, the loan officer assumed in the company's pro forma calculations that no dividend payments would be made by the Pearson Company in 1989. Each category of cash paid out is discussed separately below.

Purchases. Inventory purchases are included on the income statement as a part of a company's cost of goods sold. In the pro forma income statement for the Pearson Company, the bank has assumed flat sales for the company and has also assumed that the company's cost of goods sold will remain at $3,850,000, unchanged from 1988. Figures provided by the company show the breakdown of this total into purchases, direct labor and overhead, and depreciation (a noncash expense). According to this breakdown (shown in Exhibit 8.2), total purchases for the year are estimated at $2,695,000, spread out evenly over the entire 12 months. This translates into purchases totaling $225,000 per month except that, as an adjustment required because of rounding, December's purchases are projected at $220,000:

$$(\$225,000 \times 11) + \$220,000 = \$2,695,000.$$

However, the actual timing of a company's payments must also be considered in creating a cash budget. The Pearson Company's pro forma balance sheet shows purchase turns averaging 57 days in 1989. This means that if purchases are to amount to approximately $225,000 per month, the company will actually pay $22,000 (about one-tenth, or 3 days' worth, of the purchases) in the first month following the purchases and $203,000 (the remainder) in the second month. *Note that in calculating cash budgets, all months are assumed to have 30 days.*

The Pearson Company ended fiscal year 1988 owing $559,000 in trade payables because it had been paying suppliers an average of 76 days after purchases. However, both the company and the bank concluded (for different reasons) during their pro forma analysis that payables will be paid in 57 days in the coming year. Therefore, the $559,000 the company owes as of the first of the year will presumably be paid in the first 57 days of January and February 1989.

To calculate the amount paid in January, the loan officer simply divides 30 days by 57 days:

$$30 \div 57 = 0.53.$$

The next step is to multiply 0.53 by $559,000, the amount owed in trade payables:

$$0.53 \times \$559,000 = \$296,000.$$

This, then, is the amount of cash projected to be paid out for purchases in January 1989. In February, the remaining portion of the year-end's accounts payable should be paid. This amount is calculated by subtracting the amount to be paid in January ($296,000) from the amount owed ($559,000):

$$\$559,000 - \$296,000 = \$263,000.$$

However, in February, the Pearson Company must also pay an additional $22,000, or 3 days' worth of January's purchases:

$$\$263,000 + \$22,000 = \$285,000.$$

As of the end of February 1989, all of the accounts payable included in the company's 1988 balance sheet will have been paid.

In March, the amount paid is the amount owed for purchases for the remaining 27 days of January ($203,000) and 3 days of February ($22,000). Since the Pearson Company is expected to make purchases totaling $225,000 per month, this is also the amount of cash expected to be paid out each month from March through December 1989.

Direct labor and overhead. Labor and overhead expenses are included on the income statement as part of a manufacturer's cost of goods sold. Nevertheless, they are typically shown as a separate account on the company's cash budget. Again, since the loan officer is assuming that the company's sales and its cost of goods sold will be the same in 1989 as in 1988, the lender uses the figures provided by the company (as shown in Exhibit 8.2) which show that direct labor and overhead totaled $1,035,000 in 1988. This equals about $86,000 per month, except that a rounding adjustment in December brings that month's figure to $89,000.

$$(\$86,000 \times 11) + \$89,000 = \$1,035,000.$$

Officers' salaries. The next category of cash paid out on the cash budget is officers' salaries. According to the bank's pro forma income statement (as summarized in Exhibit 8.2), officers' salaries are also expected to remain unchanged from 1988. The $165,000 total for the year includes monthly salaries totaling $13,000 and a cash bonus of $9,000 payable in December. Thus the cash budget shows officers' salaries at $13,000 per month, except in December when they total $22,000.

$$(\$13,000 \times 12) + (\$9,000 \text{ bonus}) = \$165,000.$$

Selling expenses. The next category of cash paid out on the cash budget is selling expenses. The bank's 1989 pro forma income statement has projected selling expenses to remain unchanged from 1988 at $220,000. However, the pro forma balance sheet shows accruals as of year-end 1989 to be $5,000 above 1988 levels ($67,000 versus $62,000, as shown by Exhibit 8.3). Since the loan officer knows from past experience that the Pearson Company's accruals primarily represent sales commissions, the loan officer reduces the company's projected cash selling expenses from $220,000 to $215,000. The cash budget shows this as cash disbursements of $18,000 for the first 11 months of the year and $17,000 in December (again, a balancing mechanism required because of rounding):

$$(\$18,000 \times 11) + \$17,000 = \$215,000.$$

General and administrative expenses. In the pro forma income statement, the loan officer has projected the company's general and administrative expenses at $770,000 in 1989, considerably higher than projected by management in its pro forma income statement. The loan officer assumes these will be cash expenses with the exception of depreciation. Thus, $120,000 of depreciation (recall that the other $120,000 in depreciation was included in cost of goods sold) must be subtracted from $770,000 to arrive at $650,000 in cash expenses to be paid monthly. The cash budget shows entries of $54,000 per month for 11 months plus $56,000 in December (for rounding purposes):

$$(\$54,000 \times 11) + \$56,000 = \$650,000.$$

Often a company will list individual expense categories comprising its general and administrative expenses—such as operating expenses, supplies, repairs, travel, entertainment, accounting, and utilities. The cash budget for the Pearson Company, however, shows only the monthly totals.

Interest expense. The bank's pro forma income statement projects $144,000 as the Pearson Company's interest expense in 1989 based on existing and projected term debt. This equals $12,000 per month of interest payments. If interest were due quarterly or semiannually (rather than monthly), it would be shown as cash paid out in those months when it fell due.

Income taxes. The bank's pro forma income statement projects 1989 income taxes of $119,000. However, since the company is required to pay only 90 percent of its estimated tax liability for the year, the bank assumes the company will make quarterly payments totaling $107,000 ($119,000 × .90) or payments of $27,000 in April, June, and September, and $26,000 in December (again, because of rounding). In addition, the company's balance sheet shows $54,000 in current-year income taxes remaining unpaid as of December 1988 (as shown in Exhibit 8.3). This amount, expected to be paid in March 1989, is also included in the cash budget as an income tax payment. Thus the total amount of income tax projected to be paid in 1989 is $161,000.

Cash Paid Out—Subtotal

The monthly subtotal of cash paid out represents the amount of cash projected to be paid for operations during 1989 not including projected payments of loan principal and capital purchases. The amount of cash to be paid out during the year is projected to total $5,201,000.

Loan principal payments. The Pearson Company's pro forma balance sheet (as summarized in Exhibit 8.3) shows current maturities of long-term debt in 1989 at $310,000 (based on the assumption that the company's current loan request will be approved). For cash budgeting purposes, the loan officer assumes level principal payments throughout the year, or monthly payments of about $26,000 per month (except $25,000 in November and December due to rounding):

$$(\$26,000 \times 10) + (\$25,000 \times 2) = \$310,000.$$

Capital purchases. The company's only projected capital purchase for 1989 is the casting mold scheduled to be purchased at a cost of $600,000 in January (assuming the loan request is approved).

Total Cash Paid Out

The loan officer has now accounted for all the Pearson Company's anticipated cash expenditures for the year. The company's projected cash outlays, listed for each month on line 6, total $6,111,000.

Cash Position

This line of the cash budget, calculated by subtracting total cash paid out (line 6) from total cash available (line 4), shows that the Pearson Company's cash outflows will exceed its cash inflows plus cash on hand in January by $57,000.

Minimum Ending Cash

The Pearson Company states that the minimum amount of cash it needs for ongoing operations is $125,000. This figure is entered for each month on line 8 since any excess cash will be used to repay the company's accumulated short-term debt.

Additional Funding Requirement

This is the amount of cash the company needs to maintain its stated minimum cash position of $125,000. It is calculated by subtracting the company's cash position (line 7) from its minimum cash requirement (line 6). It shows that the company needs to borrow $182,000 immediately to maintain its cash position at $125,000 during January. Lesser amounts of cash will also be required periodically throughout the year—for example, $36,000 in February and $30,000 in March. Amounts shown in parentheses—such as ($24,000) for May—indicate repayments of previous months' funding requirements.

Cumulative Funding Requirement

The cumulative amount of funding required to maintain the company's minimum cash position is calculated by adding the cumulative funding requirement from the previous month to the additional funding requirement for the current month. For the first month of the cash budget—in this case, January—the cumulative funding requirement is equal to the additional funding requirement for that month ($182,000). The cash budget shows that by April the Pearson Company will have had to borrow a total of $251,000. From thereon, as the company's cash position improves and it is able to begin repaying the bank, its cumulative funding requirement decreases to a low of $135,000 in November. Thus, whereas the cumulative funding requirement at year-end if $148,000 (this differs from the $149,000 shown as notes payable to banks on the bank-prepared pro forma balance sheet because of rounding error), the company's permanent funding requirement is actually $135,000, according to the cash budget projections.

RECONCILIATION OF PRO FORMA AND CASH BUDGET FIGURES

At this point, the loan officer should verify that the cash budget remains consistent with the pro forma income statement and balance sheet. This is accomplished by checking the key accounts affected by the cash budget.

In line with the pro forma income statement created by the loan officer (as summarized in Exhibit 8.2), the cash budget includes revenues of approximately $5,500,00. Because the bank has predicted flat sales and the same average collection period for accounts receivable, the company's collections from credit accounts should approximate the company's projected sales of $5,500,000. The cash budget and the pro forma income statement both show officers' salaries totaling $165,000, selling expenses of $220,000 (less accruals of $5,000), general and administrative expenses of $770,000 (less depreciation of $120,000), interest expense of $144,000, and estimated income taxes of $119,000 expensed as follows: $107,000 (paid in quarterly installments) and $12,000 accrued but unpaid at year-end (an amount carried on the pro forma balance sheet as current-year income taxes).

In line with the cash account of the company's pro forma balance sheet (as summarized in Exhibit 8.3), the cash budget shows a minimum cash requirement of $125,000. Accounts receivable, which are expected to remain at $916,000 throughout the year (turning 6.0 times, or every 61 days), represent 2 months of sales; the company's purchases-to-payables ratio on the pro forma balance sheet is 6.4, or 57 days. Thus the company can anticipate having 57 days of trade accounts payable as of December 31, 1989, totaling $421,000—or a daily payables rate of $7,386 ($421,000 ÷ 57). This differs slightly from the daily purchase rate for the year of $7,486 ($2,695,000 ÷ 360). The difference results from rounding and the use of a 365-day year for the pro forma calculations versus a 360-day year for the cash budget calculations. Because the company's accruals are projected to increase by $5,000 in 1989 from a level of $62,000 at year-end 1988, cash selling expenses are reduced by that amount. Current maturities of long-term debt have been projected at $310,000 for 1989. And the balance sheet shows $12,000 for current-year income taxes; this is the amount of 1989 tax expense remaining to be paid in 1990.

INTERPRETATION OF THE CASH BUDGET

Although the Pearson Company does not have a seasonal sales cycle, the cash budget shows the company's borrowing need peaking at $251,000 (the cumulative funding requirement for April 1989), significantly more than the $149,000 in additional debt that was calculated by the loan officer in the notes payable to banks account on the pro forma balance sheet. Recall, too, that company management had identified *no* funding need beyond the $500,000 loan for the purchase of the casting mold. This cash flow inadequacy results from the company's having to make a $100,000 cash down payment for the new piece of equipment and the accelerated payment of its trade purchases—an average of 19 days faster than in the previous year—in order to bring the company's payment record in line with the newly expected payables turns.

Thus the cash budget shows that the Pearson Company needs to borrow $182,000 immediately (over and above the $500,000 loan amount) and will need to borrow a total of $251,000 by April. This includes about $135,000 in permanent funding needs and $116,000 in short-term financing which will be repaid by November. Because the budget shows a low borrowing need of $135,000, this is considered to be a permanent need, while the remainder is expected to be self-liquidating.

The loan officer should now determine the interest cost associated with the needed short-term loan and add it to the interest already shown on the cash budget. The loan officer should also structure the $135,000 as long-term debt. The additional payments of interest and principal may further alter the results of the cash budget.

The Pearson Company's cash budget demonstrates the timing and magnitude of the company's interim cash needs given the assumptions provided by the bank's pro forma analysis in Chapter 7. Without the cash budget, the loan officer might well have overlooked a significant financing requirement.

■ ■ ■ ■ Identifying Seasonal Financing Needs

The Pearson Company has level sales throughout the year. For a company with seasonal sales, the cash budget is an even more critical tool of financial analysis. Seasonal financing requirements arise in response to increases in a company's inventory and accounts receivable associated with periodic peaks in sales, production, or purchasing. Such an interim need may not be apparent from a company's year-end financial statements since a true short-term need will be self-liquidating—that is, the assets being financed will convert to cash to repay debt. The company should be able to pay the interim loan during the course of an operating cycle—that is, the period during which cash converts into inventory and then receivables and, through the collection of receivables, converts back to cash. If the company cannot pay back its interim loan by converting its assets into cash during the operating cycle, its borrowing need is not short term. Since seasonal borrowing is self-liquidating, the company does not have to be profitable to repay the debt, provided its cash flow is not negative.

The monthly cash budget is an excellent tool for identifying the cause, timing, and magnitude of a company's peak borrowing needs during interim periods between fiscal year-end statements. By determining the company's period of peak borrowing needs, the loan officer can better evaluate the bank's potential exposure to loan loss. The amount and quality of the company's assets that are available to secure indebtedness or to convert into cash can be determined by constructing a pro forma balance sheet at the peak period. The balance sheet will indicate to the lender whether the borrowing is needed to support accounts receivable or inventory. This is important to the lender because each asset has a different amount of risk associated with it. The application of cash budget analysis to seasonal working capital needs is illustrated in the following example of a variety store called the Grab Bag.

Assumptions for the Grab Bag's Cash Budget
for the Year Ending January 31, 1989

Income Statement Assumptions

Sales Projection for FY 1989	$1,200,000

- Sales vary seasonally as follows: 10% of sales occur in October ($120,000); 10% in November ($120,000); 20% in December ($240,000); sales are expected to be level at $80,000 per month for the other 9 months of the year. January 1988 sales also totaled $80,000.
- Sales are 50% cash and 50% on 30-day terms.
- Sales are expected to remain flat (at 1988 levels) during the first half of 1989.

Cost of goods sold = 50% of sales	$600,000
General and administrative expenses ($42,000 per month except $46,000 in the peak selling months—October through December).	$516,000
Depreciation	$ 36,000
Taxes	(None assumed)

Balance Sheet Assumptions

Ending cash (1/31/88)	$ 62,000
Minimum cash requirement	$ 50,000
Accounts receivable turn	30 days
Inventory (1/31/88)	$160,000

- The company maintains a 4 months' supply of inventory at all times.
- Purchases represent total cost of goods sold.

Fixed assets	(No purchases anticipated)
Accounts payable (1/31/88)	$ 40,000

- All suppliers are paid promptly on 30-day terms.

CONSTRUCTION OF THE CASH BUDGET

The primary assumptions used to prepare and construct the Grab Bag's cash budget are shown in Exhibit 8.5. Exhibit 8.6 shows the cash budget resulting from these assumptions.

Cash on Hand

The cash budget for Grab Bag begins with the ending cash from its previous year ($62,000) as the amount of cash on hand in February 1988. Thereafter the cash on hand at the beginning of each month reflects the company's cash position (line 7) at the end of the preceding month except when the cash position drops below $50,000 (the company's minimum cash requirement) or when the excess cash must be used to repay previously incurred short-term debt.

Cash Receipts

According to the income statement assumptions provided by the company (Exhibit 8.5), Grab Bag's sales are highly seasonal, with 40 percent of its sales occurring in October through December. Total sales for the 1989 fiscal year (which begins in February 1988 and ends in January 1989) are expected to total $1,200,000. Since half the company's sales are cash and half are on 30-day terms, cash receipts must be divided between cash sales and collections from credit accounts. Thus, December's sales of $240,000 show up on the cash budget as $120,000 in cash receipts in December and $120,000 in collections in January.

Cash Paid Out

The company's cost of goods sold consists only of its purchases, according to the data provided by the company, as shown in Exhibit 8.5. Moreover, its cost of goods sold equals half of its sales (that is, it takes a 100 percent markup on all inventory sold)—or $600,000 for fiscal year 1989. Inventory purchases are made 4 months in advance of sales. Thus the company's purchases begin to build up in July and reach a high of $120,000 in September in preparation for its peak end-of-year sales period.

The Grab Bag categorizes all of its operating expenses as general and administrative expenses. These are expected to total $516,000 for the year. They are incurred on a fairly level basis throughout the year

Cash Budget

Grab Bag
Cash Budget for the Year Ending January 31, 1989
(in thousands of dollars)

	Feb.	Mar.	Apr.	May	June	July	Aug.	Sept.	Oct.	Nov.	Dec.	Jan.	Total
1. Cash on hand (Beginning of month)	62	60	58	56	54	52	50	50	50	50	50	68	
2. Cash receipts: Cash sales	40	40	40	40	40	40	40	40	60	60	120	40	600
Collections from credit accounts	40	40	40	40	40	40	40	40	40	60	60	120	600
3. Total cash receipts	80	80	80	80	80	80	80	80	100	120	180	160	1,200
4. Total cash available (Before cash out)(1 + 3)	142	140	138	136	134	132	130	130	150	170	230	228	
5. Cash paid out: Purchases (merchandise)	40	40	40	40	40	60	60	120	40	40	40	40	600
General and administrative expenses	42	42	42	42	42	42	42	42	46	46	46	42	516
6. Total cash paid out	82	82	82	82	82	102	102	162	86	86	86	82	1,116
7. Cash position (4 minus 6)	60	58	56	54	52	30	28	(32)	64	84	144	146	
8. Minimum ending cash ($50,000 or greater)	60	58	56	54	52	50	50	50	50	50	68	146	
9. Additional funding requirement (or repayment) (8 minus 7)	-0-	-0-	-0-	-0-	-0-	20	22	82	(14)	(34)	(76)	-0-	
10. Cumulative funding requirement	-0-	-0-	-0-	-0-	-0-	20	42	124	110	76	-0-	-0-	
Essential operating data (Noncash-flow information):													
Sales volume (dollars)	80	80	80	80	80	80	80	80	120	120	240	80	
Accounts receivable (end of month)	40	40	40	40	40	40	40	40	60	60	120	40	
Inventory on hand (end of month)	160	160	160	160	180	200	280	280	260	240	160	160	
Accounts payable (end of month)	40	40	40	40	60	60	120	40	40	40	40	40	
Depreciation	3	3	3	3	3	3	3	3	3	3	3	3	

except for a small increase during the peak sales season (October through December), as shown in the cash budget.

Cash Position

The company's cash position at the end of each month equals its total cash available (line 4) minus total cash paid out (line 6). Only one month (September) does the loan officer foresee the company's outflows exceeding its inflows. However, in July and August the company's end-of-month cash position will be below its minimum cash requirement of $50,000.

Additional Funding Requirement

The cash budget shows that the Grab Bag will need short-term seasonal financing totaling $124,000 in July through September. This will enable it to purchase sufficient inventory for its end-of-year sales period. It will be able to begin paying the loan back in October and will have it completely repaid in December, according to the cash budget.

Essential Operating Data

The Grab Bag's cash budget also includes relevant non-cash-flow information on a month-to-month basis. These accrual-basis figures—sales volume, accounts receivable, inventory on hand, etc.—underlie the cash-basis figures shown in the cash budget.

INTERPRETATION OF THE CASH BUDGET

The cash budget enables the loan officer to identify an important interim funding need that would not be apparent from the Grab Bag's year-end pro forma balance sheet (which should show a cash account of $146,000 at year-end—well above its $50,000 minimum cash requirement). According to line 9 of the cash budget, the loan officer foresees no borrowing need until July, at which time the company begins building up its inventory for the October to December sales season. In July, August, and September, the Grab Bag will have to borrow $20,000, $22,000, and $82,000, respectively—$124,000 total—to maintain its minimum cash requirement of $50,000. The cash budget shows that the Grab Bag's total cumulative borrowing needs will total $124,000 in

September, by which time its cash flow will be sufficient to begin repaying the short-term loan. The loan will be completely repaid by December.

The company's essential operating data at the bottom of the cash budget shows projected inventory reaching a high of $280,000 in August and September. This is $120,000 greater than the company's "normal" inventory level of $160,000. The cash budget shows inventory beginning to sell at a faster pace in October, but the company's receivables also mount. At this point, the company's total accounts receivable and inventory are projected to be $120,000 greater than at normal levels. However, October's projected increase in cash sales also becomes available to begin reducing the company's short-term loan. In December (the month with highest sales), inventory is quickly reduced and receivables are projected to reach a yearly high of $120,000. The combination of more cash sales, conversion of larger amounts of receivables (reflecting high November sales), and lower inventory is expected to generate enough cash in December to completely repay the loan.

This illustrates the principle of a self-liquidating seasonal loan and how the lender's risk changes from lending for inventory to providing funds for accounts receivable increases.

▋▋▋▋▋▋▋ Summary

The monthly cash budget is a very important tool of financial analysis which helps the loan officer identify the cause, timing, and magnitude of a company's peak borrowing needs during interim periods that may not show up on its pro forma financial statements. For example, financing required to purchase inventory for seasonal sales increases can be identified. In addition, the company's ability to repay the additional debt requirement will be apparent.

Cash budgets are also used to determine whether borrowing needs are truly short-term or whether they represent permanent funding needs. In self-liquidating loans, the assets being financed are converted to cash to repay the debt. In longer term loans, the debt is repaid from the profits of the business. Thus a cash budget can help lenders avoid the pitfall of inadvertently lending for the short term when the borrower actually has a long-term need.

A cash budget also helps the loan officer monitor a company's cash flow and can serve as an early warning signal that the company's cash flow is less than expected, which may affect its ability to repay a loan.

The timing of cash flows relative to sales and accounts receivable, inventory purchases and accounts payable, and other expenses are crucial components of a company's cash flow and must be taken into consideration in constructing a cash budget. These and other assumptions must be in line with the company's past performance and with management's plans for the year (such as plans to make capital purchases, to tighten up on its credit policies, or to carry more or less inventory). In addition, the lender's assumptions used in constructing the cash budget should be consistent with its analysis of the company's pro forma financial statements.

Questions

1. What is a monthly *cash budget*, and how is it used in financial analysis?

2. Why is a cash budget prepared on a cash, rather than an accrual, basis?

3. Why is a cash budget a good supplement to pro forma financial statements?

4. How is depreciation expense taken into consideration in preparing a cash budget?

5. How are cash budgets useful in determining a company's interim funding needs? How are seasonal loans repaid?

Exercises

E-1

A company's cash balance at the beginning of January 1989 is $193,200. The company expects to collect 50 percent of its receivables during the month of sale, 40 percent in the following month, and the remainder in the second month after sale. Purchases of raw material are estimated at 70 percent of the revenue billed for the next month. Half the purchases will be paid for during the month of purchase and the other half in the following month. Various operating costs amounting to $92,000 will be paid monthly. Bank loans will be obtained if necessary to maintain a minimum cash balance of $180,000.

Prepare a cash budget for the company for the first 6 months of 1989 using the following projected sales figures:

1988	
November	$368,000
December	414,000

1989	
January	$368,000
February	414,000
March	460,000
April	598,000
May	736,000
June	828,000
July	920,000

E-2

Based on the cash budget constructed in the preceding exercise, will bank loans be required to maintain the desired minimum balance? If so, when and how much will the company have to borrow?

E-3

Again, based on the cash budget, will the company have the ability to repay any borrowed funds?

9 Other Analytical Techniques

Learning Objectives

After studying this chapter, you should be able to

- describe and apply working investment analysis calculations
- explain and apply the concept of sustainable growth
- explain and apply sensitivity analysis in projecting future results from best to worst situations
- calculate break-even points and understand their use in financial analysis
- apply the concept of operating leverage in financial analysis

▌▐▐▌▐ ▌▐ ▌ Introduction

The techniques of financial analysis presented thus far are the basic tools of the trade. This chapter covers some more advanced techniques including the concepts of working investment analysis, sustainable growth, sensitivity analysis, break-even calculations, and operating leverage. Although these techniques are discussed only briefly here, they are invaluable to the loan officer in refining and focusing the financial analysis process. The proficient loan officer learns to select the most appropriate advanced techniques and apply them along with the standard techniques to make sound lending decisions that benefit both the customer and the bank.

▌▐▐▌▐ ▌▐ ▌ Working Investment Analysis

Working investment analysis focuses on the working assets of a company and how their growth is financed as sales grow. It provides the loan officer with a quick means of projecting the financing required when a company's working assets increase to support its growth in sales. As a company's sales grow, the base level of its working assets (accounts receivable and inventory) normally grows proportionately. Accounts payable and accruals also increase while providing the basic financing for the growing accounts receivable and inventory levels. However, that portion of working assets that is not supported by the company's payables and accruals must be financed by other sources, specifically debt or equity.

Earlier chapters have shown that the loan officer can project the financing required to support an increased working investment using pro forma statements and cash budgets. Working investment analysis is a shortcut that the loan officer can use to quickly appraise the potential financial consequences of the company's growth plans. This approach is especially useful for companies with a heavy investment in accounts receivable and inventory. It is not, however, intended to replace the more accurate and detailed analytical procedures already discussed.

A company's working investment represents the difference between its working assets and its working liabilities as illustrated by the following equations:

Working assets = Accounts receivable + Inventory.
Working liabilities = Accounts payable + Accruals.
Working investment = Working assets − Working liabilities.

A company's working investment is typically expressed as a percentage of sales. Assuming that the relationship between sales and inventory, accounts receivable, and accounts payable remains fairly stable, the working investment percentage can be applied to the company's projected sales levels to determine the projected amount of working investment and the additional financing required.

The following information, obtained from a hypothetical company's most recent financial statements, is used to demonstrate the working investment calculations:

Sales	$1,000,000
Accounts receivable	$ 100,000
Inventory	$ 200,000
Accounts payable	$ 80,000
Accruals	$ 20,000
Net profit margin (Net profit ÷ sales)	2%

This company's working investment is calculated as follows:

Accounts receivable	$ 100,000
Inventory	+ 200,000
Total working assets	$ 300,000
Accounts payable	$ 80,000
Accruals	+ 20,000
Total working liabilities	$ 100,000
Total working assets	$ 300,000
Total working liabilities	− 100,000
Working investment	$ 200,000

The company's working investment expressed as a percentage of sales is calculated as follows:

$$\text{Working investment percentage} = \frac{\text{Working investment}}{\text{Sales}} \times 100$$

$$= \frac{\$200,000}{\$1,000,000} \times 100$$

$$= 0.20 \times 100$$
$$= 20\%.$$

If the company anticipates a sales increase of 20 percent in the next fiscal year (that is, total sales of $1,200,000), the additional working investment that will be required can be calculated as follows:

$$\text{New working investment} = \text{Projected sales} \times \text{Working investment percentage}$$
$$= \$1,200,000 \times 20\%$$
$$= \$240,000.$$

The company will need an additional $40,000 in working investment for its projected 20 percent increase in sales:

New working investment	$ 240,000
Previous working investment	− 200,000
Increase in working investment	$ 40,000

If it is assumed that the company's net cash flow is represented only by net profit (since new fixed asset expansion will be supported by depreciation), then the company's net capital need can be calculated as follows:

$$\text{Cash flow} = \text{Net profit margin} \times \text{Projected sales}$$
$$= 2\% \times \$1,200,000$$
$$= \$24,000.$$

$$\text{Net capital need} = \text{Increase in working investment} - \text{Cash flow}$$
$$= \$40,000 - \$24,000$$
$$= \$16,000.$$

This assumes that the company has not already earmarked its profits to reduce existing debt or to purchase capital expenditures, but that the profits are available to support the increased working investment requirement. If this is the case, a net capital need of $16,000 remains that must be financed.

This quick calculation of a company's projected net capital need in support of increased sales helps the loan officer compare the company's borrowing requirements with available financing alternatives. The financing alternatives are increasing bank debt, injecting equity into the company, increasing the percentage of working investment in accounts payable, or decreasing the working investment in accounts receivable and inventory. To determine the effect of different scenarios, the loan officer can vary the assumptions used. It should be emphasized that working investment calculations cannot replace pro forma statements and cash budgets; they are, however, useful in providing a rough measure that can quickly and easily predict the consequences of a company's growth or decline in sales on several key balance sheet components.

▪▪▪▪ Sustainable Growth

A company's growth depends on both its ability to fund increasing asset requirements and the availability of adequate equity to support the company's increasing levels of debt. Sustainable growth measures a company's ability to expand its sales assuming that profitability, asset requirements, and dividend payout ratios remain constant with sales and that the company maintains its ratio of debt to equity at existing levels. The calculation of sustainable growth is based on four underlying assumptions:

- To increase sales, total assets must increase.
- Increased assets are financed by retained earnings (net profits) and external debt.
- Net profit margins are constant.
- The dividend payout ratio (if any) is constant.

Using these assumptions, a company's sustainable growth rate can be derived using this formula:

$$g = \frac{p(1-d)\ (1+L)}{t - p(1-d)\ (1+L)}$$

where p = Net profit margin (Net profit ÷ Sales)
t = Assets ÷ Sales
L = Debt-to-worth ratio (Debt ÷ Net worth)
d = Dividend payout ratio (Dividends ÷ Net profit)
g = Sustainable growth rate.

To illustrate, assume that a company has $500,000 in assets, $1,000,000 in sales, a debt-to-worth ratio of 1.0, a dividend payout ratio of 0, and a net profit margin of 2 percent. Using the sustainable growth formula, the following calculation results:

$$g = \frac{0.02(1-0)\ (1+1)}{0.5 - 0.02(1-0)\ (1+1)}$$

$$= \frac{0.02(1)\ (2)}{0.5 - 0.02(1)\ (2)}$$

$$= \frac{0.04}{0.46}$$

$$= 8.7\%$$

where p = 0.02
t = $500,000 ÷ $1,000,000 = 0.5
L = 1.0
d = 0.

A sustainable growth rate of 8.7 percent means that the company can increase its sales by 8.7 percent and still maintain its current debt-to-worth ratio. However, assume the company is projecting a sales increase of 25 percent. Unless higher financial leverage (an increased debt-to-worth ratio) is acceptable, other adjustments would have to be made by reducing the company's assets-to-sales ratio, by improving the net profit margin, or by injecting equity into the company.

The equation can be solved for L (leverage, or debt-to-worth ratio) by using the following formula:

$$L = \frac{gt}{p(1+g)} - 1.$$

The effect on leverage of a 25 percent increase in sales can be calculated simply by plugging the appropriate values into the formula as follows:

$$L = \frac{0.25(0.5)}{0.02\ (1+0.25)} - 1$$

$$= \frac{0.125}{0.025} - 1$$

$$= 4.$$

To sustain a 25 percent growth rate, the company's debt-to-worth ratio would have to be 4:1 rather than the desired ratio of 1:1.

Sustainable growth incorporates assumptions about the company's total assets and debt-to-worth ratio not contained in the working investment formula. These assumptions are useful for a company whose fixed assets must increase proportionally with sales, although the result will be misleading if no direct correlation exists between sales and total assets. The formula also demonstrates the effect of growth on the company's financial leverage—which is usually one of the primary constraints on growth. Working investment and sustainable growth calculations can be used together effectively to project a company's capacity for growth and the amount of debt financing required to support that growth.

■ ■ ■ ■ Sensitivity Analysis

Sensitivity analysis enables the loan officer to test the validity of financial projections by analyzing a range of scenarios, including the "worst case." It is readily apparent that the validity of financial projections used in pro formas and cash budgets depends on the loan officer's underlying assumptions about the company. Deriving appropriate assumptions is complicated by several factors, including the following:

- Each company has particular characteristics that contribute to its vulnerabilities.

- Projections are based on imperfect information about an uncertain future.

- The combinations and permutations involved in deriving assumptions can be extensive.

Yet the stakes are high—both for the borrower and the lender. Despite the difficulty of accurately projecting a company's future financial stability, this is the basis upon which loans must be committed. Previous chapters have stressed the importance of using conservative projections. Sensitivity analysis is another means of hedging against uncertain projections.

Sensitivity analysis enables the loan officer to see how changing key assumptions would potentially affect the company's financial results. For example, management's sales projection could be reduced by 20 percent to determine the possible downside vulnerability of the company. A lender's projections are usually based on the *most likely* scenario. A more conservative approach is to look at a *worst-case* scenario. The operating parameters are then established between the most pessimistic and most likely scenarios, and probabilities and consequences can be applied along the scale. If even the worst-case scenario results in acceptable financial performance, the lending decision is easy. However, if the results of a worst-case scenario are disastrous, the loan officer must make additional assumptions to determine how bad the situation can become before the company (and the loan) will be adversely affected. Other techniques presented in this chapter using working investment, break-even points, and sustainable growth analysis can help the loan officer in this assessment.

To determine a worst-case scenario, the loan officer must select those factors that, based on past experience, have made the company most vulnerable. For example, companies with cyclical demands for their products typically experience a significant reduction in sales during a recession. The percentage decrease in a company's sales in past recessions could serve as an indication of the potential downside effects and could be used as the basis for a worst-case analysis. Obviously, making such projections for a company with numerous areas of vulnerability is difficult and suggests the need for significant offsetting strengths.

AN EXAMPLE OF SENSITIVITY ANALYSIS

Exhibit 9.1 demonstrates how sensitivity analysis can be applied to working investment analysis to determine the range of possibilities between "most likely" and "worst-case" scenarios for the Duffy Paper Company. This set of scenarios was chosen because the loan officer has concluded that the company's greatest vulnerability is too rapid growth. Rapid growth requires increased financing to support the increase in working assets. The key assumption of the scenarios for Duffy Paper Company, then, concerns the rate of sales growth and the company's ability to control working assets, liabilities, and profitability.

Scenario 1 of Exhibit 9.1 presents management's projections for the company. The Duffy Paper Company has grown rapidly in recent years, with sales increases of 25 to 30 percent per year. Management anticipates a slowing of this growth accompanied by a greater emphasis on financial controls. Thus, accounts receivable and inventory turns are expected to decrease from the existing levels of 43 and 118 days, respectively. Management also predicts that accounts payable turnover will decrease to at least 45 days (probably of necessity since the industry average is 30 days).

Scenarios 2 and 3 show the range of performance the loan officer thinks is most likely to occur, while Scenario 4 presents the loan officer's estimate of the worst case. This worst-case scenario is based on accounts receivable and inventory turns remaining close to current levels while accounts payable are considerably reduced (as the result of pressure throughout the industry). The worst-case scenario also includes substantial sales growth due to continuing market demand and very conservative estimates of profitability (0.75 percent profit margin compared to a current profit margin of 1.25 percent).

These four scenarios result in widely varying financing requirements—ranging from $181,280 for Scenario 1 to $307,102 for Scenario 4. Since the loan officer anticipates the company's performance will be in the range of Scenarios 2 and 3, indicating a total financing

Most Likely to Worst-Case Scenarios

Duffy Paper Company
Financial Projections for 1989

	Scenario			
	1	2	3	4
	Management's Projections	"Most Likely" Range		"Worst-Case" Scenario
Sales	$936,000	$975,000	$1,014,000	$1,053,000
Accounts receivable (average collection period)	100,000 (39)	111,000 (42)	125,000 (45)	130,000 (45)
Inventory (days inventory)	200,000 (111)	220,000 (118)	230,000 (118)	240,000 (118)
Accounts payable (days payable)	80,000 (45)	70,000 (37)	60,000 (31)	50,000 (25)
Accruals	20,000	15,000	10,000	5,000
Working investment	200,000	246,000	285,000	315,000
Net profit (margin)	18,720 (2%)	14,625 (1.5%)	10,140 (1%)	7,898 (.75%)
Financing required	$181,280	$231,375	$ 274,860	$ 307,102

need of $231,375 to $274,860, the loan officer would perform an additional analysis addressing the company's ability to handle that level of debt and the potential downside protection if the worst-case scenario were realized.

This example illustrates how the loan officer can selectively apply sensitivity analysis to the key factors that affect a company's most vulnerable operating assumptions. It can help to better focus the analysis and to determine the potential impact of various analytical assumptions.

▌▌▌▌ Break-Even Analysis

A company's break-even point is that level of sales at which total revenues equal total costs. Below the break-even point, the company is losing money. At the break-even point, the company has neither a profit nor a loss; its net income is zero. It also is unable to repay any current maturities of long-term debt. The break-even point is affected by three factors: fixed costs, variable costs, and selling price.

FIXED VS. VARIABLE COSTS

A company's costs that remain constant and do not vary with increases or decreases in sales or production levels are called *fixed costs*. Examples of fixed costs include property taxes, rent, insurance, salaries of office staff and executives, utilities, maintenance costs, and interest and principal payments. Although payments of loan principal are not shown as an expense on the income statement, it is treated as a fixed cost in break-even analysis. Utility companies, airlines, and manufacturing companies with large production facilities usually have a high proportion of fixed costs. Exhibit 9.2 illustrates that fixed costs remain constant regardless of the company's production or sales level.

A company's costs that vary relative to its level of sales or production are called *variable costs*. Examples of variable costs include purchases of raw material (for a manufacturer) or of inventory (for a retailer or wholesaler), hourly employee wages, and sales commissions. Service and other labor-intensive companies usually have high variable costs. Exhibit 9.3 illustrates that variable costs rise as the production level or sales level increases.

EXHIBIT 9.2 ■■■■■■■■■■■■■■■■■■■■■■■■■■■■■■■■

Fixed Costs

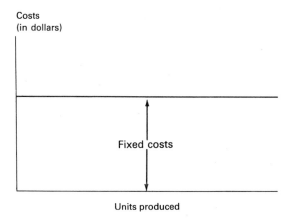

EXHIBIT 9.3 ■■■■■■■■■■■■■■■■■■■■■■■■■■■■■■■■

Variable Costs

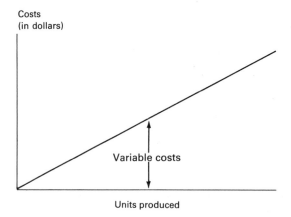

SIMPLE BREAK-EVEN ANALYSIS

To illustrate the impact of fixed costs, variable costs, and selling price on a company's break-even point, consider Pat's Flashlight Company. A young entrepreneur started selling flashlights out of her home. Flashlights were purchased for 75 cents and resold for $1.00. The cost of the flashlights is a variable cost since the total cost is proportional to the number of flashlights bought (100 flashlights cost 100 times as much as 1 flashlight). Since there are no fixed costs associated with the venture, the company has exceeded its break-even point with the sale of one unit; 25 percent of every sale is net income. This is also the company's *contribution margin*, which is defined as that portion of the sales available to cover fixed costs and to produce net income. It is calculated as follows:

Selling price per unit	$1.00
Variable cost per unit	0.75
Contribution margin per unit	$0.25

Now suppose that sales improve dramatically and Pat has to hire a part-time secretary for $5,000 per year. This is a fixed cost (since it does not vary with the company's sales) that can be covered by 25 cents of each sales dollar (the company's contribution margin). The company must now sell 20,000 flashlights to reach its break-even point. This is calculated as follows:

$$\frac{\text{Fixed costs}}{\text{Contribution margin}} = \text{Break-even point (units)} \times \text{Selling price per unit}$$
$$= \text{Break-even point (dollar amount of sales)}$$

$$\frac{\$5,000}{0.25} = 20,000 \text{ units} \times \$1 \text{ per unit} = \$20,000.$$

Pat soon needs more space to store flashlights and handle correspondence and rents a building for $1,000 per year (another fixed cost). The company's fixed costs are now $6,000 per year, further increasing the break-even point. The company must now sell 24,000 flashlights to reach the break-even point. This is calculated as follows (using the same formula as before):

$$\frac{\$6,000}{0.25} = 24,000 \text{ units} \times \$1 \text{ per unit} = \$24,000.$$

As sales grow, Pat hires a commissioned salesperson so that she can stay in the office filling orders and managing shipments. The salesperson is paid 5 percent on all sales (a variable cost). Variable costs are now 80 cents per unit. This reduces the company's contribution margin from 25 cents on each flashlight sold to 20 cents and further increases the break-even point. Now 30,000 flashlights must be sold to break even. This is calculated as follows:

$$\frac{\$6,000}{0.20} = 30,000 \text{ units} \times \$1 \text{ per unit} = \$30,000.$$

As sales continue to grow, the company begins selling to larger stores and encounters greater competition. To meet the competition, the company lowers its price from $1 to 90 cents. This further reduces the company's contribution margin, from 20 cents to 10 cents, and greatly increases the break-even point (calculated as follows):

$$\frac{\$6,000}{0.10} = 60,000 \text{ units} \times \$.90 \text{ per unit} = \$54,000.$$

This sequence of events demonstrates how fixed costs, variable costs, and selling price all influence a company's break-even point. As shown, the break-even point is derived by dividing the company's total fixed costs by the contribution margin. The contribution margin represents that portion of the sales dollar available to cover fixed costs and to produce net income.

In the preceding calculations of the break-even points for Pat's Flashlight Company, the contribution margin per unit was calculated by subtracting the variable cost per unit from the selling price per unit. The contribution margin can also be calculated as a percentage by using the concept of variable cost percentage—the ratio of variable costs to sales. The variable cost percentage is calculated either by dividing the total variable costs by total sales or by dividing the average variable cost per unit by average revenue per unit. The contribution margin is then calculated using the following formula:

$$\text{Contribution margin} = 1 - \text{Variable cost percentage}$$

where

$$\text{Variable cost percentage} = \text{Variable cost per unit} \div \text{Selling cost per unit } or$$
$$= \text{Total variable costs} \div \text{Total sales.}$$

The break-even point too can be calculated either in terms of dollar amount of sales or number of units that must be sold, using the following formulas:

$$\text{Break-even point (sales)} = \frac{\text{Fixed costs}}{1 - \text{Variable cost percentage}} = \frac{\text{Fixed costs}}{\text{Contribution margin (\%)}}$$

$$\text{Break-even point (units)} = \frac{\text{Fixed costs}}{\text{Sales price per unit} - \text{Variable cost per unit}} = \frac{\text{Fixed costs}}{\text{Contribution margin per unit}}.$$

MORE SOPHISTICATED BREAK-EVEN ANALYSIS

Another example of break-even analysis can be demonstrated with a company called the Footstep Shoe Company. Exhibit 9.4 shows a calculation of this company's break-even point in terms of dollar amount of sales and number of units (pairs of shoes) sold. It shows that the Footstep Shoe Company needs to generate almost $4 million in sales before it makes a profit. However, beyond this point the company will earn 27 cents on every dollar of sales. The break-even analysis also shows that for each pair of shoes sold beyond 99,167 units, the company's profit is $10.80.

Exhibit 9.5 graphically illustrates the Footstep Shoe Company's break-even point. It shows that the break-even point is where the company's total costs equal the company's total revenues and also shows the profit potential as sales increase above the break-even point.

The break-even point formulas allow the loan officer to solve for any one of the three variables (sales, variable costs, and fixed costs) if the other two are known. For example, the loan officer knows variable costs of the Footstep Shoe Company are 73 cents per sales dollar. Thus if sales of $3,967,000 are assumed, the level of fixed costs that the company can support and still break even is calculated as follows:

Footstep Shoe Company

Footstep Shoe Company
Break-Even Analysis

Variable costs (per sales dollar)

Direct material	$0.45
Direct labor	0.23
Selling expenses	0.05
Total (variable cost percentage)	$0.73

Product information

Variable cost per unit	$29.20
Sales price per unit	$40.00

Fixed costs

Rent	$ 14,000
Office salaries	51,000
General and administrative expenses	655,000
Suburban warehouse	156,000
Rural warehouse	195,000
Total	$1,071,000

Break-even calculations:

$$\text{Break-even point (sales)} = \frac{\$1,071,000}{1 - 0.73} = \frac{\$1,071,000}{0.27} = \$3,967,000$$

$$\text{Break-even point (units)} = \frac{\$1,071,000}{\$40 - \$29.20} = \frac{\$1,071,000}{\$10.80} = 99,167 \text{ units}$$

■ ■

Assumptions:
Sales = $3,967,000.
Variable costs = $0.73 per sales dollar
= 0.73 × $3,967,000
= $2,896,000.

Fixed costs calculation:
Fixed costs = Sales − Variable costs
= $3,967,000 − $2,896,000
= $1,071,000.

If the loan officer knows the company's fixed costs and sales level, the variable costs that the company can support and still break even can also be determined:

Assumptions:
Sales = $3,967,000.
Fixed costs = $1,071,000.

Variable costs calculation:
Variable costs = Sales − Fixed costs
= $3,967,000 − $1,071,000
= $2,896,000.

Variable cost percentage = $2,896,000 ÷ $3,967,000
= 73%.

MORE APPLICATIONS OF BREAK-EVEN ANALYSIS

Debt payment. Knowing the break-even point can be important even if it is assumed that the company will be profitable. For example, the break-even level of sales does not enable a company to repay its current maturities of term debt. Current maturities must be paid with after-tax dollars. By adjusting the current maturities for the applicable tax rate, the loan officer can derive an adjusted dollar factor that is added to the company's fixed costs to yield a break-even point that allows for debt repayment. Obviously, this break-even point assumes the company makes a profit. Depreciation is disregarded in this formula on the assumption that it is required for additional capital expenditures.

EXHIBIT 9.5 ■■■■■■■■■■■■■■■■■■■■■■■■■■■■■■■■■

**Footstep Shoe Company
Break-Even Analysis Chart**

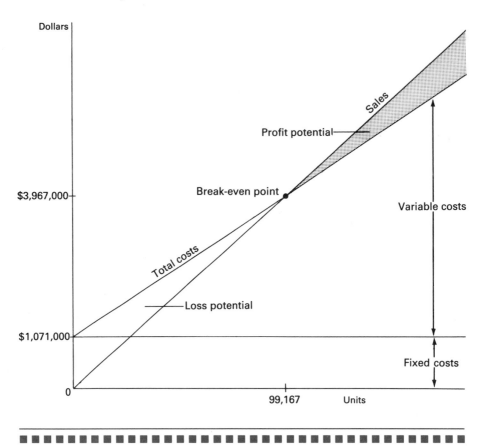

Assume that the Footstep Shoe Company has the same fixed and variable costs as shown in Exhibit 9.4 and discussed previously. If the loan officer assumes the company has $100,000 in current maturities of term debt and the company's tax rate is 40 percent, the following formula and calculations are used to adjust the current maturities for after-tax dollars.

Step 1:

$$\text{Tax-adjusted current maturities} = \frac{1}{(1 - \text{Tax rate})} \times \text{Current maturities}$$

$$= \frac{1}{(1 - 0.40)} \times \$100,000$$

$$= \frac{1}{0.60} \times \$100,000$$

$$= \$167,000.$$

Step 2:

$$\text{Break-even sales (with debt service)} = \frac{\text{Fixed costs} + \text{Tax-adjusted current maturities}}{\text{Contribution margin}}$$

$$= \frac{\$1,071,000 + \$167,000}{0.27}$$

$$= \$4,585,000.$$

Thus the break-even point for Footstep Shoe Company in terms of sales is $4,585,000, including debt service, compared to $3,967,000 without debt service.

Break-even analysis can also be applied in conjunction with a company's profit margin, dollar profit, and sales price per unit.

Profit margin. Suppose that the loan officer who is analyzing Footstep Shoe Company wants to build in a 10 percent profit margin. The contribution margin at break-even point has been calculated to be 27 percent. However, the 10 percent pretax profit margin must be treated as a variable cost. Therefore, the contribution margin becomes 27 percent minus 10 percent, or 17 percent. The new break-even point incorporating a 10 percent profit margin is then calculated as follows:

$$\text{Break-even point} = \text{Fixed costs} \div \text{Contribution margin}$$
$$= \$1,071,000 \div 0.17$$
$$= \$6,300,000.$$

Dollar profit. If the Footstep Shoe Company wants a fixed dollar profit at the end of the production year, the loan officer can treat the profit as a fixed cost. If $300,000 is management's profit target, the new break-even point is calculated as follows:

$$\text{Break-even point} = \frac{\text{Fixed costs} + \text{Annual profit}}{\text{Contribution margin}}$$

$$= \frac{\$1,071,000 + \$300,000}{0.27}$$

$$= \$5,078,000.$$

Sales price per unit. According to the product information supplied by the company (Exhibit 9.4), the variable costs for producing shoes total $29.20 per pair of shoes, and fixed costs total $1,071,000. If the Footstep Shoe Company wants to generate $300,000 in profit at a production level of 99,167 pairs of shoes (its break-even point assuming a selling price of $40 per pair of shoes), it will have to raise its selling price. The required price increase can be calculated using the following formula:

$$\text{Contribution margin} = \frac{\text{Fixed costs} + \text{Annual profit}}{\text{Product volume at break-even point}}$$

$$= \frac{\$1,071,000 + \$300,000}{99,167 \text{ units}}$$

$$= \$13.83.$$

The price of shoes must equal the company's variable costs plus its contribution margin: $29.20 + $13.83 = $43.03. Management must then determine whether the market will support a $43 pair of shoes, or whether the company's costs must be reduced to reduce the price.

APPLICATIONS OF BREAK-EVEN ANALYSIS

Break-even analysis can be very useful to financial analysis. The loan officer can use break-even analysis to test assumptions about the levels of fixed costs, variable costs, and selling price that can be supported at a company's break-even sales levels. As such, break-even analysis depends upon a realistic determination of the amount and nature of a company's costs. In summary, break-even analysis helps the loan officer and company management to

- determine the level of sales at which no profit or loss exists
- determine if the company's projected sales can support its fixed and variable costs
- determine the level of sales necessary for the company to repay debt
- determine the effect of changes in the company's cost structure or sales price on break-even sales

Finally, break-even analysis provides an important link between a company's income statement and balance sheet. Through pro forma analysis the loan officer can determine the level of assets and the amount of debt and capital required to support the break-even point for sales.

▋▋▋▋▋ Operating Leverage

Another analytical technique that is based on an understanding of a company's cost structure—fixed versus variable costs—involves an assessment of its operating leverage. The ratio of fixed costs to total costs determines a company's level of operating leverage. (Do not confuse *operating leverage* with *financial leverage* which, as seen in Chapter 6, relates to the company's debt-to-worth ratio.) As seen in the preceding discussion of break-even points, a high ratio of fixed costs to total costs implies low variable costs, which results in a high contribution margin. As sales move above the break-even point, the profits of a company with a high proportion of fixed costs (a high degree of operating leverage) increase dramatically. Since fixed costs are covered at the break-even point, the company then takes the full amount of the contribution margin (which is high) to the bottom line.

To illustrate, take a company with fixed costs of $50,000 and a variable cost percentage of 50 percent (that is, variable costs equal half of total sales). Using the formula of fixed costs divided by the contribution margin (1 minus the variable cost percentage), the break-even point is calculated as follows:

$$\text{Break-even point (sales)} \quad = \quad \frac{\$50,000}{1 - 0.50} \quad = \quad \$100,000.$$

As sales increase above $100,000, 50 cents of each additional sales dollar becomes profit. If the company's cost structure is such that it has fixed costs of $25,000 and a variable cost percentage of 75 percent, the break-even point would be the same, calculated as follows:

$$\text{Break-even point (sales)} \quad = \quad \frac{\$25,000}{1 - 0.75} \quad = \quad \$100,000.$$

However, in this case, each dollar of sales above the break-even point provides only 25 cents of profit. Clearly, a company with high operating leverage and a low variable cost percentage, as in the first example, experiences a much greater increase in profitability as sales increase than a company with low operating leverage and high variable costs.

The downside is that above the break-even point, a company with high operating leverage performs admirably; but when sales decrease below the break-even point, the company loses a significant amount on each dollar of sales—and losses mount rapidly. In the preceding example, the company with a variable cost percentage of 50 percent will lose 50 cents on each dollar if its sales are below break-even.

The effects of high and low operating leverage can be illustrated graphically, as shown in Exhibit 9.6. It is apparent that an equal increase in unit sales beyond the break-even point produces much greater profitability for the company with high operating leverage than for the company with low operating leverage. However, an equal decrease in sales volume also produces much greater losses. An understanding of operating leverage and the potential impact of sales increases and decreases on companies with different cost structures suggests the following conclusions:

EXHIBIT 9.6 ■■■■■■■■■■■■■■■■■■■■■■■■■■■■■■■■■■■

Effects of High and Low Operating Leverage

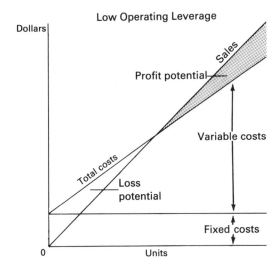

Low Operating Leverage

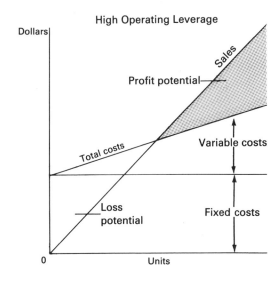

High Operating Leverage

- A company with high operating leverage and high vulnerability to decreased sales represents a great potential loan risk.

- A company with high operating leverage may be able to earn its way out of an unprofitable situation by increasing sales only moderately.

- A company with low operating leverage may be unable to earn its way out of an unprofitable situation. The additional sales required to reach the break-even point may be so great that the company's balance sheet cannot support its working asset requirements.

- A company with low operating leverage can withstand substantially greater sales decreases before becoming unprofitable.

Operating leverage is a critical concept in financial analysis because it influences profits and cash flow and thus a company's ability to grow, remain solvent, and repay debt.

Summary

The loan officer must be able to determine which of the advanced analytical techniques presented in this chapter—working investment analysis, sensitivity analysis, sustainable growth, break-even analysis, and operating leverage—are appropriate in a given situation. These techniques are usually applied along with the more basic techniques presented in the previous chapters—income statement analysis, balance sheet analysis, funds flow analysis, use of ratios, pro forma analysis, and cash budgets—to form a complete analytical picture.

Working investment analysis provides the loan officer with a quick way of roughly calculating the financial consequences of growth in a company's working assets (accounts receivable and inventory). This enables the lender to easily assess the level of financing required based on various sales projections.

Sustainable growth measures a company's ability to grow within the constraints of a given debt-to-worth ratio. It assumes that increased sales require increased fixed assets, which is not true for all companies. However, it does show the effect of growth on a company's financial leverage—which is usually a primary constraint on growth.

Sensitivity analysis allows the lender to test the validity of projections, such as those used in creating pro forma financial statements, by analyzing a range of scenarios including the "worst case." It allows the lender to focus on a company's primary areas of vulnerability (such as too rapid growth) to see how changed assumptions would affect the company's financial performance.

Break-even analysis is based on an understanding of fixed costs and variable costs. A company's break-even point, which can be expressed either in terms of dollar amount of sales or number of units sold, is that level of operations at which a company has a net income of zero—no profit and no loss. In break-even calculations, the contribution margin is that portion of sales available to cover fixed costs and to produce net income. One important use of break-even analysis is to determine what level of sales is necessary to enable the company to repay its term debt.

Operating leverage is also concerned with a company's cost mix (fixed versus variable costs). A company with high operating leverage (a high ratio of fixed costs to total costs) shows large increases in profits as sales move beyond the break-even point. However, a company with high operating leverage that is vulnerable to decreased sales represents a high credit risk.

The loan officer's proficiency in using these more advanced techniques will increase only with experience. Thus the various formulas and calculations presented in this chapter should not be regarded as useful only in unusual circumstances. Rather, they should be used routinely to further the scope of financial analysis. This will enable the loan officer to become comfortable using them and, in time, to judge which techniques are useful in a given situation.

* * *

This text provides a solid foundation in the various steps of financial analysis that must underlie any lending decision. The loan officer should not, however, expect to become proficient in financial analysis on the basis of the materials presented in this text alone. Rather, the basic skills learned here must be honed through diligent application, further study, and practical experience. In addition, many other skills that are crucial in commercial lending, such as structuring and negotiating loans, must also be acquired. Only with this breadth of knowledge and experience can the loan officer expect to make sound lending decisions that will benefit both the bank and those companies seeking financing.

Questions

1. Describe working investment analysis using the formulas for working assets and working liabilities.

2. How is the working investment percentage used in financial analysis?

3. Explain how the concept of sustainable growth is used in financial analysis.

4. List the four basic assumptions that underlie the analysis of sustainable growth.

5. Explain how the concept of sensitivity analysis is used as a part of financial analysis.

6. Describe the significance of the worst-case analysis in sensitivity analysis.

7. Explain the meaning and significance of a company's break-even point.

8. What factors influence a company's break-even point?

9. Define fixed costs, variable costs, and contribution margin.

10. Give the formulas for the break-even point for sales and the break-even point for product volume in units.

11. Describe the use of break-even analysis in evaluating a profitable company.

12. Describe the cost structure of a company with high operating leverage.

13. Compare the potential effect on earnings of a sales decline for companies with high and low operating leverage.

Exercises

E-1

Calculate the working investment and the working investment percentage for a company using the following information:

Sales	$2,000,000
Accounts receivable	$150,000
Inventory	$250,000
Accounts payable	$100,000
Accruals	$30,000
Net profit margin	3%

E-2

Using the information from Exercise E-1 and assuming the company anticipates a 25 percent sales increase, what is the additional permanent equity or debt requirement to fund its increased working investment?

E-3

Calculate and compare the financing required for increased working investment using the following operating information for the current year and projections for the coming year:

Operating Information from 1988 Financial Statements

Sales	$1,000,000
Accounts receivable	$150,000
Accounts receivable turn	54 days
Inventory	$100,000
Inventory turn	72 days
~~Accruals~~	~~$80,000~~
Net profit margin	2%
Accruals	30,000
A/P	80,000

Range of Projections for 1989

	1	2	3
Sales growth	25%	20%	15%
Accounts receivable turn	45 days	50 days	60 days
Inventory turn	60 days	70 days	75 days
Accounts payable	$80,000	$90,000	$100,000
Accruals	$40,000	$50,000	$20,000
Net profit margin	2.0%	2.5%	3.0%

E-4

Calculate a company's sustainable growth using the following information. If sales are expected to increase 30 percent during the next fiscal year, what will be the resulting leverage (debt-to-worth ratio)?

Assets	$300,000
Sales	$750,000
Total debt	$200,000
Dividend payout ratio	20%
Net profit margin	3%

E-5

A company has a vacant plant equipped sufficiently to produce a number of different products. Fixed costs for this plant are $250,000 a year. The company is considering using this plant to manufacture a new product that will sell for $10 each and has variable costs for materials, labor, overhead, and other expenses of $7.50 per unit. Management is confident that the market for this product is 2 million units per year. Physical capacity of the plant is 15,000 units per month or 180,000 units per year. Answer the following questions:

a. What is the company's break-even point in terms of dollars of sales and number of units sold?

b. With production and sales at capacity, what would the company's pretax profit be?

c. If the company wants to make a 10 percent profit margin (pretax), what is the minimum number of units that must be sold?

d. What is the minimum number of units that must be sold if the company wants to realize a profit of $150,000?

e. Assume the company has the same fixed and variable costs as described. However, in addition, the company will have $20,000 in current maturities of term debt due for a piece of equipment that must be purchased for production of the product. Assume that the company's tax rate is 40 percent. How does this affect the break-even point?

E-6

To determine the potential effects of changes in a company's operating leverage (the proportion of fixed costs to total costs), calculate profit or loss for the company described in the previous exercise, assuming sales of 150,000 units and 50,000 units. Use the following assumptions:

Fixed costs	$250,000
Variable costs	$7.50 per unit
Selling price	$10.00 per unit
Break-even point	$250,000 ÷ 2.50 =
	100,000 units or $1,000,000

a. Now change the company's cost structure as follows: fixed costs equal $350,000 and variable costs equal $6.50 per unit. Again calculate the profit or loss resulting from sales of 150,000 units and 50,000 units.

b. From this exercise, what can you conclude about the effects of increased operating leverage on profitability?

Appendix: A Case Study

Learning Objectives

After studying this appendix, you should be able to

- carry out in sequential order the various steps in a comprehensive financial analysis
- understand the importance of conducting a financial analysis as efficiently as possible without overanalyzing
- see clearly that credit decisions often rest ultimately on the loan officer's subjective interpretation of the technically manipulated data

▌▐▐▐▐▐▐ Introduction

The final section of the text is a case study demonstrating a comprehensive financial analysis of a commercial loan applicant—the Alpha Company. The case study is used to review and illustrate the efficient use of the various analytical tools presented in this text. Thus the loan officer first gathers background materials relating to the company and its industry before proceeding with an analysis of the company's past performance using a common-sized comparative income statement and balance sheet and a funds flow statement supplied by Alpha Company management. The lender then considers the company's future performance as projected by a company-provided pro forma income statement and balance sheet and cash budget. The loan officer next prepares new pro forma financial statements and a revised cash budget as part of the sensitivity analysis of the company, and also analyzes the company's operating leverage and its implications. All of these analytical techniques together help the lender assess the company's financial condition and creditworthiness and reach a conclusion concerning its request for additional financing.

One important reason for presenting this case study is to help the beginning loan officer learn to conduct a financial analysis as efficiently as possible. This entails gathering the facts, interpreting them, and reaching a conclusion with as little wasted effort as possible. Among other things, this means selecting the appropriate analytical techniques and not overanalyzing. Although this is something that requires experience and practice, there are five factors that should be taken into consideration in determining the extent of analysis that is appropriate:

- the firm's relative strengths and weaknesses
- the amount of financing involved
- the level of uncertainty about the future
- the potential impact of anticipated changes
- the skill of the analyst

The case study presented here is closely based on an actual situation, and the student is encouraged to step into the role of the loan officer and to come to his or her own decision as to whether the bank should extend the Alpha Company additional credit—and if so, under what terms—

before reading the actual outcome of the case. This will enable the student to test his or her own judgment and to see to what extent the final lending decision is often a subjective one—that financial analysis does not necessarily result in an obvious "right" answer.

■ ■ ■ ■ Case Background

In November 1988, the Third National Bank in Charlotte, North Carolina, reviewed its lending relationship with the Alpha Company, an old and valued customer. The company's September 30, 1988, fiscal results revealed a loss of $175,000—the first loss in the company's history. The company requested that, for fiscal 1989, the Third National Bank review its present $2.5 million loan agreement and consider additional financing requirements indicated in the analysis. The company also provided the bank with fiscal 1989 projections to substantiate the increase.

THE COMPANY

The Alpha Company manufactures patio doors for the residential, multifamily, and mobile home industries. Its sales mix for the last 5 years is shown in Exhibit A.1.

The Alpha Company is in a highly competitive business. More than 250 companies engage in patio door manufacturing, most of them operating seasonally. The Alpha Company ranks among the top 10 firms in both of its patio door lines. It also leads in its other two product lines (closet doors and a new entry-door system).

The company has grown from a privately owned basement operation started in the late 1950s to a publicly traded, over-the-counter company. Its major plant is in Charlotte, although it brought another large facility on line in Kansas City in February 1988. The new facility is part of management's plan to shift capacity toward the multifamily home market (apartments and condominiums), which is the direction that housing market trends and Alpha Company sales have been going, as shown in Exhibit A.2.

Sales Mix for the Alpha Company

	1984	1985	1986	1987	1988
Aluminum-framed patio doors	37%	37%	32%	32%	25%
Wood-framed patio doors	28%	33%	37%	40%	42%
Steel bifold closet doors	35%	30%	31%	28%	16%
Entry-door system*	-0-	-0-	-0-	-0-	17%

*This product was first introduced to the market in fiscal 1987.

Changes in U.S. Housing Mix by Percentage

Years	Single-Family Homes	Multifamily Homes	Mobile Homes
1964-69	83	10	7
1970-75	67	25	8
1976-81	55	31	14
1982-87	44	35	21

Note: These are not the actual figures for the years shown.

A geographical breakdown of its sales shows that 81 percent of the Alpha Company's sales are east of the Mississippi River, with an additional 10 percent in Canada. The company's 17 full-time salespersons market to 600 building supply customers who maintain an inventory of Alpha Company products. The salespersons also market directly to large multifamily and commercial contractors. The company's largest customer, Americana Homes, Inc., accounting for nearly 12 percent of Alpha Company's total sales, decided in 1988 to discontinue carrying the Alpha Company door line. The Alpha Company expects to lose this account altogether in 1989. At the same time, it significantly increased its sales to a Canadian company, which had represented 3 percent of Alpha's total sales in 1987 but increased to 11 percent in 1988. None of the remaining accounts represents more than 3 percent of the Alpha Company's total sales.

The company's sales are seasonal, peaking in the early months of the calendar year in anticipation of late spring and summer construction.

The Alpha Company's financial vice president resigned in 1988. He had provided the company with strong expense control systems and accurate forecasting. The company has recently hired a replacement from a competitor.

1988 FISCAL RESULTS

Despite an expected 12 percent decline in housing starts in 1988, the Alpha Company projected a 10 percent sales increase in 1988 based on an anticipated increase in its market share. Instead, housing starts actually declined by 37 percent because of a nationwide recession. Most of that decline occurred in the multifamily home market, as shown in Exhibit A.3. The Alpha Company's sales of doors to multifamily home builders dropped by 42 percent, while its sales to single-family home builders increased by 7 percent.

Despite the weak market, the Alpha Company's materials, labor costs, and distribution expenses skyrocketed, shrinking its profit margins. The company also had to bear the expenses associated with the start-up of the Kansas City plant (only 7 months in operation by fiscal year-end) and a 3-month shutdown of the Charlotte facility due to a lack of sales.

Housing Starts in the U.S., 1983–1987

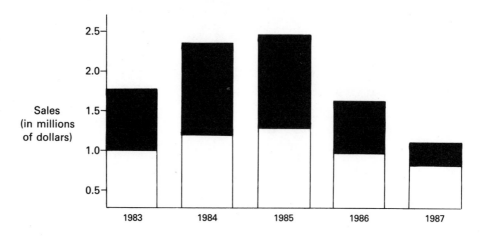

Note: These are not the actual figures for the years shown.

■ Multifamily homes
☐ Single-family homes

■ ■

Nevertheless, the company managed to maintain its previous sales level despite these disastrous market conditions. It was able to do so by increasing its market share—the result of a strong sales effort, geographic expansion, increased product acceptance, and the introduction of new products. The company may also have engaged in price-cutting to maintain its market share.

The Alpha Company projects a strong recovery in 1989, including 50 percent more sales, based on the following changes:

- a market recovery that will spur housing starts from approximately 1.1 million in 1988 to 1.5 million in 1989

- geographic expansion into Texas and Canada

- expansion of wood-door production to meet the strong demand for these products in Texas and Canada

- sales of steel products to new markets

- full use of all production facilities

- introduction of new products

BANK RELATIONSHIP

The Third National Bank has been the Alpha Company's only bank since the company's inception. The bank has helped the company negotiate insurance company term debt and has assisted in a public stock offering. The present relationship is limited to a $2.5 million seasonal working capital line of credit. The company was unable to pay off this debt in 1988. The loan officer must determine why the company failed to pay the seasonal line of credit—and if, and how, it will be able to repay it this year.

▮▮▮▮▮ Past Performance

In any lending situation, the loan officer must determine the depth and breadth of the analysis. The depth of analysis determines how extensively the available information is analyzed. This should be limited to what is necessary to reach the given objectives. The breadth of analysis

Income Statement

Alpha Company
Income Statement
for the Fiscal Years Ending Sept. 30, 1985–1988
(in thousands of dollars)

	FYE 9/30/85	%	FYE 9/30/86	%	FYE 9/30/87	%	FYE 9/30/88	%
Net sales	15,469	100	19,578	100	20,540	100	20,055	100
Cost of goods sold	11,043	71	14,370	73	15,194	74	15,703	78
Gross profit/revenues	4,426	29	5,208	27	5,346	26	4,352	22
Selling expenses	1,016	7	1,259	6	1,529	7	1,443	7
General and administrative expenses	1,553	10	1,888	10	2,410	12	2,485	13
Total operating expenses	2,569	17	3,147	16	3,939	19	3,928	20
Operating profit	1,857	12	2,061	11	1,407	7	424	2
Interest expense	138	1	241	2	635	3	833	4
Profit before tax	1,719	11	1,820	9	772	4	(409)	(2)
Income taxes	665	4	806	4	103	1	(234)	(1)
Net profit after tax	1,054	7	1,014	5	669	3	(175)	(1)
Ratios:								
Net profit-to-worth	N/A		20.17		11.68		Neg.	
Net profit-to-total assets	N/A		12.12		8.85		Neg.	
Cash flow-to-current maturities	28.31		18.95		9.51		Neg.	
Times interest earned	13.46		8.59		2.22		.51	
Notes:								
Dividends	97		144		144		717	
Depreciation	770		760		750		859	

■ ■

involves determining how many analytical tools should be applied to the information. In all situations, an analysis of the income statement, balance sheet, and funds flow statement should be performed to examine trends and to interpret the basic ratios.

This section analyzes the Alpha Company's past performance using these basic tools. As an analysis progresses, questions and issues often arise that require clarification. Some of these can be answered through further analysis, but others may require answers or additional information from management. Questions should be noted as they arise and, at the completion of the analysis, any that remain unanswered should be directed to the company's management.

Before proceeding further, the loan officer must spread and common-size the income statements and balance sheets, complete the funds flow statement, and calculate the basic ratios.

INCOME STATEMENT ANALYSIS

Exhibit A.4 shows the Alpha Company's income statements for the past 4 years. Although the company's sales dropped off only very slightly, its gross margin declined four points from 1987 to 1988, resulting in a $1,000,000 decline in gross profit. That decline presumably resulted from a combination of the company's inability to pass on skyrocketing costs, its fight to maintain its market share, and increased overhead costs associated with its increased capacity. The $1,000,000 decline in gross profit, combined with a $200,000 increase in interest expenses, resulted in a pretax loss of $409,000 in fiscal year 1988. The impact of the loss was softened by tax benefits which resulted in a $175,000 after-tax loss.

The loan officer can get a clearer picture of the company's income picture by requesting the following information:

- an historic breakdown of sales by geographic regions to verify the assertion concerning geographic expansion

- a sales breakdown by unit volume to determine to what extent past increases in sales revenues reflected additional volume of sales compared with price increases

- a breakdown of the components of cost of goods sold to determine the cause of the increase in that account

Balance Sheet

Alpha Company
Balance Sheet
(in thousands of dollars)

	FYE 9/30/85	%	FYE 9/30/86	%	FYE 9/30/87	%	FYE 9/30/88	%
Assets								
Cash	202	2	109	1	409	2	548	3
Accounts receivable—								
net	3,056	34	3,422	34	3,662	21	4,161	23
Inventory	1,933	22	2,661	26	4,095	23	4,118	23
Income tax refund	—	—	—	—	297	2	426	2
Current assets	5,191	58	6,192	61	8,463	48	9,253	51
Fixed assets—net	3,336	38	3,503	35	8,285	47	8,294	47
Other assets	355	4	378	4	725	5	442	2
Noncurrent assets	3,691	42	3,881	39	9,010	52	8,736	49
Total assets	8,882	100	10,073	100	17,473	100	17,989	100
Liabilities and Net Worth								
Notes payable to banks	1,500	17	400	4	1,800	10	2,500	14
Accounts payable—								
trade	709	8	558	6	1,530	9	1,434	8
Accruals	623	7	558	6	519	3	589	3
Current maturities—								
long-term debt	61	1	86	—	134	1	147	1
Current-year income								
taxes	207	2	289	3	—	—	—	—
Current debt	3,100	35	1,891	19	3,983	23	4,670	26
Long-term debt—								
secured	995	11	2,355	23	6,762	39	6,615	37
Total debt	4,095	46	4,246	42	10,745	62	11,285	63
Reserve—deferred								
income taxes	194	2	364	4	740	4	963	5
Capital stock—common	1,200	14	1,200	12	1,200	7	1,320	7
Paid-in surplus	1,524	17	1,524	15	1,524	9	2,049	12
Retained earnings	1,869	21	2,739	27	3,264	18	2,372	13
Net worth	4,593	52	5,463	54	5,988	34	5,741	32
Total liabilities and								
net worth	8,882	100	10,073	100	17,473	100	17,989	100
Working capital	2,091		4,301		4,480		4,583	
Ratios:								
Quick/current	1.05/1.67		1.87/3.27		1.10/2.12		1.10/1.98	
Debt-to-worth	.89		.78		1.79		1.97	
Sales-to-receivables								
(days)	—		60		63		71	
Cost of sales-to-								
inventory (days)	—		58		81		95	
Purchases-to-payables								
(days)	—		16		25		34	

■■

- a breakdown of the company's variable and fixed costs and operating expenses (to help determine what portion of the margin decline resulted from increased manufacturing capacity)

BALANCE SHEET ANALYSIS

Exhibit A.5 shows the Alpha Company's balance sheets for the past 4 years. A significant decline in liquidity and an increase in debt-to-net worth, or financial leverage, are apparent from 1986 to 1987. These changes resulted primarily from the company's expansion of its production capacity in excess of its ability to generate internal cash flow to fund that expansion. The company consequently funded most of the increase with debt, a portion of which was in the form of short-term notes payable. This partial funding of fixed assets with short-term debt presents a problem because the company does not appear to have the liquidity or cash flow to repay the debt within a short period. Although 1988 operating cash flow of $684,000 (loss of $175,000 plus depreciation charges of $859,000—as shown in Exhibit A.4) would be sufficient to pay the next year's current maturities of $147,000, it is insufficient to retire a substantial portion of the $2,500,000 in notes payable. To determine the precise magnitude of cash flows, the loan officer must analyze the funds flow statement.

FUNDS FLOW STATEMENT ANALYSIS

The funds flow statement shown in Exhibit A.6 verifies the results of the analysis of the income statement and balance sheet. The Alpha Company's operating inflows over the 1987 to 1988 period were sufficient to fund the company's operating outflows, but did not provide excess cash for discretionary use (net positive operating flow of $698,000 versus discretionary outflows of $7,325,000 for 1987 and 1988). Most of the discretionary outflows occurred in 1987 and represented fixed asset purchases and dividend payments. The purchases were financed by a combination of long-term debt and short-term notes payable. Although dividends increased sharply—from $144,000 in 1987 to $717,000 in 1988—capital accounts were credited with $645,000 in an unidentified

Comparative Funds Flow Statement

Alpha Company
Comparative Funds Flow Statement
(in thousands of dollars)

	FYE 9/30/86	FYE 9/30/87	FYE 9/30/88
Operating Funds			
Net income	1,014	669	(175)
Add: Depreciation/amortization	760	750	859
Change in deferred tax liability	170	376	223
Change in accounts receivable	(366)	(240)	(499)
Change in inventory	(728)	(1,434)	(23)
Change in other current assets	—	(297)	(129)
Change in accounts payable	(151)	972	(96)
Change in accruals	(65)	(39)	70
Change in current-year income tax	82	(289)	—
Net operating flow	716	468	230
Discretionary Funds			
Change in other noncurrent assets	(23)	(347)	283
Increase in fixed assets	(927)	(5,532)	(868)
Dividends paid	(144)	(144)	(717)
Net discretionary flow	(1,094)	(6,023)	(1,302)
Financing Funds			
Change in notes payable to banks	(1,100)	1,400	700
Change in commercial long-term debt	25	48	13
Change in long-term debt	1,360	4,407	(147)
Increase in capital accounts	—	—	645
Net financing flow	285	5,855	1,211
Change in cash/marketable securities	93	(300)	(139)
Summary			
Net operating flow	716	468	230
Net discretionary flow	(1,094)	(6,023)	(1,302)
Net financing flow	285	5,855	1,211
Change in cash/marketable securities	93	(300)	(139)

transaction, thus alleviating the negative impact of such a large dividend. The loan officer should discuss the nature of this transaction with management.

Up until this point, the analysis has indicated that the company has maintained or increased its market position and thus its revenue stream. However, an increase in capacity that exceeded present requirements and the cost pressures of a soft market have resulted in an operating loss. The company's balance sheet leverage was affected because the company's ambitious fixed asset expansion program was financed largely by debt. Also, liquidity was adversely affected by the use of short-term debt to finance a portion of the fixed asset increase. This suggests the possible need to restructure the company's debt. In addition, operating cash flow must increase in the future if the company is to amortize the debt it has incurred.

▌▌▌▌▌ Projected Performance

The analysis of the Alpha Company's past performance gives direction to the analysis of the company's projected performance. It is already apparent that the company has significant debt. The next analytical steps will help the loan officer develop an opinion regarding the company's repayment ability and its future financing requirements. The pro forma financial statements aid in this process and in projecting the resulting balance sheet structure. The cash budget highlights the timing and magnitude of the company's interim funds requirements, which are primarily seasonal, while sensitivity analysis measures the potential impact of the lender's downside assumptions. Finally, the analysis of the Alpha Company's operating leverage and working investment requirements indicates its potential earnings ability and its capacity to generate cash.

PRO FORMA STATEMENT AND CASH BUDGET ANALYSIS

The Alpha Company's new financial vice president supplied the bank with a pro forma income statement, balance sheet, and cash budget.

Pro Forma Income Statements

Alpha Company
Pro Forma Income Statements
(in thousands of dollars)

	Company-Prepared Pro Forma		Bank-Prepared Pro Forma	
	FYE 9/30/89	%	*FYE 9/30/89*	%
Net sales	30,000	100	25,910	100
Cost of goods sold	21,900	73	20,002	77
Gross profit/revenues	8,100	27	5,908	23
Selling expenses	1,600	5	1,300	5
General and administrative expenses	3,440	12	3,500	14
Total operating expenses	5,040	17	4,800	19
Operating profit	3,060	10	1,108	4
Interest expense	1,116	4	1,276	5
Profit before tax	1,944	6	(168)	(1)
Income taxes	864	3	(74)	—
Net profit after tax	1,080	3	(94)	—
Ratios:				
Net profit-to-worth	17.39		Neg.	
Net profit-to-total assets	9.39		Neg.	
Cash flow-to-current maturities	12.08		4.10	
Times interest earned	2.74		.87	
Notes:				
Dividends	144		144	
Depreciation	840		840	

■ ■

These are shown in Exhibits A.7 and A.8 (along with the bank's revised pro forma financial statements), and in Exhibit A.9, respectively.

The company's pro forma income statement (shown in Exhibit A.7) projects a profit of $1,080,000 for 1989, a strong rebound from fiscal 1988. However, this still amounts to only 3 percent of sales compared to levels of 7 percent and 5 percent in 1985 and 1986. The improved gross margin projected for 1989 (27 percent versus 22 percent) presumably is based on the company's increased production capacity and full use of the new Kansas City plant. The higher utilization would enable the company to spread its fixed manufacturing costs over more units of production.

Even if the company's operating performance improves as markedly as management predicts, there remains an apparent funding imbalance that the loan officer must address. The company-prepared pro forma balance sheet (shown in Exhibit A.8) was balanced using the notes payable to banks account, which nevertheless shows a projected decrease from $2,500,000 as of September 30, 1988, to $1,117,000 by September 30, 1989. Although Alpha management is projecting all required funding as notes payable, the loan officer may see the company's needs as long term. Although the notes payable will still not be fully paid, the general balance sheet position shows improvement as measured in terms of liquidity and leverage. It shows the current ratio (current assets to current liabilities) increasing from 1.98 to 2.53 and the debt-to-worth ratio decreasing from 1.97 to 1.57. In addition to a reduction in short-term debt, the company-prepared pro forma analysis shows internally generated funds being used to support increased working capital needs—accounts receivable and inventory.

In preparing the cash budget (Exhibit A.9), company management assumed a $300,000 minimum cash balance. The short-term funding requirement begins with the $2,500,000 in notes payable and $147,000 in current maturities of long-term debt from the company's balance sheet. The cash budget shows interim short-term financing needs increasing to $5,136,000 by February 1989. This results from a level production policy that creates a seasonal inventory buildup before the peak selling season. Thus, inaccurate sales forecasts could lead to overproduction of inventory. This risk is increased in a cyclical and competitive industry such as this one, which is directly tied to the housing market.

Pro Forma Balance Sheets

Alpha Company
Pro Forma Balance Sheets
(in thousands of dollars)

	Company-Prepared Pro Forma		Bank-Prepared Pro Forma	
	FYE 9/30/89	%	FYE 9/30/89	%
Assets				
Cash	300	2	300	2
Accounts receivable—net	4,200	23	3,780	21
Inventory	5,639	31	5,117	29
Income tax refund	—	—	557	3
Current assets	10,139	56	9,754	55
Fixed assets—net	7,634	42	7,634	43
Other assets	442	2	442	2
Noncurrent assets	8,076	44	8,076	45
Total assets	18,215	100	17,830	100
Liabilities and Net Worth				
Notes payable to banks	1,117	6	3,153	18
Accounts payable—trade	1,958	11	735	4
Accruals	782	4	758	4
Current maturities—long-term debt	147	1	147	1
Current debt	4,004	22	4,793	27
Long-term debt—secured	6,468	36	6,468	36
Total debt	10,472	58	11,261	63
Reserve—deferred income taxes	1,066	6	1,066	6
Capital stock—common	1,320	7	1,320	7
Paid-in surplus	2,049	11	2,049	12
Retained earnings	3,308	18	2,134	12
Net worth	6,677	36	5,503	31
Total liabilities and net worth	18,215	100	17,830	100
Working capital	6,135		4,961	
Ratios:				
Quick/current	1.12/2.53		.97/2.04	
Debt-to-worth	1.57		2.05	
Sales-to-receivables (days)	51		56	
Cost of sales-to-inventory (days)	81		84	
Purchases-to-payables (days)	28		20	

Company-Prepared Cash Budget

Alpha Company
Company-Prepared Cash Budget
for the Fiscal Year Ending September 30, 1989
(in thousands of dollars)

	Oct.	Nov.	Dec.	Jan.	Feb.	Mar.	Apr.	May	Jun.	Jul.	Aug.	Sept.	Total
Cash on hand	548	300	300	300	300	300	300	300	300	300	300	300	3,848
Cash receipts	2,080	2,081	1,100	1,500	2,200	3,200	3,600	3,500	3,400	2,700	2,400	2,200	29,961
Total cash available	2,628	2,381	1,400	1,800	2,500	3,500	3,900	3,800	3,700	3,000	2,700	2,500	33,809
Cash paid out													
Purchases	1,076	631	545	545	545	545	545	545	545	545	545	925	
Payroll	725	725	725	725	725	725	725	725	725	725	725	725	
Manufacturing overhead	316	505	505	505	505	505	505	505	505	505	505	505	
Selling, gen. and adm. exp.	380	400	400	400	400	400	400	400	400	400	400	400	
Interest expense	93	95	94	106	116	117	110	97	85	76	72	71	
Income tax	0	(426)	0	190	0	190	0	0	190	0	0	191	
Cash dividends	0	0	36	0	0	36	0	0	36	0	0	36	
Subtotal	2,590	1,930	2,305	2,471	2,291	2,518	2,285	2,272	2,486	2,251	2,247	2,853	28,499
Loan principal payments	0	0	36	0	0	37	0	0	37	0	0	37	
Capital purchases	15	15	15	15	15	15	15	15	15	15	15	15	
Total cash paid out	2,605	1,945	2,356	2,486	2,306	2,570	2,300	2,287	2,538	2,266	2,262	2,905	28,826
Cash position	23	436	(956)	(686)	194	930	1,600	1,513	1,162	734	438	(405)	
Minimum ending cash	300	300	300	300	300	300	300	300	300	300	300	300	
Additional funding requirement (or repayment)	277	(136)	1,256	986	106	(630)	(1,300)	(1,213)	(862)	(434)	(138)	705	
Cumulative funding requirement	2,924	2,788	4,044	5,030	5,136	4,506	3,206	1,993	1,131	697	559	1,264	

■■■■■■■■■■■■■■■■■■■■■■■■■■■■■■■■■■■■■■■

SENSITIVITY ANALYSIS

The focus of sensitivity analysis is to determine the company's points of greatest vulnerability and to enable the loan officer to change critical assumptions affecting those areas. Because of its high fixed costs and cyclicality, the Alpha Company is very vulnerable to decreased sales. Consequently, the loan officer prepares more conservative pro forma financial statements and a revised cash budget, as shown in Exhibits A.7, A.8, and A.10, based on discussions with the Alpha Company's management.

Instead of projecting sales of $30,000,000 in 1989, as management did in its pro forma income statement, the loan officer uses a more conservative sales figure of $25,910,000 in the bank-prepared pro forma income statement (which is shown along with the company's projections in Exhibit A.7). Thus the results of the bank's pro forma analysis are dramatically different from those produced by the company. The bank's pro forma income statement shows lower gross profit margin (23 percent rather than 27 percent) and increased interest costs, resulting in an after-tax loss of $94,000 (rather than a $1,080,000 net profit as projected by the company). The bank's pro forma balance sheet (which is compared with the company's pro forma figures in Exhibit A.8) shows a year-end level of notes payable to banks of $3,153,000 and a debt-to-worth ratio of 2.05. Thus, whereas management projected a decrease in short-term debt and an improved debt-to-worth ratio during 1989, the bank foresees an increase in notes payable and leverage compared to the past year.

The cash budget constructed by the loan officer (Exhibit A.10), which is based on the revised pro forma financial statements, shows the company's cumulative funding requirement peaking in March at $5,814,000, nearly $700,000 higher than the company's peak borrowing projections (as seen in its cash budget—Exhibit A.9). Because the company maintains level production, inventory builds up rapidly at the low side of the marketing cycle. In order to get the $5.8 million in short-term financing down to a more manageable level as quickly as follows, the loan officer feels that at the end of March, the company should cut production and prices by 10 percent. This will help reduce the buildup in inventory and is consistent with management's past and stated strategy of maintaining or increasing its market share. By discounting prices, the loan officer anticipates the company will be able to increase its sales volume for the last 6 months of the fiscal year, although revenues will be lower. By lowering production, the company's purchases, wages, and manufacturing overhead will also be reduced, further helping its cash flow and debt repayment ability. The cash budget prepared by the loan officer, which includes these assumptions, projects the company's minimum debt level (which occurs in August following the collection of accounts receivable from the seasonal sales peak) at $3,111,000 compared to a low of $559,000 in the company's projections. These differences reflect the bank's lower sales forecasts and its assumption of increased interim working investment required to support inventory.

A company with this much potential for debt accumulation under these assumed conditions should have either a strong balance sheet (high liquidity and low leverage) or a strong earnings potential. A strong balance sheet provides the capacity to withstand cyclical swings, while strong earnings potential is needed to ensure that profitability during cyclical peaks more than offsets losses during the low points in the cycle. The Alpha Company's vulnerability to the downside risk of decreased sales, combined with a highly leveraged balance sheet, mandates a strong earnings potential. Analysis of operating leverage and working investment, which are the next analytical steps, will provide the loan officer with insight into the company's upside earnings potential.

OPERATING LEVERAGE AND WORKING INVESTMENT ANALYSIS

When the Alpha Company opened its Kansas City plant in 1988, it anticipated dramatic sales increases. Despite the lackluster results in 1988, management believes sales of $30,000,000 in 1989 and $40,000,000 in 1990 should be easily attainable provided the expected strong housing market develops. Since the new plant is currently operating at only 50 percent of capacity (a sufficient level of production to meet the company's $30,000,000 sales projection), the lender should explore the potential effects of operating leverage on earnings for sales at the $40,000,000 level.

The loan officer first needs to determine the percentage of variable costs in the company's cost of goods sold (COGS). This is calculated based on the normal monthly disbursements shown in the company's

Bank-Prepared Cash Budget

Alpha Company
Bank-Prepared Cash Budget
for the Fiscal Year Ending September 30, 1989
(in thousands of dollars)

	Oct.	Nov.	Dec.	Jan.	Feb.	Mar.	Apr.	May	Jun.	Jul.	Aug.	Sept.	Total
Cash on hand	548	300	300	300	300	300	300	300	300	300	300	300	3,848
Cash receipts	2,080	2,081	1,100	1,300	1,800	2,500	3,000	2,800	3,060	2,430	2,160	1,980	26,291
Total cash available	2,628	2,381	1,400	1,600	2,100	2,800	3,300	3,100	3,360	2,730	2,460	2,280	30,139
Cash paid out													
Purchases	1,076	631	545	545	545	545	545	518	490	490	490	490	
Payroll	725	725	725	725	725	725	655	655	655	655	655	655	
Manufacturing overhead	316	505	505	505	505	505	505	480	480	480	480	480	
Selling, gen. and adm. exp.	380	400	400	400	400	400	380	360	360	360	360	360	
Interest expense	93	95	94	106	118	123	124	116	109	100	97	96	
Income tax	0	(426)	0	190	0	190	0	0	0	0	0	0	
Cash dividends	0	0	36	0	0	36	0	0	36	0	0	36	
Subtotal	2,590	1,930	2,305	2,471	2,293	2,524	2,209	2,129	2,130	2,085	2,082	2,117	26,865
Loan principal payments	0	0	36	0	0	37	0	0	37	0	0	37	
Capital purchases	15	15	15	15	15	15	15	15	15	15	15	15	
Total cash paid out	2,605	1,945	2,356	2,486	2,308	2,576	2,224	2,144	2,182	2,100	2,097	2,169	27,192
Cash position	23	436	(956)	(886)	(208)	224	1,076	956	1,178	630	363	111	
Minimum ending cash	300	300	300	300	300	300	300	300	300	300	300	300	
Additional funding requirement (or repayment)	277	(136)	1,256	1,186	508	76	(776)	(656)	(878)	(330)	(63)	189	
Cumulative funding requirement	2,924	2,788	4,044	5,230	5,738	5,814	5,038	4,382	3,504	3,174	3,111	3,300	

■■■

cash budget (Exhibit A.9) that are components of cost of goods sold—namely, purchases (or materials), $545,000; payroll (or labor), $725,000; and manufacturing overhead, $505,000. These are each expressed as a percentage of $1,775,000—the normal monthly disbursement for cost of goods sold (called the *cost of goods sold percentage* in the following calculation). In this case, materials and labor are considered to be 100 percent variable, while manufacturing overhead (according to management estimates) is 15 percent variable. Thus the percentage of the cost of goods sold that is variable is calculated as follows:

Item	Variable Percentage		Cost of Goods Sold Percentage		Percentage of COGS That Is Variable
Materials	100%	of	31%	=	31%
Labor	100%	of	41%	=	41%
Manufacturing overhead	15%	of	28%	=	4% (rounded)
					76%

The next step is to determine the percentage of variable costs in the company's sales. Since the company projects the cost of goods sold in a strong year (1989) to be 73 percent of sales, as shown in Exhibit A.7, the variable costs in the cost of goods sold represent 73 percent × 76 percent, or 55 percent of sales. The company's pro forma income statement also estimates selling expense (another variable cost) as 5 percent of sales. Total variable cost can then be calculated as follows:

Item	Variable Percentage of Sales
Cost of goods sold	55%
Selling expense	5%
Total variable costs	60%

Having calculated the variable costs associated with the Alpha Company's operations, its fixed costs (still using the figures in the company's pro forma income statement—Exhibit A.7) are easily determined. Since the company's cost of goods sold has been calculated to be 76 percent variable, it follows that 24 percent of its cost of goods sold consists of fixed costs:

24% of the cost of goods sold = 0.24 × $21,900,000 =	$5,256,000
General and administrative expenses	3,440,000
Total fixed costs	$8,696,000

The loan officer uses this information to calculate the operating profit that would result from a sales level of $40,000,000:

Sales	$40,000,000
Less: Variable costs (60% of sales)	− 24,000,000
Gross profit	16,000,000
Less: Fixed costs	− 9,000,000 (rounded)
Operating profit before interest expense	$ 7,000,000

To determine how much of this operating profit would be available for debt service and reduction, the loan officer must next determine the working investment required for the increased level of sales. The September 30, 1989, pro forma balance sheet prepared by Alpha Company management (Exhibit A.8) shows a working investment (Accounts receivable + Inventory − Accounts payable − Accruals) of $7,099,000. At a $30,000,000 sales level, this amounts to a working investment of approximately 24 cents for each dollar of sales. Thus, a $10,000,000 increase in sales should require a $2,400,000 increase in working investment.

The $7,000,000 in net operating profit calculated above is used to determine the cash available for debt retirement or further investment as follows:

Operating profit	$7,000,000
Less: Interest expense (assumed no change)	1,116,000
Profit before tax	5,884,000
Less: Estimated income tax (46%)	2,707,000
Profit after tax	3,177,000
Plus: Depreciation (unchanged)	840,000
Less: Increase in working investment	2,400,000
Less: Fixed asset purchases*	180,000
Cash available for debt retirement	$1,437,000

*From the company's 1989 cash budget (Exhibit A.9): Capital purchases total $15,000 × 12 = $180,000.

This calculation shows that an increase in sales from $30,000,000 to $40,000,000 would create free cash of $1,437,000, which could be used for debt retirement or other purposes. Thus there appears to be significant upside earning potential, which could justify the risk involved in continuing to finance the Alpha Company. The company is experiencing rapid growth and has significant excess production capacity, both of which would explain the relatively high operating leverage.

Although a very strong upside potential exists for the company, the loan officer cannot ignore the downside—excessive debt accumulation. The question is how much financial leverage is too much. Although no clear answer exists, the loan officer can examine alternative performance scenarios and consider the risks involved for each and their probability of occurrence.

The bank's more conservative scenario for the Alpha Company assumes a net loss for the coming year, with bank debt approximately $2,000,000 higher than that projected by management. It also assumes a balance sheet with somewhat higher financial leverage and less liquidity. On the other hand, using the company's own assumptions for a second year (that is, for 1990) results in significant profit and cash flow opportunities arising from the available operating leverage and sufficient excess cash flow to more than offset the increased debt brought on during the past year.

■ ■ ■ ■ Summary

The comprehensive (yet necessarily brief) financial analysis of the Alpha Company described here illustrates the various financial analysis concepts presented in the text. The company had just experienced its first unprofitable year in some 30 years of operations, largely the result of a nationwide recession that disrupted the housing market. Moreover, the company had opened a new plant during the year and lost a major account. The company has asked the bank to consider an additional loan on top of its existing $2,500,000 seasonal working capital line of credit (which remained unpaid as of the end of the company's 1988 fiscal year).

The loan officer began by looking at the history of the company and its position in the highly competitive market for patio doors. The lender's assessment of the company's past performance involved spreading and common-sizing the company's income statements and balance sheets for the past 4 years, as well as calculating the principal ratios and analyzing the company's funds flow for the past 3 years. The overall conclusion of the loan officer at this point was that in a potentially disastrous year, the company had fought an uphill battle and experienced only a slight decline in sales, but because of increased expenses this had resulted in a net loss for the year. It was also apparent that the company needed to convert at least part of its bank debt to term debt, especially since it had used short-term debt to finance its fixed asset expansion during the previous year.

The loan officer then looked at the pro forma income statement and balance sheet and cash budget supplied by the company, which projected a strong recovery—including a 50 percent increase in sales during the current year. The loan officer decided to reformulate the company's pro forma financial statements and cash budget using a more conservative sales projection. This sensitivity analysis showed that the company could experience another after-tax loss and a still higher level of debt in the coming year, thus effectively demonstrating the downside risk in further lending to this company.

The loan officer next did an analysis of the company's operating leverage and working investment to see what would happen if the company's sales projections proved correct and the company actually did double its sales over the next 2 years (as management strongly believed it could). This analysis showed that, because the production capacity for this much-increased level of sales was already in place, this scenario would result in a significant amount of cash becoming available for debt retirement or for other purposes. Thus the company appeared to have significant upside earnings potential to balance the downside risk.

The lender was left to choose between two courses of action. Presumably the bank would not simply advance the company an increased line of credit since this would not take into account the change in the company's lending needs from temporary to permanent financing. However, the bank could grant the requested increase and at the same time restructure the borrowing arrangement. Such a restructuring of debt could provide the bank an opportunity to specify terms and conditions that would give it some measure of control in the company's operations. Alternatively, the company could attempt to terminate its relationship with the Alpha Company by requesting payment in full of all outstanding debt. This would be the proper course if the lender concluded that the company's strengths did not sufficiently outweigh its weaknesses to overcome the uncertainties faced by the company. The lender would then have to consider the means of expected payment—and assess the probability of the bank's being repaid in full.

The credit decision ultimately rested on the loan officer's subjective judgment of the viability of the company's market and the capability of its management. The analytical process provided direction and focus, helping the loan officer isolate and examine the major factors affecting the company's potential performance and creditworthiness so that the likelihood of a sound lending decision was enhanced. But even this comprehensive financial analysis could not, in the end, supply a definitive answer as to what action the lender should take.

Questions

1. Explain the concept of efficient analysis. What factors influence the amount of analysis required in a given situation?

2. What did the loan officer conclude on the basis of the analysis of the Alpha Company's past performance—that is, the income statement, balance sheet, and funds flow analysis?

3. What questions did the loan officer attempt to answer about the Alpha Company's future performance, and what tools were used to answer those questions?

4. What are the implications of the Alpha Company's high operating leverage?

5. What did the loan officer's sensitivity analysis reveal?

6. What uncertainties does the Alpha Company face, and what are its strengths and weaknesses in dealing with those uncertainties?

7. Based on the available information, what would your decision be?

▌▌▌▌▌ Addendum: Actual Results of the Case Study

In the actual situation, the bank increased its loan amount to the Alpha Company to $3,000,000, divided into two parts—a short-term seasonal line of credit and a permanent working capital loan. The permanent working capital loan was extended on a revolving basis in order to allow

Actual Results—Income Statement

Alpha Company
Income Statement
(in thousands of dollars)

	FYE 9/30/89	%	FYE 9/30/90	%
Net sales	30,135	100	40,572	100
Cost of goods sold	22,652	75	28,973	71
Gross profit/revenues	7,483	25	11,599	29
Selling expenses	1,747	6	2,267	6
General and administrative expenses	2,932	10	3,635	9
Total operating expenses	4,679	16	5,902	15
Operating profit	2,804	9	5,697	14
Interest expense	794	2	628	1
Profit before tax	2,010	7	5,069	13
Income taxes	855	3	2,316	6
Net profit after tax	1,155	4	2,753	7
Ratios:				
Net profit-to-worth	16.75		29.2	
Net profit-to-total assets	5.78		12.7	
Reconciliation of Net Worth:				
Net worth—beginning	5,741		6,896	
Add: Net profit	1,155		2,753	
Less: Dividends	—		224	
Retained earnings—increase	1,155		2,529	
Net worth—increase	1,155		2,529	
Net worth—ending	6,896		9,425	

Actual Results—Balance Sheet

Alpha Company
Balance Sheet
(in thousands of dollars)

	FYE 9/30/89	%	FYE 9/30/90	%
Assets				
Cash	935	5	689	3
Accounts receivable (net)	6,106	30	8,123	38
Inventory	4,193	21	4,642	21
Current assets	11,234	56	13,454	62
Fixed assets (net)	8,413	42	7,937	37
Deferred charges/prepaid expenses	104	5	115	1
Intangibles	107	5	53	—
Other assets	130	1	93	—
Noncurrent assets	8,754	44	8,198	38
Total assets	19,988	100	21,652	100
Liabilities and Net Worth				
Notes payable to banks	2,500	12		
Accounts payable (trade)	1,395	7	1,720	8
Accruals	805	4	1,184	5
Current maturities of long-term debt	162	1	186	1
Current-year income taxes	621	3	1,635	8
Current debt	5,483	27	4,725	22
Long-term debt (unsecured)	4,544	23	4,419	20
Capitalized leases	1,891	10	1,871	8
Total long-term debt	6,435	33	6,290	29
Total debt	11,918	60	11,015	51
Reserve—Deferred income taxes	1,174	6	1,212	6
Capital stock—common	1,320	7	1,320	6
Paid-in surplus	2,049	10	2,049	9
Retained earnings	3,527	18	6,056	28
Net worth	6,896	34	9,425	43
Total liabilities and net worth	19,988	100	21,652	100
Working capital	5,751		8,729	
Ratios:				
Quick/current	1.28/2.05		1.86/2.85	
Debt-to-worth	1.72		1.18	
Sales-to-receivables (days)	4.94 (74)		4.99 (73)	
Cost of sales-to-inventory (days)	5.40 (68)		6.24 (58)	

■ ■

the company to increase its sales to take advantage of its inherent operating leverage before beginning to generate cash flow to retire the debt. The new loan agreement also placed a number of restrictions on the company's operations.

As can be seen from Exhibits A.11 and A.12, the Alpha Company's performance in 1989 and 1990 was remarkably close to management's projections, and its profitability continued from that point forward. The company's strengths saw it through the economic recession and the loan officer's decision to extend the company additional credit allowed it to take advantage of the renewed demand for housing.

Exercises

E-1

Read the following case and analyze it, using the questions at the end of the case material as a guide.

Introduction

In January 1989, the Samson National Bank of Chicago was reviewing a $1,200,000 loan request from its customer, Nevgin Corp. The loan would be used to purchase capital equipment that would allow Nevgin to diversify into a new product line. The company had provided Samson National Bank with historical financial information as well as future performance expectations in support of its request.

The Company

Nevgin was established in 1985 as an engineering/marketing firm that manufactures and sells air-pollution sampling instruments. The instruments are used to insure compliance with environmental regulations. The company's products are sold both domestically and internationally, with domestic sales representing 70 percent of total volume. Products are sold direct and through manufacturers' representatives to regulatory agencies, industries, hospitals, research institutes, and others. Nevgin currently controls approximately 65 percent of the total market.

Competition is limited because of the highly specialized nature of the products and the limited growth potential of the market. Product design is dictated primarily by regulatory requirements.

Nevgin is owned and operated by Michael L. Raas and Thomas P. Johnson. Both are considered excellent managers, working nights and weekends to make the company successful. Raas is a C.P.A., while Johnson spent 9 years with the Environmental Protection Agency as an air quality engineer.

The company would like to diversify into a line of water-pollution sampling instruments. This market is different from the air sampling market in the following ways:

- Different technology is required. Air sampling devices are primarily mechanical, while most water pollution devices depend upon chemical reaction. In addition, support instrumentation involving electronic microprocessing is critical to water sampling, while such instrumentation plays no significant role in air sampling.

- The water sampling market has greater growth potential than that for air sampling. Concern for water quality is only now developing, thus the market is still in a growth stage. Also, it appears that water pollution will be the concern of a larger group of potential customers since it is controlled primarily at the local level.

- The water sampling market is characterized by established competition. RAMOR Corp., a subsidiary of ASAD Electronics, now controls 80 percent of the market.

- Marketing requirements are different. Air-sampling product purchases are controlled by corporate purchasing agents, while many water-sampling product purchases are controlled by government bodies at various levels.

Recent Operations

Nevgin's 1988 sales of air samplers was flat, as construction of new manufacturing facilities by traditional customers continued to be weak.

The company began manufacturing its own product in 1987, having previously subcontracted all work out. Production problems were encountered in 1987, but a new production manager and improved operating methods drastically improved the situation in 1988.

The company's tax position is extremely favorable due to regulations relating to its international sales position. Foreign taxes are credited against domestic liabilities. Management does not expect that situation to change with the new product line.

Future Expectations

Management expects sales growth to be strong as a consequence of the introduction of its new product line. Margins should improve as a consequence of demand for the new product and manufacturing efficiencies.

A new production manager and a change to a centralized warehousing system are expected to allow the company to increase its sales while maintaining inventories at year-end 1988 levels.

Bank Relationship

Samson's loan relationship with Nevgin began with its financing the start-up of the company in 1985. Present debt consists of two term loans originally totaling $575,000, with $280,000 presently outstanding. The bank also extends a $100,000 line of credit for working capital needs. The debt is secured by substantially all of the company's assets.

1. Analyze Nevgin's past performance using the case information and exhibits. Evaluate the company's strengths and weaknesses in terms of its liquidity, profitability, leverage, and cash flow. What uncertainties has the company historically faced? What other information would be helpful in analyzing past performance?

2. Construct a pro forma income statement and balance sheet and a cash budget for Nevgin Corporation for 1989. Assume the following:

a. Sales are—

Jan.	Feb.	Mar.	Apr.	May	June
$209 M	$207 M	$220 M	$231 M	$236 M	$248 M

July	Aug.	Sept.	Oct.	Nov.	Dec.
$248 M	$258 M	$267 M	$267 M	$270 M	$270 M

Receivables are collected in 45 days.

b. Purchases are—

Jan.	Feb.	Mar.	Apr.	May	June
$99 M	$98 M	$104 M	$109 M	$112 M	$117 M

July	Aug.	Sept.	Oct.	Nov.	Dec.
$117 M	$122 M	$125 M	$125 M	$127 M	$127 M

Purchases are payable in 30 days.

c. Operating expenses, including interest, are—

Jan.	Feb.	Mar.	Apr.	May	June
$72 M	$71 M	$76 M	$80 M	$82 M	$85 M

July	Aug.	Sept.	Oct.	Nov.	Dec.
$85 M	$89 M	$91 M	$91 M	$93 M	$93 M

Operating expenses are payable in the month incurred.

d. Existing current maturities are amortized quarterly:

March	June	Sept.	Dec.
$34 M	$34 M	$35 M	$35 M

e. The new capital assets are acquired in March for $1,200,000 funded 100 percent by term debt. The new debt will be repaid in equal quarterly installments over 5 years with the first payment in June.

f. The company has a minimum cash balance requirement of $100,000.

g. For the pro forma income statement and balance sheet, assume—

- Cost of goods sold equals 47 percent of sales.

- No taxes will be payable.

- All operating costs incurred during the year are expensed on the income statement.

- Depreciation expense equals $110,000.

- The balance sheet category "other assets" does not change.

- All profits are retained by the firm.

3. Use sensitivity analysis to evaluate the company's ability to meet its projections. What are the critical financial variables? How do the projections for those variables compare to historical performance? What reasons exist for such variance? What uncertainties does the company face in the new market?

4. Accepting these 1989 projections as valid, what factors are critical in determining Nevgin Corporation's ability to continue amortizing the new loan in subsequent years?

5. Summarize the critical issues of the loan decision, financial and nonfinancial, in terms of the Strengths − Weaknesses > Uncertainties equation. What conditions should be negotiated with the borrower if the loan is made?

Nevgin Corp.
Comparative Income Statement
(in thousands of dollars)

	YE 12/31/85	%	YE 12/31/86	%	YE 12/31/87	%	YE 12/31/88	%
Net sales	826	100	1,845	100	2,108	100	2,234	100
Cost of goods sold	250	30	855	46	1,127	53	1,090	49
Gross profit/revenues	576	70	990	54	981	47	1,144	51
General and admin. expenses	—	—	501	27	618	29	794	36
Depreciation and amortization	—	—	47	3	46	2	15	1
Management contract fee	—	—	201	11	201	10	41	2
Total operating expenses	272	33	749	41	865	41	850	39
Operating profit	303	37	241	13	116	6	294	12
Interest expense	—	—	52	3	88	4	75	2
Profit before tax	303	37	189	70	28	2	219	10
Income taxes	—	—	68	4	5	—	—	—
Extraordinary items net of tax	—	—	68	4	5	—	—	—
Net profit after tax	303	37	189	10	28	2	219	10
Ratios:								
Net profit-to-worth		93.52%		95.45%		96.10%		49%
Net profit-to-total assets		46.76%		18.71%		24.03%		24%
Cash flow-to-curr. mat.		2.32%		3.95%		1.74%		1.70%
Times interest earned		N/A		4.63%		1.32%		3.92%
Recon. of Net Worth:								
Net worth—beginning				$324		$198		$226
Add: Net profit				189		28		219
Dividends				115		—		—
Retained earnings—incr.				74		28		219
Capital accts.—decrease				(200)		—		1
Net worth—decrease				(126)		28		220
Net worth—ending				198		226		446
Noncash mgmt. contr. fee				201		201		41
Deprec./amort.		$20		48		51		15

Nevgin Corp.
Comparative Balance Sheet
(in thousands of dollars)

	12/31/85	%	12/31/86	%	12/31/87	%	12/31/88	%
Assets								
Cash	69	11	98	10	121	15	83	9
Accounts receivable (net)	143	22	235	23	289	35	278	30
Inventory (FIFO)	314	48	428	42	410	50	521	56
Current assets	526	81	761	75	820	100	882	95
Fixed assets (net)	25	4	6	1	3	—	23	2
Patents	97	15	37	4	—	—	—	—
Mgmt. contract fees	—	—	201	20	—	—	—	—
Other	—	—	5	—	—	—	24	3
Noncurrent assets	122	19	249	25	3	—	46	5
Total assets	648	100	1,010	100	823	100	929	100
Liabilities and Net Worth								
Notes payable to banks	—	—	200	20	—	—	—	—
Accounts payable (trade)	42	6	194	19	155	19	203	22
Current maturities of long-term debt	139	21	111	11	161	19	138	15
Current debt	181	27	505	50	316	38	341	37
Long-term debt (secured)	200	31	289	28	279	34	142	15
Subordinated debt	—	—	—	—	2	—	—	—
Due to stockholders	—	—	18	2	—	—	—	—
Total long-term debt	200	31	307	30	281	34	142	15
Total debt	381	58	812	80	597	72	483	52
Capital stock—common	1	—	—	—	—	—	1	—
Paid-in surplus	20	3	81	8	81	10	81	9
Retained earnings	303	47	117	12	145	18	364	39
Net worth	324	50	198	20	226	28	446	48
Total liabilities and net worth	648	100	1,010	100	823	100	929	100
Working capital	345		256		504		541	
Ratios:								
Quick/current	1.17/2.91		.66/1.51		1.30/2.59		1.06/2.59	
Debt-to-worth	1.18		4.10		2.64		1.08	
Sales-to-receivables (days)	6.93 (53)		7.85 (46)		7.29 (50)		8.04 (45)	
Cost of sales-to-inventory (days)	.96 (380)		2.00 (1.83)		2.75 (133)		2.09 (175)	

183

Nevgin Corp.
Comparative Funds Flow Statement
(in thousands of dollars)

	YE 12/31/86	YE 12/31/87	YE 12/31/88
Operating Funds			
Net income	189	28	220*
Add: depreciation/amortization	48	51	15
Change in accounts receivable	(92)	(54)	11
Change in inventory	(114)	18	(111)
Change in accounts payable	152	(39)	48
Net operating flow	183	4	183
Discretionary Funds			
Change in other noncurrent assets	(146)	243	(24)
Add to fixed assets	(29)	(48)	(35)
Reduction in capital account	(315)	—	—
Net discretionary flow	(490)	195	(59)
Financing Funds			
Change in notes payable to bank	200	(200)	—
Change in current maturities of long-term debt	(28)	50	(23)
Change in long-term debt	107	(26)	(139)
Change in reserves/minority interest	57	—	—
Increase in capital account			
Net financing flow	336	(176)	(162)
Change in cash and marketable securities	29	23	(38)
Summary			
Net operating flow	183	4	183
Net discretionary flow	(490)	195	(59)
Net financing flow	336	(176)	(162)
Change in cash and marketable securities	29	23	(38)

---

*Income statement profit is 219, but balancing adjustment results in addition to retained earnings of 220.

Index